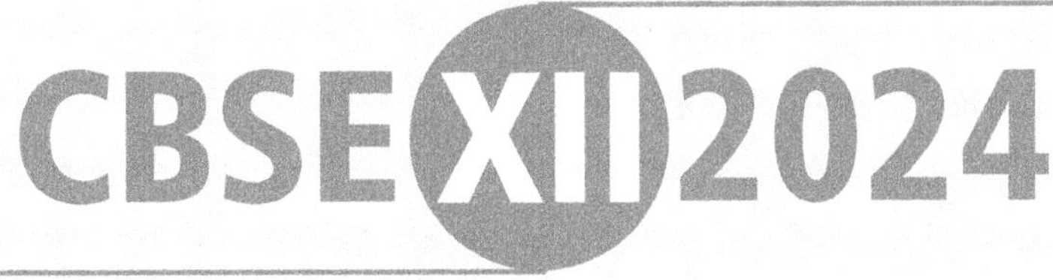

CBSE XII 2024

Chapter and Topic-Wise
Solved Papers
2011-2023

English Core

(All Sets : Delhi & All India)

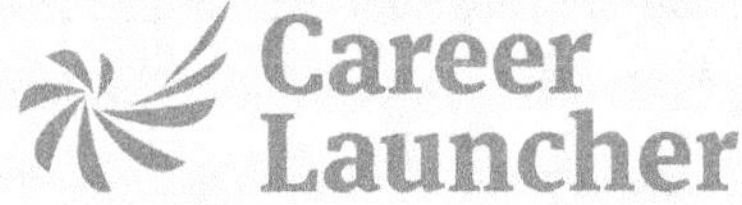

Title   : CBSE Class XII : Chapter and Topic-wise Solved Papers 2011-2023 :
                 English Core (All Sets - Delhi & All India)

Language   : English

Editor's Name   : Amit Singh

Copyright ©   : 2023 CLIP

Typeset & Published by :

Career Launcher Infrastructure (P) Ltd.

A-45, Mohan Cooperative Industrial Area, Near Mohan Estate Metro Station, New Delhi - 110044

Marketed by :

G.K. Publications (P) Ltd.

Plot No. 9A, Sector-27A, Mathura Road, Faridabad, Haryana-121003

ISBN   : 978-93-56812-65-9

Printer's Details : Print in India, New Delhi.

For product information :

Visit *www.gkpublications.com* or email to *gkp@gkpublications.com*

English

Note: CBSE Class 12th 2021 Board exams cancelled due to Covid-19.

PREFACE

English is a compulsory but overlooked subject. Sadly, students often lose marks in other subjects because they struggle with English, which is the question paper medium. Your basic concepts of English need to be in place if you want to excel in the Board Examination. At Career Launcher, our goal is not only to help you maximize your scores in Class XII English Board Exam, but also to lay a strong foundation in the subject to help you get ahead in your college and professional career. The question paper pattern of Class XII English paper has kept students on their toes by throwing unexpected questions which require in-depth chapter reading and conceptual clarity. Bearing in mind this unpredictable nature of English Exam, we've come up with Chapter-wise Solved Papers for English for Class XII - to help you prepare better and face the Boards with confidence.

Exclusively designed for the students of CBSE Class XII by highly experienced teachers, the book provides solutions to all actual questions of English Board Exams conducted from 2011 to 2023. The solutions have been prepared exactly in coherence with the latest marking pattern; after a careful evaluation of previous year trends of the questions asked in Class XII Boards and actual solutions provided by CBSE.

The book follows a two-pronged approach to make your study more focused. The questions have been arranged Chapter-wise so that you can begin your preparation with the areas that demand more attention, followed by break-down as per the marking pattern. This division will equip you with the ability to gauge which questions require more emphasis and answer accordingly.

We hope the book provides the right exposure to Class XII students so that you not only ace your Boards but mold a better future for yourself. And as always, Career Launcher's school team is behind you with its experienced gurus to help your career take wings.

Let's face the Boards with more confidence!

Wishing you all the best,

Team CL

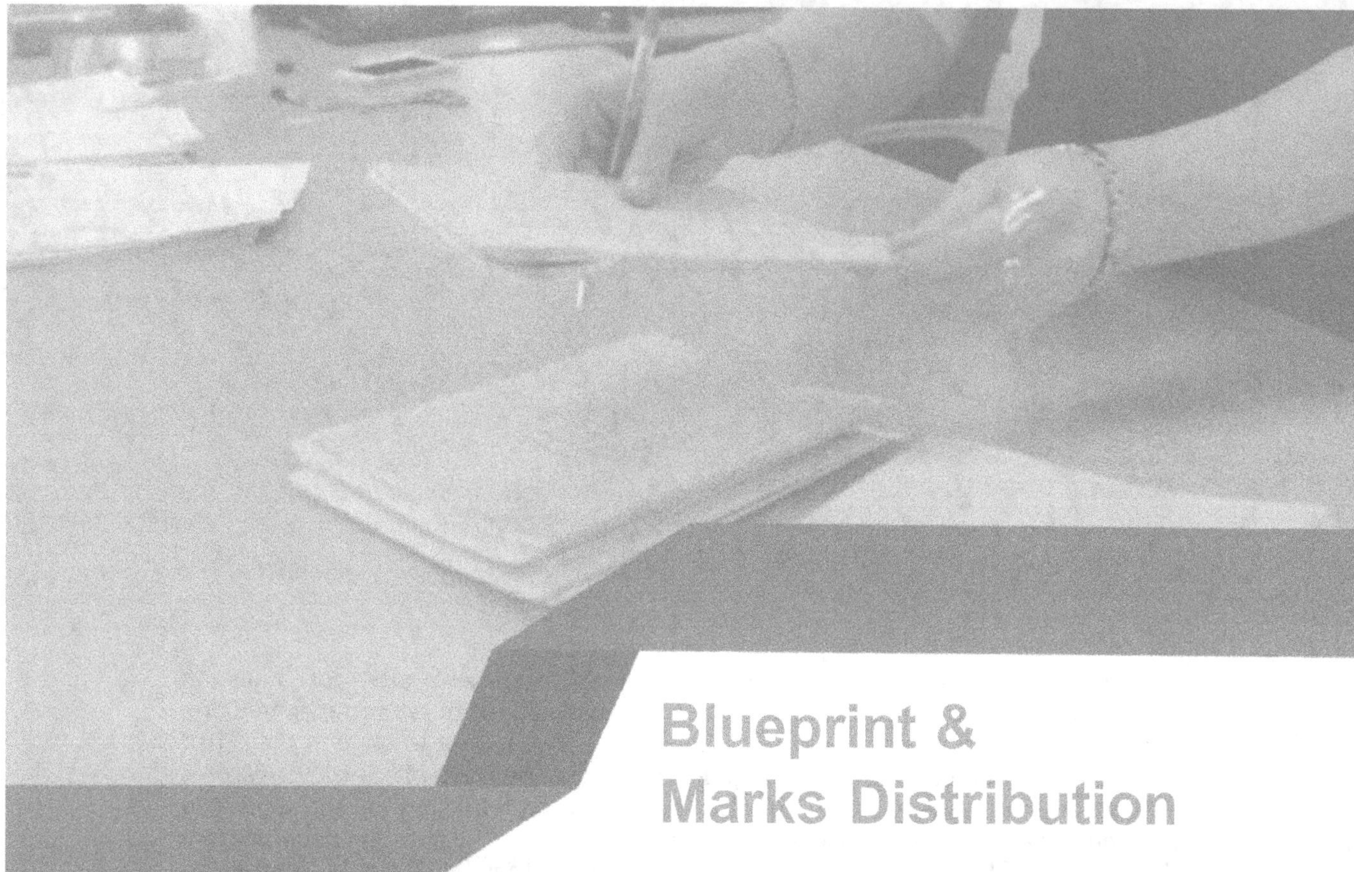

Blueprint & Marks Distribution

Class 12th English 2023-24 Question Paper Design

Section	Competencies	Total marks
Reading Skills	Conceptual understanding, decoding, Analyzing, inferring, interpreting, appreciating, literary, conventions and vocabulary, summarizing and using appropriate format/s.	20
Creative Writing Skills	Conceptual Understanding, application of rules, Analysis, Reasoning, appropriacy of style and tone, using appropriate format and fluency, inference, analysis, evaluation and creativity.	20
Literature Text Books and Supplementary Reading Texts	Recalling, reasoning, critical thinking, appreciating literary convention, inference, analysis, creativity with fluency.	40
	TOTAL	80
	Assessment of Listening and Speaking Skills	10
	Internal Assessment – Listening – Speaking – Project Work	5 5 10
	GRAND TOTAL	100

SECTION A

Reading Skills

Reading Comprehension through Unseen Passage   20 Marks

I.   One unseen passage to assess comprehension, interpretation and inference. Vocabulary and inference of meaning will also be assessed. The passage may be factual, descriptive or literary.   (10x1 = 10 Marks)

II. One unseen case-based passage with verbal/visual inputs like statistical data, charts etc.   (10x1 = 10 Marks)

Note: The combined word limit for both the passages will be 700-750 words.

Multiple Choice Questions / Objective Type Questions will be asked.

SECTION B

III. **Creative Writing Skills**   20 Marks

The section has Short and Long writing tasks.

i.   Notice up to 50 words. One out of the two given questions to be answered. (5 Marks: Format : 1 / Organisation of Ideas: 1/Content : 2 / Accuracy of Spelling and Grammar : 1).

ii. Formal/Informal Invitation and Reply up to 50 words. One out of the two given questions to be answered. (5 Marks: Format : 1 / Organisation of Ideas: 1/Content : 2 / Accuracy of Spelling and Grammar :1).

iii. Letters based on verbal/visual input, to be answered in approximately 120-150 words. Letter types include application for a job with bio data or resume. Letters to the editor (giving suggestions or opinion on issues of public interest) . One out of the two given questions to be answered . (5 Marks: Format : 1 / Organisation of Ideas: 1/Content : 2 / Accuracy of Spelling and Grammar :1).

iv. Article/ Report Writing, descriptive and analytical in nature, based on verbal inputs, to be answered in 120-150 words. One out of the two given questions to be. (5 Marks: Format : 1 / Organisation of Ideas: 1/Content : 2 / Accuracy of Spelling and Grammar :1).

SECTION C

This section will have variety of assessment items including Multiple Choice Questions, Objective Type Questions, Short Answer Type Questions and Long Answer Type Questions to assess comprehension, analysis, interpretation and extrapolation beyond the text.

i.   One Poetry extract out of two from the book Flamingo to assess comprehension, interpretation, analysis and appreciation.   (6x1=6 Marks)

ii. One Prose extract out of two from the book Vistas to assess comprehension, interpretation, analysis and appreciation.   (4x1=4 Marks)

iii. One prose extract out of two from the book Flamingo to assess comprehension, interpretation and analysis.   (6x1=6Marks)

iv. Short answer type question (from Prose and Poetry from the book Flamingo), to be answered in 40-50 words. Questions should elicit inferential responses through critical thinking. Five questions out of the six given are to be answered.   (5x2=10 Marks)

v.   Short answer type question, from Prose (Vistas), to be answered in 40 - 50 words. Questions should elicit inferential responses through critical thinking. Any 2 out of 3 questions to be done.   (2x2=4 Marks)

vi. One Long answer type question, from Prose/Poetry (Flamingo), to be answered in 120-150 words. Questions can be based on incident / theme / passage / extract / event as reference points to assess extrapolation beyond and across the text. The question will elicit analytical and evaluative response from student. Any 1 out of 2 questions to be done.   (1x5=5 Marks)

vii. One Long answer type question, based on the chapters from the book Vistas, to be answered in 120-150 words to assess global comprehension and extrapolation beyond the text. Questions to provide evaluative and analytical responses using incidents, events, themes as reference points. Any 1 out of 2 questions to be done.

(1x5=5 Marks)

Prescribed Books

1. **Flamingo: English Reader** published by National Council of Education Research and Training, New Delhi

   (Prose)

   - The Last Lesson
   - Lost Spring
   - Deep Water
   - The Rattrap
   - Indigo
   - Poets and Pancakes
   - The Interview
   - Going Places

(Poetry)

- My Mother at Sixty-Six
- Keeping Quiet
- A Thing of Beauty
- A Roadside Stand
- Aunt Jennifer's Tigers

2. Vistas: Supplementary Reader published by National Council of Education Research and Training, New Delhi

- The Third Level
- The Tiger King
- Journey to the end of the Earth
- The Enemy
- On the Face of It
- Memories of Childhood
    › The Cutting of My Long Hair
    › We Too are Human Beings

INTERNAL ASSESSMENT

Assessment of Listening Skills - 5 Marks
Assessment of Speaking Skills - 5 Marks
Project Work - 10 Marks

Reading

Summary

Introduction:

A comprehension passage is a text set which is used to test the reader's ability to understand the meaning which is being forwarded through the text and the title of that particular passage. Comprehension should be understood using one's own critical thinking.

One should be familiar with the entire passage to answer the questions asked in the given comprehension as the questions asked in the passage are generally in chronological relationship with the passage. It basically means that the answer to question 1 should ideally be found earlier in the passage than questions 2.

Types of Comprehension Passage:

(*i*) Factual Passages: They contain some facts like historical facts or some achievements attained by somebody. It can also be the report or description of something. It can also contain some instruction regarding something.

(*ii*) Discursive Passages : These passages are argumentative in nature as they often involve opinion.

(*iii*)Literary Passages: These are usually taken from literary pieces.

Tips to know:

Here are some important points that should be followed while attempting an unfamiliar passage:

(*i*) The passage should be read quietly.

(*ii*) To make out the correct sense the complete sentence should be read. It is important to get the main idea before reading the questions.

(*iii*)One should not get nervous with the difficult words used in the passage.

(*iv*) Answer to the given questions should be relevant and to the point and should be written in a complete sentence.

(*v*) The section of the passage which contain the answer to the asked question should be read twice to draw the correct meaning.

(*vi*) The answers should be written in own words as much as possible.

(*vii*) For answering the vocabulary questions, same parts of speech should be used as given in the question.

(*viii*) The order of the questions should be maintained.

PREVIOUS YEARS' EXAMINATION QUESTIONS

1. Read the passage given below and answer the questions that follow:

[DELHI & ALL INDIA 2011]

1. For many years now the Governments have been promising the eradication of child labour in hazardous industries in India. But the truth is that despite all the rhetoric no Government so far has succeeded in eradicating this evil, nor has any could ensure compulsory primary education for every Indian child. Between 60 and 100 million children are still at work instead of going to school and around 10 million are working in hazardous industries. India has the biggest child population of 380 million in the world; plus, the largest number of children who are forced to earn a living.

2. We have many laws that ban child labour in hazardous industries. Per the Child Labour (Prohibition and Regulation) Act 1986, the employment of children below the age of 14 in hazardous occupations has been strictly banned. But each state has different rules regarding the minimum age of employment. This makes implementation of these laws difficult.

3. Also, there is no ban on child labour in non-hazardous occupations. The act applies to the organised or factory sector and not the unorganized or informal sector where most children find employment as cleaners, servants, porters, waiters among other forms of unskilled work. Thus, child labour continues because of the implementation of the existing laws in lax.

4. There are industries, which have a special demand for child labour because of their nimble fingers, high level of concentration and capacity to work hard at abysmally low wages. The carpet industry in U.P. and Kashmir employs children to make hand-knotted carpets. There are 80,000 child workers in Jammu & Kashmir alone. In Kashmir because of the political unrest, children are forced to work while many schools are shut. Industries like gem cutting and polishing pottery and glass want to remain competitive by employing children.

5. The truth is that it is poverty which is pushing children into the brutish labour market. We have 260 million people below the poverty line in India, many of them are women. Poor and especially woman-headed families have no option but to push their little ones in this hard life in hostile conditions, with no human or labour rights.

6. There is a lobby which argues that there is nothing wrong with children working if the environment for work is conducive to learning new skills but studies have shown that the children are made to do boring, repetitive and tedious jobs and are not taught new skills as they grow older. In these hell-holes like the sweet shops of the old, there is no hope.

7. Children working in hazardous industries are prone to debilitating diseases which can cripple them for life. By sitting in cramped, damp and unhygienic spaces, their limbs become deformed for life. Inside matchstick, fireworks and glass industries they are victims of bronchial diseases and TB. Their mental and physical development is permanently impaired by long hours of work. Once trapped, they can't get out of this vicious circle of poverty. They remain uneducated and powerless. Finally, in later years, they too are compelled to send their own children to work. Child labour perpetuates its own nightmare.

8. If at all the Government was serious about granting children their rights, an intensive effort ought to have been made to implement the Supreme Court's Directive of 1997 which laid down punitive action against employers of child labour. Only compulsory primary education can eliminate child labour.

9. Surely, if 380 million children are given a better life and elementary education, India's human capital would be greatly enhanced. But that needs, as former President Abdul Kalam says, "a Second Vision".

[12 marks]

(a) (i) On which two counts has the Government not succeeded so far in respect of children? [2 marks]

(ii) What makes the implementation of child labour law difficult? [2 marks]

(iii) Why do the industries prefer child labour? [2 marks]

(iv) What are the adverse effects of hazardous industries on children? Give any two. [2 marks]

(v) What does the Supreme Court's Directive of 1997 provide? [1 mark]

(b) Find words from the passage which mean the same as the following: [3 marks]

(i) risky/dangerous (para 1)

(ii) very unfriendly (para 5)

2. Read the passage given below and answer the questions that follow: [12 marks]

[DELHI & ALL INDIA 2012]

1. While there is no denying that the world loves a winner, it is important that you recognize the signs of stress in your behaviour and be healthy enough to enjoy your success. Stress can strike anytime, in a fashion that may leave you unaware of its presence in your life. While a certain amount of pressure is necessary for performance, it is important to be able to recognise your individual limit. For instance, there are some individuals who accept competition in a healthy fashion. There are others who collapse into weeping wrecks before an exam or on comparing marks-sheets and finding that their friend has scored better.

2. Stress is a body reaction to any demands or changes in its internal and external environment. Whenever there is a change in the external environment such as temperature, pollutants, humidity and working conditions, it leads to stress. In these days of competition when a person makes up his mind to surpass what has been

achieved by other, leading to an imbalance between demands and resources, it causes psycho-social stress. It is a part and parcel of everyday life.

3. Stress has a different meaning, depending on the stage of life you are in. The loss of a toy or a reprimand from the parents might create a stress shock in a child. An adolescent who fails an examination may feel as if everything has been lost and life has no further meaning. In an adult, the loss of his or her companion, job or profession failure may appear as if there is nothing more to be achieved.

4. Such signs appear in the attitude and behaviour of the individual, as muscle tension in various parts of the body, palpitation and high blood pressure, indigestion and hyperacidity. Ultimately the result is self-destructive behaviour such as eating and drinking too much smoking excessively, relying on tranquillizers. There are other signs of stress such as trembling, shaking, nervous blinking, dryness of throat and mouth and difficulty in swallowing.

5. The professional under stress behaves as if he is a perfectionist. It leads to depression, lethargy and weakness. Periodic mood shifts also indicate the stress status of the students, executives and professionals.

6. In a study sponsored by World Health Organization and carried out by Harvard School of Public Health, the global burden of diseases and injury indicated that stress diseases and accidents are going to be the major killers in 2020.

7. The heart disease and depression-both stress diseases-are going to rank first and second in 2020. Road traffic accidents are going to be the third largest killers. These accidents are also an indicator of psycho-social stress in a fast-moving society. Other stresses like ulcers, hypertension and sleeplessness have assumed epidemic proportions in modern societies.

8. A person under stress reacts in different ways and the common ones are flight, fight and flee depending upon the nature of the stress and capabilities of the person. The three responses can be elegantly chosen to cope with the stress so that stress does not damage the system and become distressed.

9. When a stress crosses the limit peculiar to an individual, it lowers his performance capacity. Frequent crossings of the limit may result in chronic fatigue in which a person feels lethargic disinterested and is not easily motivated to achieve anything. This may make the person mentally undecided, confused and accident prone as well. Sudden exposure to unnerving stress may also result in a loss of memory. Diet, massage, food supplements, herbal medicines, hobbies, relaxation techniques and dance movements are excellent stress busters.

(*a*) (*i*) What is stress? What factors lead to stress?   [2 marks]

(*ii*) What are the signs by which a person can know that he is under stress?

[2 marks]

(*iii*) What are the different diseases a person gets due to stress?   [2 marks]

(*iv*) Give any two examples of stress busters.   [1 mark]

(*v*) How does a person react under stress?

[2 marks]

(*b*) Which words in the above passage mean the same as the following: [3 marks]

(*i*) fall down (para 1)

(*ii*) rebuke (para 3)

(*iii*) inactive (para 9)

3. Read the passage given below and answer the questions that follow:

[DELHI & ALL INDIA 2013]

1. Air pollution is an issue which concerns us all alike. One can willingly choose or reject a food, a drink or a life comfort, but unfortunately, there is little choice for the air we breathe. All, what is there in the air is inhaled by one and all living in those surroundings.

2. Air pollutant is defined as a substance which is present while normally it is not there or presents in an amount exceeding the normal concentrations. It could either be gaseous or a particulate matter. The important and harmful polluting gases are carbon monoxide, carbon dioxide, ozone and oxides of sulphur and nitrogen. The common particulate pollutants are the dust of various

inorganic or organic origins. Although we often talk of the outdoor air pollution caused by industrial and vehicular exhausts, the indoor pollution may prove to be as or a more important cause of health problems.

3. Recognition of air pollution is relatively recent. It is not uncommon to experience a feeling of 'suffocation' in a closed environment. It is often ascribed of the lack of oxygen. Fortunately, however, the composition of air is remarkably constant all over the world. There are about 7.9 per cent nitrogen and 21 per cent oxygen in the air-the other gases forming a very small fraction. It is true that carbon dioxide exhaled out of lungs may accumulate in a closed and over-crowded place. But such an increase is usually small and temporary unless the room is air-tight. Exposure to poisonous gases such as carbon monoxide may occur in a closed room, heated by burning coal inside. This may also prove to be fatal.

4. What is more common in a poorly ventilated home is a vague constellation of symptoms described as the sick-building syndrome. It is characterized by a general feeling of malaise, head-ache, dizziness and irritation of mucous membranes. It may also be accompanied by nausea, itching, aches, pains and depression. Sick building syndrome is getting commoner in big cities with the small houses, which are generally over-furnished. Some of the important pollutants whose indoor concentrations exceed those of the outdoors include gases such as carbon monoxide, carbon dioxide, oxides of nitrogen and organic substances like spores, formaldehydes, hydrocarbon aerosols and allergens. The sources are attributed to a variety of construction materials, insulations, furnishings, adhesives, cosmetics, house dust, fungi and other indoor products.

5. By-products of fuel combustion are important in houses with indoor kitchens. It is not only the burning of dried dung and fuel-wood which is responsible but also kerosene and liquid petroleum gas. Oxides of both nitrogen and sulphur are released from their combustion.

6. Smoking of tobacco in the closed environment is an important source of indoor pollution. It may not be high quantitatively, but significantly hazardous for health. It is because of the fact that there are over 3000 chemical constituents in tobacco smoke, which have been identified. These are harmful to human health.

7. Micro-organisms and allergens are of special significance in the causation and spread of diseases. Most of the infective illnesses may involve more persons of a family living in common indoor environment. These include viral and bacterial diseases like tuberculosis.

8. Besides infections, allergic and hypersensitivity disorders are spreading fast. Although asthma is the most common form of respiratory allergic disorders, pneumonia are not uncommon, but more persistent and serious. These are attributed to exposures to allergens from various fungi, moulds, hay and other organic materials. Indoor air ventilation systems; coolers, air-conditioners, dampness, decay, pet animals, production or handling of the causative items are responsible for these hypersensitivity-diseases.

9. Obviously, the spectrum of pollution is very wide and our options are limited. Indoor pollution may be handled relatively easily by an individual. Moreover, the good work must start from one's own house.

(a) (i) What is an air pollutant? [1 mark]

(ii) In what forms are the air pollutants present? [2 marks]

(iii) Why do we feel suffocated in a closed environment? [1 mark]

(iv) What is sick building syndrome? How is it increasing? [2 marks]

(v) How is indoor smoking hazardous? [1 mark]

(vi) How can one overcome the dangers of indoor air pollution? [2 marks]

(b) Find the words from the above passage which mean the same as the following: [3 marks]

(i) giddiness (para 4)

(ii) constant (para 8)

(iii) humidity (para,8)

4. Read the passage given below and answer the questions that follow: [8 marks]

The term dietary fibres refer collectively to indigestible carbohydrates present in plant foods. The importance of these dietary fibres came into the picture when it was observed that the people having a diet rich in these fibres, had low incidence of coronary heart disease, irritable bowel syndrome, dental caries and gall stones.

The foodstuffs rich in these dietary fibres are cereals and grains, legumes, fruits with seeds, citrus fruits, carrots, cabbage, green leafy vegetables, apples, melons, peaches, pears etc.

These dietary fibres are not digested by the enzymes of the stomach and the small intestine whereas most of other carbohydrates like starch and sugar are digested and absorbed. The dietary fibres have the property of holding water and because of it, these get swollen and behave like a sponge as these pass through the gastrointestinal tract. The fibres add bulk to the diet and increase transit time in the gut. Some of these fibres may undergo fermentation in the colon. In recent years, it has been considered essential to have some amount of fibres in the diet. Their beneficial effects lie in preventing coronary heart disease, and decreasing cholesterol level. The fibres like gums and pectin are reported to decrease post-prandial (after meals) glucose level in blood. These types of dietary fibres are recommended for the management of certain types of diabetes. Recent studies have shown that the fenugreek (Methi) seeds, which contain 40 per cent Burn, are effective in decreasing blood glucose and cholesterol levels as compared to other gum containing vegetables.

Some dietary fibres increase transit time and decrease the time or release of ingested food in colon. The diet having less fibre is associated with colon cancer and the dietary fibres may play a role in decreasing the risk of it.

The dietary fibres hold water so that stools are soft, bulky and readily eliminated. Therefore, high fibre intake prevents or relieves constipation. The fibres increase motility of the small intestine and the colon and by decreasing the transit time there 'is less time for exposure of the mucosa to harmful toxic substances.

Therefore, there is a less desire to eat and the energy intake can be maintained within the range of requirement. This phenomenon helps in keeping a check on obesity. Another reason in helping to decrease obesity is that the high-fibre diets have somewhat lower coefficients of digestibility.

The dietary fibres may have some adverse effects on nutrition by binding some trace metals like calcium, magnesium, phosphorus, zinc and others and therefore preventing their proper absorption. This may pose a possibility of nutritional deficiency especially when diets contain marginal levels of mineral elements. This may become important constraints on increasing dietary fibres. It is suggested that an intake of 40 grams dietary fibres per day is desirable.

(Extracted from 'The Tribune')

(a) On the basis of your reading of the above passage make notes on it in recognizable abbreviations wherever necessary. Also, suggest a suitable title.

(b) Write a summary of the above in about 80 words.   [3 marks]

5. Read the following passage and answer the questions that follow: [12 marks]

1. Too many parents these days can't say no. As a result, they find themselves raising, children, who respond greedily to the advertisements aimed right at them. Even getting what they want doesn't satisfy some kids; they only want more. Now, a growing number of psychologists, educators and parents think it's time to stop the madness and start teaching kids about what's really important: values like hard work, contentment, honesty and compassion. The struggle to set limits has never been tougher and the stakes have never been higher. One recent study of adults who were overindulged as children paint a discouraging picture of their future: when given too much too soon they grow up to be adults who have difficulty coping with life's disappointments. They also have distorted sense of entitlement that gets in the way of success in the workplace and in relationships.

2. Psychologists say that parents who overindulge their kids set them up to be more vulnerable to future anxiety and depression. Today's parents themselves raised on values of thrift and self-sacrifice, grew up in a culture where no was a household word. Today's kids want much more, partly because there is so much more to want. The oldest members of this generation were born in the late 1980s, just as pcs and video games were making them assault on the family room. They think of MP3 players and flat-screen TV as essential utilities, and they have developed strategies to get them. One survey of teenagers found that when they crave for something new most expect to ask nine times before their parents give in. By every measure, parents are shelling out record amounts. In the heat of this buying blitz, even parents who desperately need to say no find themselves reaching for their credit cards.

3. Today's parents aren't equipped to deal with the problem. Many of them, raised in the 1960s and '70s, swore they'd act differently from their parents and have closer relationships with their own children. Many even wear the same designer clothes as their kids and listen to the same music. And they work more hours; at the end of a long week, it's tempting to buy peace with 'yes' and not mar precious family time with conflict. Anxiety about future is another factor. How do well intentioned parents say no to all the sports gear and arts and language lessons they believe will help their kids thrive in an increasingly competitive world? Experts agree: too much love won't spoil a child. Too few limits will.

4. What parents need to find, is a balance between the advantages of an affluent society and the critical life lessons that come from waiting, saving and working hard to achieve goals. That search for balance must start early. Children need limits on their behaviour because they feel better and more secure when they live within a secured structure. Older children learn self-control by watching how others, especially parents act. Learning how to overcome challenges is essential to becoming a successful adult. Few parents ask kids to do chores. They

think their kids are already overburdened by social and academic pressures. Every individual can be of service to others, and life has meaning beyond one's own immediate happiness. That means parents are eager to teach values have to take a long, hard look at their own.

(a) Answer the following:
   (1) What values do parents and teachers want children to learn?   [2 marks]
   (2) What are the results of giving the children too much too soon?
   [2 marks]
   (3) Why do today's children want more?
   [1 mark]
   (4) What is the balance which the parents need to have in today's world?
   [2 marks]
   (5) What is the necessity to set limits for children?   [2 marks]

(b) Pick out words from the passage that mean the same as the following: [3 marks]
   (1) a feeling of satisfaction (para 1)
   (2) valuable (para 3)
   (3) important (para 4)

6. Read the passage given below carefully:
   [12 marks]

[DELHI & ALL INDIA 2015]

1. For four days, I walked through the narrow lanes of the old city, enjoying the romance of being in a city where history still lives — in its cobblestone streets and in its people riding asses, carrying vine leaves and palm as they once did during the time of Christ.

2. This is Jerusalem, home to the sacred sites of Christianity, Islam and Judaism. This is the place that houses the church of the Holy Sepulchre, the place where Jesus was finally laid to rest. This is also the site of Christ's crucifixion, burial and resurrection.

3. Built by the Roman Emperor Constantine at the site of an earlier temple to Aphrodite, it is the most venerated Christian shrine in the world. And justifiably so. Here, within the church, are the last five stations of the cross, the 10th station where Jesus was stripped of his clothes, the 11th where he was nailed to the cross, the 12th where he died on the cross, the 13th where the body was removed from the cross, and the 14th, his tomb.

4. For all this weighty tradition, the approach and entrance to the church is non-descript. You have to ask for directions. Even to the devout Christian pilgrims walking along the Via Dolorosa – the Way of Sorrows – first nine stations look clueless. Then a courtyard appears, hemmed in by other buildings and a doorway to one side. This leads to a vast area of huge stone architecture.

5. Immediately inside the entrance is your first stop. It's the stone of anointing: this is the place, according to Greek tradition, where Christ was removed from the cross. The Roman Catholics, however, believe it to be the spot where Jesus' body was prepared for burial by Joseph.

6. What happened next? Jesus was buried. He was taken to a place outside the city of Jerusalem where other graves existed and there, he was buried in a cave. However, all that is long gone, destroyed by continued attacks and rebuilding; what remains is the massive — and impressive — Rotunda (a round building with a dome) that Emperor Constantine built. Under this, and right in the centre of the Rotunda, is the structure that contains the Holy Sepulchre.

7. "How do you know that this is Jesus' tomb?" I asked one of the pilgrims standing next to me. He was clueless, more interested, like the rest of them, in the novelty of it all and in photographing it, than in its history or tradition.

8. At the start of the first century, the place was a disused quarry outside the city walls. According to the gospels, Jesus' crucifixion occurred 'at a place outside the city walls with graves nearby......'. Archaeologists have discovered tombs from that era, so the site is compatible with the biblical period.

9. The structure at the site is a marble tomb built over the original burial chamber. It has two rooms, and you enter four at a time into the first of these, the Chapel of the Angel. Here the angel is supposed to have sat on a stone to recount Christ's resurrection. A low door made of white marble, partly worn away by pilgrims' hands, leads to a smaller chamber inside. This is the 'room of the tomb', the place where Jesus was buried.

10. We entered in single file. On my right was a large marble slab that covered the 0riginal rock bench on which the body of Jesus was laid. A woman knelt and prayed. Her eyes were wet with tears. She pressed her face against the slab to hide them, but it only made it worse.

On the basis of your understanding of this passage answer the following questions with the help of given options: [4 marks]

(a) How does Jerusalem still retain the charm of ancient era?
   (i) There are narrow lanes
   (ii) Roads are paved with cobblestones
   (iii) People can be seen riding asses
   (iv) All of the above

(b) Holy Sepulchre is sacred to________
   (i) Christianity
   (ii) Islam
   (iii) Judaism
   (iv) Both (i) and (iii)

(c) Why does one have to constantly ask for directions to the church?
   (i) Its lanes are narrow
   (ii) Entrance to the church is nondescript
   (iii) People are not tourist- friendly
   (iv) Everyone is lost in enjoying the romance of the place

(d) Where was Jesus buried?
   (i) In a cave
   (ii) At a place outside the city
   (iii) In the Holy Sepulchre
   (iv) Both (i) and (ii)

Answer the following questions briefly:
[6 marks]

(e) What is the Greek belief about the 'stone of anointing'?

(f) Why did Emperor Constantine build the Rotunda?

(g) What is the general attitude of the pilgrims?

(h) How is the site compatible with the biblical period?

(i) Why did the pilgrims enter the room of the tomb in a single file?

(j) Why did a woman 'try to hide her tears?

(k) Find words from the passage which mean the same as: [2 marks]

(i) A large grave (para 3)

(ii) Having no interesting features/dull (para 4)

7. Read the passage given below: [10 marks]

[DELHI & ALL INDIA 2015]

1. We often make all things around us the way we want them. Even during our pilgrimages we have begun to look for whatever makes our heart happy, gives comfort to our body and peace to the mind. It is as if external solutions will fulfil our needs, and we do not want to make any special efforts even in our spiritual search. Our mind is resourceful-it works to find shortcuts in simple and easy ways.

2. Even pilgrimages have been converted into tourism opportunities. Instead, we must awaken our conscience and souls and understand the truth. Let us not tamper with either our own nature or that of the Supreme.

3. All our cleverness is rendered ineffective when nature does a dance of destruction. Its fury can and will wash away all imperfections. Indian culture, based on Vedic treatises, assists in human evolution, but we are now using our entire energy in distorting these traditions according to our convenience instead of making efforts to make ourselves worthy of them.

4. The irony is that humans are not even aware of the complacent attitude they have allowed themselves to sink to. Nature is everyone's Amma and her fierce blows will sooner or later corner us and force us to understand this truth. Earlier, pilgrimages to places of spiritual significance were rituals that were undertaken when people became free from their worldly duties. Even now some seekers take up this pious religious journey as a path to peace and knowledge. Anyone travelling with this attitude feels and travels with only a few essential items that his body can carry. Pilgrims traditionally travelled light, on foot, eating light, dried chickpeas and fruits, or whatever was available. Pilgrims of olden days did not feel the need to stay in special AC bedrooms, or travel by luxury cars or indulge themselves with delicious food and savouries.

5. Pilgrims traditionally moved ahead, creating a feeling of belonging towards all, conveying a message of brotherhood among all they came across whether in small caves, ashrams or local settlements. They received the blessings and congregations of yogis and mahatma's in return while conducting the dharma of their pilgrimage. A pilgrimage is like penance or sadhana to stay near nature and to experience a feeling of oneness with it, to keep the body healthy and fulfilled with the amount of food, while seeking freedom from attachments and yet remaining happy while staying away from relatives and associates.

6. This is how a pilgrimage should be rather than making it like a picnic by taking a large group along and living in comfort, packing in entertainment, and tampering with the environment. What is worse is giving a boost to the ego of having had a special darshan. Now alms are distributed, charity done while they brag about their spiritual experiences!

7. We must embark on our spiritual journey by first understanding the grace and significance of a pilgrimage and following it up with the prescribed rules and rituals-this is what translates into the ultimate and beautiful medium of spiritual evolution. There is no justification for tampering with nature.

8. A pilgrimage is symbolic of contemplation and meditation and acceptance, and is a metaphor for the constant growth or movement and love for nature that we should hold in our hearts.

9. This is the truth!

On the basis of your understanding of the above passage: answer the questions that follow with the help of given options: [2 marks]

(a) How can a pilgrim keep his body healthy?

   (i) By travelling light

   (ii) By eating a small amount of food

   (iii) By keeping free from attachments

   (iv) Both (i) and (ii)

(b) How do we satisfy our ego?

(i) By having a special darshan

(ii) By distributing alms

(iii) By treating it like a picnic

(iv) Both (i) and (ii)

Answer the following as briefly as possible:

[6 marks]

(*c*) What change has taken place in our attitude towards pilgrimages?

(*d*) What happens when pilgrimages are turned into picnics?

(*e*) Why are we complacent in our spiritual efforts?

(*f*) How does nature respond when we try to be clever with it?

(*g*) In olden days with what attitude did people go on a pilgrimage?

(*h*) What message does the passage convey to the pilgrims?

(*i*) Find words from the Passage which mean the same as the following:

[2 marks]

(*i*)   made/turned (para 3)

(*ii*) very satisfied (Para 4)

8. Title - Listening Verses Hearing

Read the passage given below: [12 marks]

[DELHI & ALL INDIA 2016]

1. Maharana Pratap ruled over Mewar only for 25 years. However, he accomplished so much grandeur during his reign that his glory surpassed the boundaries of countries and time turning him into an immortal personality. He along with his kingdom became a synonym for valor, sacrifice and patriotism. Mewar had been a leading Rajput kingdom even before Maharana Pratap occupied the throne' Kings of Mewar, with the cooperation of their nobles and subjects, had established such traditions in the kingdom, as augmented them magnificence despite the hurdles of having a smaller area under their command and less population. There did come a few thorny occasions where the flag of the kingdom seemed sliding down. Their flag once again heaved high in the sky thanks to the gallantry and brilliance of the People of Mewar.

2. The destiny of Mewar was good in the sense that barring a few kings, most of the rulers were competent and patriotic. This glorious tradition of the kingdom almost continued for 1500 years since its establishment, right from the reign of Bappa Rawal. In fact, only 60 Years before Maharana Pratap, Rana Sagna drove the kingdom to the pinnacle of fame. His reputation went beyond Rajasthan and reached Delhi. Two generations before him, Rana Kumbha had given a new status to the kingdom through victories and development work. During his reign, literature and art also progressed extraordinarily. Ratna himself was inclined towards writing and his works are read with reverence even today. The ambience of his kingdom was conducive to the creation of high-quality work of art and literature These accomplishments were the outcome of a longstanding tradition sustained by several generations.

3. The life of the people of Mewar must have been peaceful and prosperous during the Long span of time; otherwise such extraordinary accomplishment in these fields would not have been possible. This is reflected in their art and literature as well as their loving nature. They compensate for lack of admirable physique their firm but pleasant nature. The ambience of Mewar remains lovely thanks to the cheerful and liberal character of its people.

4. One may observe astonishing pieces of workmanship not only in the forts and palaces of Mewar but also in public utility buildings. Ruins of many structures which are still standing tall in their grandeur are testimony to the fact that Mewar was not only the land of the brave but also art flourished and creative pursuits of literature and artists did not suffer. Imagine, glorious the period must have been when the Vijaya Stambha which is the sample of our great ancient architecture even today, was constructed. In the same fort, Kirti Stambha is standing high, reflecting how liberal the then administration was which allowed people from other communities and kingdoms to come and carry out construction work. It is useless to indulge in the debate whether the Vijaya Stambha was constructed first or the Kirti Stambha. The fact is that both the capitals are standing side by side and reveal the proximity between the king and the subjects of Mewar.

5. The cycle of time does not remain the same. Whereas, the reign of Rana Sanga was crucial in raising the kingdom to the acme of glory, it also proved to be his nemesis. History took a turn. The fortune of Mewar the land of the brave, started waning. Rana tried to save the day with his acumen, which was running against the stream and the glorious traditions for sometimes.

On the basis of your understanding of the above passage answer each of the questions given below with the help of the options that follow:

[4 marks]

(a) Maharana Pratap becomes immortal because:

   (i) he ruled Mewar for 25 years.

   (ii) he added a lot of grandeur to Mewar.

   (iii) of his valour, sacrifice and patriotism.

   (iv) both (ii) and (iii).

(b) Difficulties in the way of Mewar were:

   (i) lack of cooperation of the nobility.

   (ii) ancient traditions of the kingdom.

   (iii) its small area and small population.

   (iv) the poverty of the subjects

(c) During thorny occasions:

   (i) the flag of Mewar seemed to be lowered.

   (ii) the flag of Mewar was hoisted high.

   (iii) the people of Mewar showed gallantry.

   (iv) most of the rulers heaved a sigh of relief.

(d) Mewar was lucky because:

   (i) all of its rulers were competent.

   (ii) most of its people were competent.

   (iii) most of its rulers were competent.

   (iv) only a few of its people were incompetent.

Answer the following question briefly:

[6 marks]

(e) Who is the earliest king of Mewar mentioned in the passage?

(f) What was Rana Kumbha's contribution to the glory of Mewar?

(g) What does the writer find worth admiration in the people of Mewar?

(h) How could art and literature flourish in Mewar?

(i) How did the rulers show that they cared for their subjects?

(j) What does the erection of Vijaya Stambha and Kirti Stambha in the same fort signify?

(k) Find words from the passage which mean the same as each of the following:

   (i) surprising (para 4)

   (ii) evidence (para 4)

9. Read the passage given below: [10 marks]
[DELHI & ALL INDIA 2016]

1. To ensure its perpetuity, the ground is well held by the panther both in space and time. It enjoys a much wider distribution over the globe than its bigger cousins, and procreates sufficiently profusely to ensure its continuity for all time to come.

2. There seems to be no breeding season of the panther, although its sawing and caterwauling is more frequently heard during winter and summer. The gestation period is about ninety to hundred days (ninety-two days). The litter normally consists of four cubs, rarely five. Of these, generally, two survive and not more than one reaches maturity I have never come across more than two cubs at the heels of the mother. Likewise, graziers in the forest have generally found only two cubs hidden away among rocks, hollows of trees, and other impossible places.

3. Panther cubs are generally in evidence in March. They are born blind. This is a provision of nature against their drifting away from the place of safety in which they are lodged by their mother, and exposing themselves to the danger of there being devoured by hyenas, jackals, and other predators. They generally open their eyes in about three to four weeks.

4. The mother alone rears its cubs in seclusion. It keeps them out of the reach of the impulsive and impatient male. As a matter of fact, the mother separates from the male soon after mating and forgets all about their tumultuous union. The story that the male often looks in to find out how the mother is progressing with her cubs has no foundation except in what we wish it should do at least.

5. The mother carries its cubs about by holding them by the scruff of their neck in its mouth. It trains them to stalk, and teaches them how to deliver the bite of death to the prey. The cubs learn to treat all and sundry with suspicion at their mother's heels. Instinctively the cubs seek seclusion, keep to cover and protect their flanks by walking along the edge of the forest.

6. I have never had an opportunity to watch mother panther train its cubs. But in Pilibhit forests, I once saw a tigress giving some lessons to its little ones. I was sitting over its kill of Mala. As the sun set, the tigress materialized in the twilight behind my machan. For about an - hour, it scanned and surveyed the entire area looking and listening with the gravest concern. It even went to the road where my elephant was awaiting my signal. The mahout spotted it from a distance and drove the elephant away.

7. When darkness descended upon the scene and all was well and safe, the tigress called its cubs by emitting a low howl. The cubs, two in number and bigger than a full-grown cat, soon responded. They came trotting up to their mother and hurried straight to the kill in indecent haste. The mother spitted at them-so furiously that they doubled back to its heels immediately. Thereafter, the mother and its cubs sat under cover about 50 feet (15 m) away from the kill to watch, wait to look and listen. After about half an hour's patient and fidget less vigil the mother seemed to say 'paid for'. At this signal, the cubs cautiously advanced covering their flanks, towards the kill. No longer did they make a beeline for it, as they had done before.

8. The mother sat watching its cubs eat, and mounted guard on them. She did not partake of the meals.

On the basis of your understanding of the passage complete the statements given below with the help of options that follow:

[2 marks]

(a) To protect its cubs, the mother panther hides them:
  (i) among rocks.
  (ii) in the branches of the trees.
  (iii) behind the tree trunks.
  (iv) at its heels.

(b) The male panther:
  (i) is protective of its cubs.
  (ii) trains its cubs.
  (iii) watches the progress of the mother.
  (iv) is impulsive and impatient.

Answer the following questions briefly:

[6 marks]

(c) How many cubs does the mother panther rarely deliver?

(d) What may happen if the panther cubs are not born blind?

(e) Why did the mahouts dive his elephant away?

(f) Why did the tigress spit at its cubs?

(g) From the narrator's observation, what do we learn about the nature of the tigers?

(h) Why does the panther not face the risk of extinction?

(i) Find words from the passage which mean the same as each of the following:

[2 marks]

(a) moving aimlessly (para 3)

(b) came down/fell (para7)

10. Read the passage given below and answer the questions that follow:

[DELHI & ALL INDIA 2017]

1. We sit in the last row, bumped about but free of stares. The bus rolls out of the dull crossroads of the city, and we are soon in open countryside, with fields of sunflowers as far as the eye can see, their heads all facing us. Where there is no water, the land reverts to desert. While still on level ground we see in the distance the tall range of the Mount Bogda, abrupt like a shining prism laid horizontally on the desert surface. It is over 5,000 metres high, and the peaks are under permanent snow, in powerful contrast to the flat desert all around. Heaven Lake lies part of the way up this range, about 2,000 metres above sea level, at the foot of one of the higher snow-peaks.

2. As the bus climbs, the sky, brilliant before, grows overcast. I have brought nothing warm to wear: it is all down at the hotel in Urumqi. Rain begins to fall. The man behind me is eating overpoweringly smelly goat's cheese. The bus window leaks inhospitably but reveals a beautiful view. We have passed quickly from desert through arable land to pasture, and the ground is now green with grass, the slopes dark with pine. A few cattle drink from a clear stream flowing past moss-covered stones; it is a Constable landscape. The stream hanges into a white torrent, and as we climb higher I wished more and more that I had brought with me something

warmer than the pair of shorts that have served me so well in the desert. The stream (which, we are told, rises in Heaven Lake) disappears, and we continue our slow ascent. About noon, we arrive at Heaven Lake, and look for a place to stay at the foot, which is the resort area. We get a room in a small cottage, and I am happy to note that there are thick quilts on the beds.

3. Standing outside the cottage we survey our surroundings. Heaven Lake is long, sardine-shaped and fed by snowmelt from a stream at its head. The lake is an intense blue, surrounded on all sides by green mountain walls, dotted with distant sheep. At the head of the lake, beyond the delta of the inflowing stream, is a massive snow-capped peak which dominates the vista; it is part of a series of peaks that culminate, a little out of view, in Mount Bogda itself.

4. For those who live in the resort, there is a small mess-hall by the shore. We eat here sometimes and sometimes buy food from the vendors outside, who sell kabab and naan until the last bus leaves. The kababs, cooked on skewers over charcoal braziers, are particularly good; highly spiced and well-done. Horse's milk is available too from the local Kazakh herdsmen, but I decline this. I am so affected by the cold that Mr. Cao, the relaxed young man who runs the mess, lends me a spare pair of trousers, several sizes too large but more than comfortable. Once I am warm again, I feel a pre-dinner spurt of energy – dinner will be long in coming – and I ask him whether the lake is good for swimming in.

5. "Swimming?" Mr. Cao says. "You aren't thinking of swimming, are you?"

6. "I thought I might," I confess. "What's the water like?"

7. He doesn't answer me immediately, turning instead to examine some receipts with exaggerated interest. Mr. Cao, with great off-handedness, addresses the air. "People are often drowned here," he says. After a pause, he continues. "When was the last one?" This question is directed at the cook, who is preparing a tray of mantou (squat white steamed bread rolls), and who now

appears, wiping his doughy hand across his forehead. "Was it the Beijing athlete?" asks Mr. Cao.

On the basis of your understanding of the above passage, complete the statements given below with the help of options that follow:

(*a*) One benefit of sitting in the last row of the bus was that:

  (*i*)   the narrator enjoyed the bumps.

  (*ii*) no one stared at him.

  (*iii*) he could see the sunflowers.

  (*iv*) he avoided the dullness of the city.

(*b*) The narrator was travelling to:

  (*i*)   Mount Bogda

  (*ii*) Heaven Lake

  (*iii*) a 2000 metre high snow peak

  (*iv*) Urumqi

(*c*) On reaching the destination the narrator felt relieved because:

  (*i*)   he had got away from the desert.

  (*ii*) a difficult journey had come to an end.

  (*iii*) he could watch the snow peak.

  (*iv*) there were thick quilts on the bed.

(*d*) Mount Bogda is compared to :

  (*i*)   a horizontal desert surface

  (*ii*) a shining prism

  (*iii*) a Constable landscape

  (*iv*) the overcast sky

Answer the following questions briefly:

(*e*) Which two things in the bus made the narrator feel uncomfortable?

(*f*) What made the scene look like a Constable landscape?

(*g*) What did he regret as the bus climbed higher?

(*h*) Why did the narrator like to buy food from outside?

(*i*) What is ironic about the pair of trousers lent by Mr Cao?

(*j*) Why did Mr Cao not like the narrator to swim in the lake?

(*k*) Find words from the passage which mean the same as the following:

  (*i*)   sellers (para 4)

  (*ii*) increased (para 7)

11. Read the passage given below and answer the questions that follow: [10 marks]

[DELHI & ALL INDIA 2017]

1. Thackeray reached Kittur along with a small British army force and a few of his officers. He thought that the very presence of the British on the outskirts of Kittur would terrorise the rulers and people of Kittur and that they would lay down their arms. He was quite confident that he would be able to crush the revolt in no time. He ordered that tents be erected on the eastern side for the fighting forces and a little away on the western slopes tents be put up for the family members of the officers who had accompanied them. During the afternoon and evening of 20th October, the British soldiers were busy making arrangements for these camps.

2. On the 21st morning, Thackeray sent his political assistants to Kittur fort to obtain a written assurance from all the important officers of Kittur rendering them answerable for the security of the treasury of Kittur. They, accordingly, met Sardar Gurusiddappa and other officers of Kittur and asked them to comply with the orders of Thackeray. They did not know that the people were in a defiant mood. The commanders of Kittur dismissed the agent's orders as no documents could be signed without sanction from Rani Chennamma.

3. Thackeray was enraged and sent for his commander of the Horse Artillery, which was about 100 strong, ordered him to rush his artillery into the fort and capture the commanders of the Desai's army. When the Horse Artillery stormed into the fort, Sardar Gurusiddappa, who had kept his men on full alert, promptly commanded his men to repel and chase them away. The Kittur forces made a bold front and overpowered the British soldiers.

4. In the meanwhile, the Desai's guards had shut the gates of the fort and the British Horse Artillery men, being completely overrun and routed, had to get out through the escape window. Rani's soldiers chased them out of the fort, killing a few of them until they retreated to their camps on the outskirts.

5. A few of the British had found refuge in some private residences, while some were hiding in their tents. The Kittur soldiers captured about forty persons and brought them to the palace. These included twelve children and a few women from the British officers' camp. When they were brought in the presence of the Rani, she ordered the soldiers to be imprisoned. For the women and children she had only gentleness, and admonished her soldiers for taking them into custody. At her orders, these women and children were taken inside the palace and given food and shelter. Rani came down from her throne, patted the children lovingly and told them that no harm would come to them.

6. She, then, sent a word through a messenger to Thackeray that the British women and children were safe and could be taken back any time. Seeing this noble gesture of the Rani, he was moved. He wanted to meet this gracious lady and talk to her. He even thought of trying to persuade her to enter into an agreement with the British to stop all hostilities in lieu of an inam (prize) of eleven villages. His offer was dismissed with a gesture of contempt. She had no wish to meet Thackeray. That night she called Sardar Gurusiddappa and other leading Sardars and after discussing all the issues came to the conclusion that there was no point in meeting Thackeray who had come with an army to threaten Kittur into submission to British sovereignty.

On the basis of your understanding of the above passage complete the statements given below with the help of options that follow:

(a) Thackeray was a/an:

    (i) British tourist

    (ii) army officer

    (iii) adviser to Rani of Kittur

    (iv) treasury officer

(b) British women and children came to Kittur to:

    (i) visit Kittur

    (ii) enjoy life in tents

    (iii) stay in the palace

    (iv) give company to officers

Answer the following questions briefly:

(c) Why did Thackeray come to Kittur?

(d) Why did the Kittur officials refuse to give the desired assurance to Thackeray?

(e) What happened to the Horse Artillery?

(f) How do we know that the Rani was a noble queen?

(g) How in your opinion would the British women have felt after meeting the Rani?

(h) Why did the Rani refuse to meet Thackeray?

(i) Find words from the passage which mean the same as the following:

    i.   entered forcibly (para 3)

    ii. aggressive / refusing to obey (para 2)

12. Read the passage given below   [12 Marks]

[DELHI & ALL INDIA 2018]

1. When you grow up in a place where it rains five months a year, wise elders help you to get acquainted with the rain early. They teach you that it is ignorant to think that it is the same rain falling every day. Oh no, the rain is always doing different things at different times. there is rain that is gentle, and there is also rain the falls too hard and damages the crops. Hence, the prayer for the sweet rain that helps the crops to grow.

2. The monsoon in the Naga hills goes by the native name, khuthotei (which means the rice-growing season). It lasts from May to early or mid-October. The local residents firmly believe that Durga Puja in October announces the end of rain. After that, one might expect a couple of short winter showers, and the spring showers in March and April. Finally, comes the "big rain" in May; proper rainstorms accompanied by heat-stopping lightning the ear-splitting thunder. I have stood out in storms looking at lightning arc across dark skies, a light-and-sound show that can go on for hours.

3. This is the season when people use the word sezuo or suzu to refer to the week-long rains, when clothes don't dry and smell of mould, when fungus forms on the floor and when you can't see the moon or the stars because of the rainclouds. But you learn not to complain. Rain, after all, is the farmer's friend and brings food to the table. Rituals and festivals centre around the agricultural rhythm of life, which is the occupation of about 70 percent of the population.

4. The wise learn to understand its ways. I grew up hearing my grandfather say, "It's very windy this year. We'll get good rain." If the windy season was short and weak, he worried there might not be enough rain for the crops. I learned the interconnectedness of the seasons from childhood, and marvelled at how the wind could bring rain. Another evening, many rainy seasons ago, my paternal aunt observed the new moon and worried, "Its legs are in the air, we're in for some heavy rain." She was right. That week, a storm cut off power lines and brought down trees and bamboos.

5. Eskimos boast of having a hundred names for show. Norwegians in the north can describe all kinds of snow by an equal amount of names : pudder, powder snow, wet snow, slaps, extra wet snow, tight snowfall, dry snow, and at least 95 more categories of snow. Likewise, in India we have names and names for rain. Some are common, some are passing into history.

6. The rains are also called after flowering plants and people believe that the blossoming of those plants draws out rain. Once the monsoons set in, field work is carried out in earnest and the work of uprooting and transplanting paddy in flooded terrace fields is done. The months of hard labour and June, July and August. In August, as the phrougu plant begins to bloom, a rain will fall. This August rain, also called phrogu, is a sign that the time for cultivation is over. If any new grain seeds are sown, they may not sprout; even if they do sprout, they are not likely to bear grain. The rain acts as a kind of farmer's almanac.

7. The urban population of school-goers and office-goers naturally dislike the monsoon and its accompanying problems of landslides, muddy streets and periodic infections. For non-farmers, the month of September can be depressing, when the rainfall is incessant and the awareness persists that the monsoons will last out till October. One needs to have the heart of a farmer to remain grateful for the watery

days, and be able to observe — from what seems to the inexperienced as a continuous downpour — the many kinds of rain. Some of the commonly known rain-weeks are named after the plants that alternately bloom in August and September. The native belief is that the flowers draw out the rain.

8. Each rain period has a job to fulfil: October rain helps garlic bulbs to form, while kumunyo rain helps the rice bear grain.. Without it, the ears of rice cannot form properly. End October is the most beautiful month in the Naga hills, as the fields turn gold and wild sunflowers bloom over the slopes, all heralding the harvest. prayers go up for protecting the fields from storms, and the rains to retreat because the grain needs to stand in the sun and ripen. The cycle nears completion a few weeks before the harvest, and the rain does retreat so thoroughly from the reaped furrows that the earth quickly turns hard. The months of rain become a distant memory until it starts all over again.

On the basis of your understanding of the above passage, complete the statements given below with the help of options that follows:

[4 marks]

(*a*) The rains are called after flowering plants because

   (*i*)   heavy rains kill plants

   (*ii*)   flowers grow in the rainy season

   (*iii*)   it is believed that the plants bring the rain

   (*iv*) flowers grow all the year round

(*b*) The rain is like a calendar for farmers because

   (*i*)   it tells them when to sow and when to harvest

   (*ii*)   it tells them the birthdays of their children

   (*iii*)   each month has a time for plantation

   (*iv*)   different kinds of rain tell different things

(*c*) People who live in cities don't like rain because

   (*i*)   it brings mud and sickness with it

   (*ii*)   they are not bothered about the farmers

   (*iii*)   they don't like the plants that grow during the rain

   (*iv*)   going shopping becomes difficult

(*d*) People pray asking the rain to retreat because

   (*i*)   the fungus and mould need to dry

   (*ii*)   children don't get a chance to play

   (*iii*)   the crops need the sun and heat to ripen

   (*iv*)   they like to pray

Answer the following questions briefly :

[6 marks]

(*e*) Why do the elders want you to understand the rains in the Naga hills ?

(*f*) What does Durga Puja mean to the farmers of the Naga hills?

(*g*) What kind of rain is called sezuo?

(*h*) What is the occupation of more than half the population of the Naga hills?

(*i*) How is the heart of the farmer different from that of the city person?

(*j*) When does rain become a memory in the minds of the people of the Naga hills?

(*k*) Find words from the passage which mean the same as the following   [2 marks]

   (*i*)   flowering (para 6)

   (*ii*)   nonstop (para 7)

13. Read the passage given below: [10 marks]

[DELHI 2018]

1. Every morning Ravi gives his brain an extra boost. We're not talking about drinking strong cups of coffee or playing one of those mind-training video games advertised all over Facebook. "I jump onto my stationary bike and cycle for 45 minutes to work, " says Ravi. "When I get to my desk, my brain is at peak activity for a few hours." After his mental focus comes to a halt later in the day, he starts it with another short spell of cycling to be able to run errands.

2. Ride, work, ride, repeat. It's a scientifically proven system that describes some unexpected benefits of cycling. In a recent study in the Journal of Clinical and Diagnostic Research, scientists found that people scored higher on tests of memory, reasoning, and planning after 30 minutes of spinning on a stationary bike than they did before they rode the bike. They also completed the tests faster after pedalling.

3. Exercise is like a fertilizer for your brain. All those hours spent on exercising your muscles, create rich capillary beds not only in leg and hip muscles but also in our brain. More blood vessels in your brain and muscles mean more oxygen and nutrients to help them work. When you pedal, you also force more nerve cells to fire. The result: you double or triple the production of these cells — literally building your brain. You also release neurotransmitters (the messengers between your brain cells) so all those cells, new and old, can communicate with each other for better, faster functioning. That's a pretty profound benefit to cyclists.

4. This kind of growth is especially important with each passing birthday because as we age, our brains shrink and those connections weaken. Exercise restores and protects the brain cells. Neuroscientists say, "Adults who exercise display sharper memory skills, higher concentration levels, more fluid thinking, and greater problem-solving ability than those who are sedentary."

5. Cycling also elevates your mood, relieves anxiety, increases stress resistance, and even banishes the blues, "Exercise works in the same way as psychotherapy and antidepressants in the treatment of depression, maybe better," says Dr. Manjari. A recent study analyzing 26 years of research finds that even some exercise — as little as 20 to 30 minutes a day — can prevent depression over the long term.

6. Remember: although it's healthy, exercise itself is a stress, especially when you're just getting started or getting back into riding. When you first begin to exert yourself, your body releases a particular hormone to raise your heart rate, blood pressure, and blood glucose levels, say Meher Ahluwalia, PhD, a professor of integrative physiology. As you get fitter, it takes a longer, harder ride to trigger that same response.

On the basis of your understanding of the above passage, complete the statements given below with the help of options that follows:

[2 marks]

(a) Ravi gets his brain to work at peak level by

   (i)   drinking three cups of coffee

   (ii)   playing games that need brain activity

   (iii) cycling on a stationary bike

   (iv) taking tablets to pump up his brain.

(b) When nerve cells work during exercise then

   (i)   the body experiences stress

   (ii)   the brain is strengthened by multiplying them

   (iii) you start to lose your temper

   (iv) your stationary cycle starts to beep

Answer the following questions briefly:

[6 marks]

(c) How does exercise help the brain?

(d) Whey does Ravi do a circuit of 'ride, work, ride'?

(e) What is the work of neurotransmitters?

(f) What benefits other than greater brain activity does one get from cycling?

(g) Why is exercise so important for adults?

(h) How is exercise itself a stress?

(i) Find words from the passage which mean the same as the following: [2 marks]

   (i)   manure (para 3)

   (ii)   inactive (para 4)

14. Read the passage given below: [8 marks]

[DELHI 2018]

Keeping cities clean is essential for keeping their residents healthy. Our health depends not just on personal hygiene and nutrition, but critically also on how clean we keep our cities and their surroundings. The spread of dengue and chikungunya are intimately linked to the deteriorating state of public health conditions in our cities.

The good news is that waste management to keep cities clean is now getting attention through the Swachh Bharat Mission. However, much of the attention begins and stops with the brooms and the dustbins, extending at most to the collection and transportation of the mixed waste to some distant or not so distant place, preferably out of sight.

The challenge of processing and treating the different streams of solid waste, and safe disposal of the residuals in scientific landfills, has received much less attention in municipal solid waste management than is expected from a health point of view.

One of the problems is that instead of focusing on waster management for health, we have got sidetracked into "waste for energy". If only we were to being by not mixing the biodegradable component of solid waste (close to 60 percent of the total) in our cities with the dry waste, and instead use this stream of waste for composting and producing a gas called methane.

City compost from biodegradable waste provides an alternative to farmyard manure (like cow-dung). It provides an opportunity to simultaneously clean up our cities and help improve agricultural productivity and quality of the soil. Organic manure or compost plays a very important role as a supplement to chemical fertilisers in enriching the nutrient-deficient soils. City compost can be the new player in the field.

Benefits of compost on the farm are well-known. The water holding capacity of the soil which uses compost helps with drought-proofing, and the requirement of less water per crop is a welcome feature for a water-stressed future. By making the soil porous, use of compost also makes roots stronger and resistant to pests and decay. Farmers using compost, therefore, need less quantity of pesticides. There is also evidence to suggest that horticulture crops grown with compost have better flavour, size, colour and shelf-life.

City compost has the additional advantage of being weed-free unlike farmyard manure which brings with it the seeds of undigested grasses and requires a substantial additional labour cost for weeding as the crops grow. City compost is also rich in organic carbon, and our soils are short in this.

Farmers clearly recognize the value of city compost. If city waste was composted before making it available to the farmers for applying to the soil, cities would be cleaned up and the fields around them would be much more productive.

Quite apart from cleaning up the cities of biodegradable waste, this would be a major and sustainable contribution to improving the health of our soils without further damage by excessive chemical inputs. What a marvellous change from waste to health!

The good news is that some states are regularly laying plastic roads. Plastic roads will not only withstand future monsoon damage but will also solve a city's problem of disposing of non-recyclable plastic. It is clear that if the mountains of waste from our cities were to be recycled into road construction material, it would tackle the problem of managing waster while freeing up scarce land.

(*a*) On the basis of your understanding of the above passage, make notes on it using headings and subheadings. Use recognisable abbreviations wherever necessary (minimum four) and a format you consider suitable. Also supply an appropriate title to it.

[5 marks]

(*b*) Write a summary of the passage in about 80 words. [3 marks]

15. Read the passage given below: [20 marks]

[DELHI 2019]

1. All of Earth's oceans share one thing in common: plastic pollution. Discarded plastic bags, cups, and bottles make their way into the sea. Today, it seems that no part of the ocean is safe from plastic trash. In recent years, oceanographers have searched in vain for a pristine marine environment. They have found plastic everywhere they have looked. "It is a common global problem, we can't point to a single habitat or location with no plastic."

2. Plastic harms wildlife and introduces dangerous chemicals into marine ecosystems - communities of organisms interacting with their surroundings. Once plastic enters the environment, it lasts a long time. Scientists are working to prevent plastic pollution from entering the sea.

3. When people litter, or when trash is not properly disposed of, things like plastic bags, bottles, straws, foam beverage cups get carried to the sea by winds and waterways. About 80 percent of ocean plastic originates on land. The rest comes from marine industries such as shipping and fishing.

4. In 2015, engineer Jenna Jambeck at the University of Georgia and other researchers calculated that at least 8 million tons of plastic trash is swept into the ocean from coasts every year. That's the equivalent of a full garbage truck of plastic being dumped into the sea every minute. If current trends

in plastic production and disposal continue, that figure will double by 2025. A report published by the World Economic Forum last year predicts that by 2050, ocean plastic will outweigh all the fish in the sea.

5. In today's world, plastic is everywhere. It's found in shoes, clothing, household items, electronics, and more. There are different types of plastics, but one thing they all have in common is that they're made of polymers - large molecules made up of repeating units. Their chemical structure gives them a lot of advantages: they're cheap and easy to manufacture, lightweight, water-resistant durable, and can be moulded into nearly any shape.

6. Unfortunately, some of the properties that make plastics great for consumer goods also make them a problem pollutant. Plastic's durability comes in part from the fact that unlike paper or wood, it doesn't biodegrade, or break down naturally. Instead it just fragments, or breaks into tiny pieces over time. These tiny pieces, known as microplastic, can potentially stick around for hundreds or perhaps even thousands of years.

7. Another problem with plastics is the other chemicals they contain, like dyes and flame retardants. When plastic isn't disposed of properly, these additives end up in the environment. Plastic also tends to absorb harmful chemicals from its surroundings. "It's like a sponge for persistent organic pollutants". These longlasting, toxic substances include pesticides and industrial chemicals. If plastic absorbs the chemicals, and marine organisms eat the plastic, they may be exposed to higher concentrations of these contaminants.

8. One of the biggest impacts of plastic pollution is its effect on sea life. Seals, sea turtles, and even whales can become entangled in plastic netting. They can starve to death if the plastic restricts their ability to move or eat. Or the plastic can cut into the animals' skin, causing wounds that develop severe infections.

9. Sea turtles eat plastic bags and soda-can rings, which resemble jellyfish, their favourite food. Seabirds eat bottle caps or chunks of foam cups. Plastic pieces may make an animal feel full, so it doesn't eat

enough real food to get the nutrients it needs. Plastic can also block an animal's digestive system, making it unable to eat.

10. Plastic and its associated pollutants can even make it into our own food supply. Scientists recently examined fish and shell-fish bought at markets in California and Indonesia. They found plastic in the guts of more than a quarter of samples purchased at both locations. In organisms that people eat whole, such as sardines and oysters, that means we're eating plastic too. In larger fish, chemicals from plastic may seep into their muscles and other tissues that people consume.

11. One way to keep the ocean cleaner and healthier is through cleanup efforts. A lot of plastic waste caught in ocean currents eventually washes up on beaches. Removing it can prevent it from blowing out to sea again. Beach clean-up is ocean clean-up.

12. Cleanup efforts can't reach every corner of the ocean or track down every bit of microplastic. That means it's critical to cut down on the amount of plastic that reaches the sea in the first place. Scientists are working toward new materials that are safer for the environment. For example, Jambeck and her colleagues are currently testing a new polymer that breaks down more easily in seawater.

13. "Individual actions make a big difference," says Jambeck. Disposing of plastic properly for recycling or trash collection is a key step. "And simple things like reusable water bottles, mugs, and bags really cut down on waste," she says. Skipping straws or using paper ones helps too. Ocean pollution can seem overwhelming, but it's something everyone can help address. This is a problem we can really do something about.

(a) On the basis of your understanding of the above passage, answer each of the questions given below by choosing the most appropriate option: [1 x 5 = 5]

(i) Percentage of ocean plastic that originates from land is:

   (a) 20%

   (b) 50%

   (c) 80%

   (d) 25%

(ii) In which year did Jenna Jambeck and other researchers calculate that at least 8 million tons of plastic trash is swept into ocean every year?

    (a) 2018

    (b) 2015

    (c) 2005

    (d) 2010

(iii) Plastic is not biodegradable because it is made up of:

    (a) low atomic particles

    (b) tiny particles

    (c) strong big particles

    (d) large molecule polymers

(iv) Sea turtles eat:

    (a) plastic bottles

    (b) plastic bags and soda-can rings

    (c) bottle caps

    (d) chunks of foam cups

(v) Scientists bought fish and shell-fish for examination at markets in

    (a) China and Russia

    (b) Pakistan and Afghanistan

    (c) California and Indonesia

    (d) Australia and Brazil

(b) Answer the following questions briefly :

[1 x 6 = 6]

(i) Which articles made of plastic generally cause pollution in the sea?

(ii) How does plastic in oceans harm marine ecosystems?

(iii) How is microplastic formed?

(iv) Why is plastic compared to a sponge?

(v) What is the biggest impact of plastic pollution on sea life?

(vi) How are scientists trying to reduce the plastic pollutants ?

(c) Answer any three of the following questions in 25-30 words each: [2 x 3 = 6]

(i) How does plastic waste enter the oceans?

(ii) How is it true to say that plastic is everywhere in today's world?

(iii) Which property of plastic makes it a problem pollutant?

(iv) What has scientist Jambeck suggested for having cleaner and healthier oceans?

(d) Pick out the words/phrases from the passage which are similar in meaning to the following: [1 x 3 = 3]

(i) unsafe (para 2)

(ii) rubbish/junk (as a noun) (para 3)

(iii) shaped/formed (para 5)

16. Read the passage given below: [10 marks]

[DELHI 2019]

1. Getting enough sleep is as important as taking time out to relax. A good night's sleep is essential for preserving the health of your brain and gives you the best chance to meet the coming day with a razor sharp mind. An average person needs about six to eight hour sleep a night - SIX to eight hour sleep a night - although it is also true that you need slightly less than this, as you grow older-another advantage of aging stress and sleep deprivation often feed on each other, since stress tends to make it harder for you to fall asleep at night and sleep deprivation in itself causes stress.

2. Eventually, too little sleep can dramatically interfere with the performance of your memory - something you obviously want to prevent. If you are not getting enough sleep, try going to bed 30 to 60 minutes earlier than your normal bed time for a few days. Lie down on the bed and try to relax by dissociating yourself from your daily routine work. This is normally enough to catch up on any sleep deprivation.

3. If, however, you suffer from insomnia you should seek the advice of your doctor. The chances are it is already affecting your ability to remember and recall information - and if you are struggling to improve your memory scores, this could be at the root of your problem. Prolonged periods of insufficient sleep can deplete your immune system, make you more accident prone and even cause depression - this can also reinforce a more negative outlook on life, which can contribute to your stress burden. The good news is that your memory and mood should automatically improve once you improve your sleep patterns. Tackle your sleep issues and everything else should fall into place.

4. Because stress management is so essential to maximize your brain power, if you are not in the habit of setting aside time to relax, make it a priority to do so. Even a

minute or two of deep breathing can start to work wonders. Often the best ideas and memories can come to you when you are in a state of relaxation as it is during these moments that your brain stores, processes and plays with the information it has received.

5. Meditation has long been part of religious and spiritual life, specially in Asia. Today, more and more people are adopting it in Western countries also, for its value in developing peace of mind and lowering stress. There is some evidence that regular meditation can have real sleep gain and health benefits particularly in terms of protecting your brain against aging.

(a) On the basis of your understanding of the above passage, make notes on it using headings and subheadings. Use recognizable abbreviations (wherever necessary - minimum four) and a format you consider suitable. Also supply an appropriate title to it. **[5 marks]**

(b) Write a summary of the above passage in about 100 words. **[5 marks]**

17. Read the following passage : **[8 marks]**

[DELHI 2020]

(1) How does television affect our lives? It can be very helpful to people who carefully choose the shows that they watch. Television can increase our knowledge of the outside world; there are high quality programmes that help us understand many fields of study, science, medicine, the different arts and so on Morever, television benefits very old people, who can't leave the house, as well as patients in hospitals. It also offers non-native speakers the advantages of daily informal language practice. They can increase their vocabulary and practice listening.

(2) On the other hand, there are several serious disadvantages of television, of course, it provides us with a pleasant way to relax and spend our free time, but in some countries people watch television for an average of six hours or more a day. Many children stare at the TV screen for more hours a day than they spend on anything else, including

studying and sleeping. It's clear that TV has a powerful influence on their lives and that its influence is often negative.

(3) Recent studies show that after only thirty seconds of television viewing, a person's brain 'relaxes' the same way that it does just before the person falls asleep. Another effect of television on the human brain is that it seems to cause poor concentration Children who view a lot of television can often concentrate on a subject for only fifteen to twenty minutes. They can pay attention only for the amount of time between commercials.

(4) Another disadvantage is that television often causes people to become dissatisfied with their own lives. Real life does not seem so exciting to these people. To many people, television becomes more real than reality and their own lives seem boring. Also many people get upset or depressed when they can't solve problems in real life as quickly as television actors seem to.

(5) Before a child is fourteen years old, he or she views eleven thousand murders on the TV. He or she begins to believe that there is nothing strange about fights, killings and other kinds of violence. Many studies show that people become more violent after viewing certain programmes. They may even do the things that they see in a violent show.

(a) On the basis of your reading of the above passage make notes on it using Headings and Sub-headings. Use recognizable abbreviations (minimum four) and a format you consider suitable. Supply a suitable title to it. **[4 marks]**

(b) Make a summary of the above passage in about 80 words. **[4 marks]**

Directions (Q. 18 to 27) : Read the passage given below. **[10 marks]**

[DELHI Term I, 2022]

1. What's the one thing that you associate with your college days? For me, it was consuming copious amounts of chai. A cup of tea was a panacea to all troubles and the companion to all joys. In this exclusive interview, we caught up with 65-year-old Deepak Garg, owner of Ganga Dhaba, a spot that every officer from National Academy of Administration has visited multiple times.

2. Deepak begins, "My family has been here for almost 90 years. It was my grandfather who first started working here as the supplier to the hotel that existed then." In 1964, when Deepak was all of eight, he lost his father and the responsibility of raising four children, fell on his mother.

3. "Our growing up years were a huge struggle. My mother used to teach home science at a local balwadi school, and which was also where my siblings and I studied," he says. In 1978, Deepak says that he started a food joint that he named Om Chinese restaurant. "In those days, there was a huge liking for Chinese food and hence the name and the choice of cuisine," he says.

4. For almost 17 years, things continued and then Deepak got a Public Call Office (PCO) installed for the Officer Trainees. The business did so well that soon he had installed more than ten telephones, with separate cabins, to allow them some privacy while they made and received their calls.

5. "The OTs who would talk on the PCO from here would always refer to the place as 'Ganga Dhaba'. It was because this place is so close to the Ganga hostel inside the academy, that slowly the name changed and it became Ganga Dhaba. "Since it was the OTs that gave us our identity, we decided to change the name and call it Ganga Dhaba," he says.

6. There have been instances when Deepak and his family members have learnt dishes from the OTs. He says, "So many dishes on our menu today are because some officer came in and decided to teach us how to make them".

7. We have seen two generations of officers, served the parents, who now as the parents come back to drop their children at the academy and tell us to take care of them. What more can we ask for? While the money we make is not great, the respect and the love we have accumulated over the years is what keeps us going," says Deepak, proudly (400 words)

Based on your understanding of the passage, answer any eight out of the ten questions by choosing the correct options :

18. What, according to the author, gave him solace during his bad times in his college days?

    (a) Friends

    (b) Family

    (c) Tea

    (d) Telephone

19. Read the following statements :

    (i) Mr. Deepak named his food joint Om Chinese.

    (ii) Chinese food was then popular among people.

    (a) (ii) is the cause for (i)

    (b) (i) is the cause for (ii)

    (c) (i) is true and (ii) is false

    (d) (i) is false and (ii) is true

20. 'Soon he had installed ten telephones.'

    In the light of the above statement select the option that lists the right inference.

    (a) He was kind enough to do social service for the OTs.

    (b) He was successful and flourishing in his business.

    (c) He expanded his canteen to accommodate more people.

    (d) He switched his business from canteen to telephone booths.

21. The gesture of changing the name of the food joint to 'Ganga Dhaba' speaks of Deepak's

    (a) wavering mind

    (b) tendency to change with times

    (c) respect and tribute to OTs

    (d) dogmatic approach

22. '..... his family members learnt dishes from OTs.'

    Choose the option that lists the inference with reference to the above statement.

    (a) OTs were equally good connoisseurs of food.

    (b) his family was mediocre in cooking.

    (c) his family had close association and good rapport with OTs.

    (d) his family wanted to learn more recipes to expand their business.

23. As per paragraph 7, select the option that sums up the personality of Deepak Garg.

    (a) He is a struggler, lacks business acumen to make his business profitable.

    (b) He is a very social and friendly person and enjoys good relationship with OTs.

    (c) A responsible son who shared the burden of his family.

    (d) A person who upholds dignity and esteem in life, not materialistic.

24. "......OTs that gave us our identity." He means to say

    (a) His canteen was in the vicinity of OTs hostel.

    (b) The canteen was named after the OTs hostel.

    (c) It was OTs who helped his family to learn new recipes.

    (d) It was OTs who patronized his canteen business.

25. Choose the option that aptly defines Deepak Garg's life story "from struggling childhood days to becoming a successful businessman".

    (a) Where there is a will, there is a way.

    (b) Make Ray while the Sun shines.

    (c) A good fire make a good cook.

    (d) Despair gives courage to a coward.

26. "....... many dishes on our menu today are because some officer came in and decided to teach us."

    Choose the option that rightly reflects the tone of the speaker.

    (a) Ignorance

    (b) Humility

    (c) Pride

    (d) Regret

27. ".......tell us to take care of them."

    Choose the option that lists the appropriate reason behind the statement.

    (a) Parents make a request as they stay away from their children.

    (b) Deepak Garg can take care as he stays close to the hostel.

    (c) Parents trust and respect Deepak Garg's hospitality.

    (d) Parents pay Deepak Garg for the facilities he offers.

28. Read the passage given below :   [8 marks]

    [DELHI Term II, 2022]

    1. Very often, we did not take the first step towards a good cause because we say to ourselves, "The task is so big. What can I do alone?" So nothing gets done. There is much talk about environmental protection, air pollution and saving our forests. Do we really care ? If we do, here are a few things we can do to make our surroundings more pleasant.

    2. It is good to adopt a two-uses-attitude! By putting an article to a second use, we are giving it a longer lease of life and using up less raw material from nature. One of the worst things we do is the abuse of paper. The clean sides of envelopes can be used to write small notes, lists and reminders around the house. The more paper we use, the more trees will have to be cut down. For the same reason, we should avoid the use of paper napkins or paper plates. Cloth napkins are just as good, for they can be washed and used over and over again.

    3. Another area which need the most urgent attention is effective garbage disposal. People who are conscious about it follow rules and laws strictly. As a result, their neighbourhoods are clean and beautiful. Similarly, each one of us can contribute to a cleaner environment. All kitchen waste should be collected separately. Those of you who have green fingers can turn this into valuable manure. Dig a pit and put the kitchen waste into it. When the pit is a little over half full, cover it up with mud. Let nature do the rest. Within three or six months, we will have a good garden manure. It can also be done as a community project by digging a large pit in the colony. Do take help of all the members, for nothing succeeds like co-operation.

    4. A lot of people don't care about the environment because they don't understand the adverse effect that society has on it. It is important to convince people to care about the environment. The first step would be to convince people to change by providing simple alternative solutions and ways of doing things. The internet is a powerful tool and a group on social media of like-minded people can be formed. People can share environmental stories and issues, as well as pool in solutions and alternatives to educate one another. With the current state that our planet is in, it is imperative that people actively care about the environment and most importantly to act now.

    Based on your understanding of the passage, answer ANY EIGHT questions from the nine given below :

    (i) Why don't we take the first step towards a good cause ?

(ii) What is a two-uses-attitude ?

(iii) What can we do to avoid the abuse of paper ? (any two points)

(iv) What is the result of an effective way of garbage disposal ?

(v)   What procedure can one adopt or kitchen waste ?

(vi) How can making of garden manure be done as community project ?

(vii) How long does it take to make good garden manure ?

(viii) Select a suitable word from the passage which means - being concerned or interested. (Para 3)

(ix) Pick out the word from the passage which means– completely necessary ? (Para 4)

29. Read the passage given below :   [10 marks]
                                       [DELHI 2023]

(1) When we think of the game of cricket, we come to the conclusion that it is primarily a game that depends on outstanding physical activities, good hand-eye co-ordination, speed, skill and strength. It provides entertainment and generates strong feelings of excitement. A good match of cricket or of any other game neither adds to the existing stock of human knowledge nor reveals any secret of existence. It does not carry any deep meaning but most people, particularly the lover of sports attach deep emotions and numerous meanings to it. Games are thought of as a metaphor for life. They are supposed to teach many lessons. In fact, more is said and written about a cricket match than about scientific findings or great philosophy.

(2) This is because games, like a morality play, in which settings and rules are made by us, can easily make people test their fair and foul conduct, principles of reward and punishment, and emotions of joy and disappointment. They can make us experience the thrill of war without exposing us to its dangers. A man watching a cricket match on T.V. and munching popcorn is like a surrogate warrior. In fact, games provide us with a safe outlet for our aggressiveness. If games become aggressive, they lose the

very purpose of providing entertainment and purging us of our aggressiveness. They can calm our impatience without creating any conflict.

(3) Commentators, journalists, politicians and analysts can do a great favour to the competing teams by keeping the excitement within limits. The teams should play without being dominated by feelings of national honour and shame. Excellent performance of the players of both teams should be enjoyed and appreciated.

Winning or losing in a game should not be taken seriously. A game is fun if it is played with true spirit of sportsmanship.

Based on your understanding of the passage, answer the questions given below :

(i)   Complete the sentence by choosing an appropriate option :

Most people conclude that cricket is primarily a game because _______.

(a) it is played as a match

(b) it requires two teams

(c) it includes physical activity

(d) it depends only on skill and strength

(ii) Comment on the writer's reference to that cricket does not reveal any secret of existence.

(iii) List two responses which watching a game of cricket gives rise to.

(iv) Select the option that conveys the opposite of 'destroy' from words used in the passage.

(a) reveals

(b) experience

(c) genet-ate

(d) purging

(v)   The writer would not agree with the given statements based on paragraph 2, EXCEPT

(a) Rules of any game are made by people.

(b) Watching a cricket match makes the viewer believe that he is fighting a battle?

(c) It is necessary for a game to be aggressive in order to build excitement.

(d) A game can test people's sense of fair judgement.

(vi) With reference to the passage, a spectator is compared to a 'surrogate warrior'.

Choose the option that best describes this phrase :

(a) a spectator who is paid to watch.

(b) a spectator who is in pain while watching the match.

(c) a spectator who enjoys the match as an armchair soldier.

(d) a spectator who makes judgement about reward and punishment.

(vii) Why does the writer compare games to a morality play ?

(viii) Complete the given sentence with an appropriate inference with respect to the following :

The writer says that games can calm our impatience without creating any conflict by ____________.

(ix) The writer advises the players that games should not become aggressive because ____________.

(x) Select the most suitable title for the above passage.

(a) Excellent Performance by Cricketers

(b) The Benefits of Playing Cricket

(c) Cricket – The King of Games

(d) The True Spirit of Playing Games

Unseen Passage

30. Read the passage given below :   (12 Marks)

[DELHI 2020]

Donated Organs and their Transportation

(1) Once an organ donor's family gives its consent and the organs are matched to a recipient, medical professionals are faced with the onerous challenge of transporting organs while ensuring that the harvested organ reaches its destination in the shortest possible time. This is done in order to preserve the harvested organs and involves the police and especially the traffic police department.

(2) The traditional method of transporting organs by road is referred to as a "green corridor". This process entails police escorting an ambulance, so as to move around traffic - usually a specific traffic lane is chosen and all signals on the route stay green to ensure it to reach its destination in the shortest possible time. A 'green-corridor' is a route cleared and cordoned off by the traffic police to ensure the smooth and steady transportation of harvested organs, on most occasions, to those awaiting a life-saving transplant. Organs tend to have a very short preservation time, such as the heart which has to be harvested and transplanted within four hours or the lungs which can be preserved for only six hours once they are harvested.

(3) The first green corridor in India was created by Chennai Traffic Police in September 2008 when they accomplished their task of enabling an ambulance to reach its destination within 11 minutes during peak hour traffic. That organ saved a nine-year-old girl whose life depended on the transplant.

(4) Similarly, such green corridors have been created by traffic police of various cities such as Pune, Mumbai, Delhi NCR etc. Personnel are stationed at selected points to divert, control and clear the traffic giving way to the ambulance. Apart from this, a motorcade of police vehicles accompanies the ambulance ensuring that it does not face any problems. Delhi Traffic Police provided a green corridor from IGI Airport to Institute of Liver and Biliary Sciences in Vasant Kunj for transportation of a liver. The distance of 14 kms was covered in 11 minutes.

(5) Experts point out the lack of a robust system to transport organs to super-specialty hospitals in least possible time. National Organ & Tissue Transplant Organisation (NOTTO), the country's apex organ donation agency, is now framing a proposal to airlift cadaver organs and will send a report to the Union Health Ministry. "Cadaver organs have a short life and so transplant should be done within a few golden hours," Director (NOTTO) expressed, "Therefore, we are preparing a proposal for airlifting organs at any given moment."

(6) Most states do not have enough well-trained experts to retrieve or perform transplant procedures. Also, there is an acute shortage of advanced healthcare facilities to carry out a transplant. So, it is referred to other big centres in metropolitan cities. Organs retrieved from Aurangabad, Indore, Surat, Pune are sent to Mumbai as these cities do not have super-specialty healthcare centres, informed officials.

(7) "In India, about fifty thousand to one lakh patients are suffering from acute heart failure and need heart transplant at any point of time. In a private set-up, a heart transplant costs Rs. 15-20 lakhs, which is followed up by postoperative medication of about Rs. 30,000 per month lifelong."

A. On the basis of your understanding of the above passage, answer any five of the following questions by choosing the most appropriate options :   (1 × 5 = 5)

(a) The first green corridor in India was created in:
  (i) New Delhi   (ii) Chennai
  (iii) Mumbai   (iv) Pune

(b) The organization which is framing a proposal to airlift cadaver organs is :
  (i) Union Health Ministry
  (ii) Regional Organ and Tissue Transplant Organisation
  (iii) National Organ and Tissue Transplant Organisation
  (iv) State Organ and Tissue Transplant Organisation

(c) The onerous task the author is talking about in Para 1 is:
  (i) finding organ donors.
  (ii) finding doctors capable of performing transplants
  (iii) to carry the harvested organ in the shortest possible time,
  (iv) to arrange the requisite facilities for the transplant.

(d) Most of the people do not go for the heart transplant as ;
  (i) it is very risky.
  (ii) it is very painful.
  (iii) it may cause death of the receipient.
  (iv) the cost is prohibitive.

(e) Most states refer organ transplant cases to big hospitals because :
  (i) they don't have well trained experts.
  (ii) the patients don't trust local doctors.
  (iii) the state hospitals are very crowded.
  (iv) they don't have a pool of harvested organs.

(f) Heart retrieved from a body is alive only for _______ hours.
  (i) two   (ii) three
  (iii) four   (iv) five

B. Answer the following questions briefly :
                                        (1 × 5 = 5)

(a) What is a 'green corridor' ?
(b) Why is smooth transportation of the retrieved organ necessary ?
(c) What opinion do you form of Chennai Police with regard to the transportation of the harvested heart ?
(d) What does the author mean by 'a few golden hours' ?
(e) How much does a heart transplant cost a patient in a private hospital ?

C. Pick out the words from the passage which mean the same as the following :   (1 × 2 = 2)
(a) save (para 1)
(b) achieved / carried out (para 3)

Case Based Passage

Directions (31 to 36) : Read the passage given below :   [DELHI Term I, 2022]

1. Air pollution is a major threat to human health. The United Nations Environment Programme has estimated that, globally, 1.1 billion people breathe in unhealthy air. The Word Health Organization (WHO) has estimated that urban air pollution is responsible for approximately 800,000 deaths and 4.6 million people lose their lives every year around the globrle.

2. Traffic and transportation problems, inadequate drainage facilities, lack of open spaces, carbon emission, and the accumulation of waste aggravate the problem. Air pollution is associated with increased risk of acute respiratory infections (ARI), the principal cause of infant and child mortality in developing countries.

3. Urban air quality in most mega cities has been found to be critical and Kolkata is no exception to this. An analysis of ambient air quality in Kolkata was done by applying the Exceedance Factor (EF) method, where the presence of listed pollutants' (RPM, SPM, NO_2, and SO_2) annual average concentration are classified into four different categories; namely critical, high, moderate, and low pollution. Out of a total of 17 ambient air quality monitoring stations operating in Kolkata, five fall under the critical category, and the remaining 12 locations fall under the high category of NO_2 concentration, while for RPM, four record critical, and 13 come under the high pollution category. The causes of high concentration of pollutants in the form of NO_2 and RPM have been identified in earlier studies as vehicular emission (51.4%), followed by industrial sources (24.5%) and dust particles (21.1%).

4. Later, a health assessment was undertaken with a structured questionaire at some nearby dispensaries which fall under areas with different ambient air pollution levels. Three dispensaries have been surveyed with 100 participants. It shows that respondents with respiratory diseases (85.1%) have outnumbered waterborne diseases (14.9%) and include acute respiratory infections (ARI) (60%), chronic obstructive pulmonary diseases (COPD) (7.8%), upper track respiratory infection (UTRI) (1.2%), Influenza (12.7%), and acid-fast bacillus (AFB) (3.4%).

5. To live a healthy life and have better well-being, practising pollution-averting activities in one's day-to-day activities is needed. These pollution-averting practices can only be possible when awareness among the masses is generated that the air, they breathe outdoors, is not found to be safe.

Pollution in India

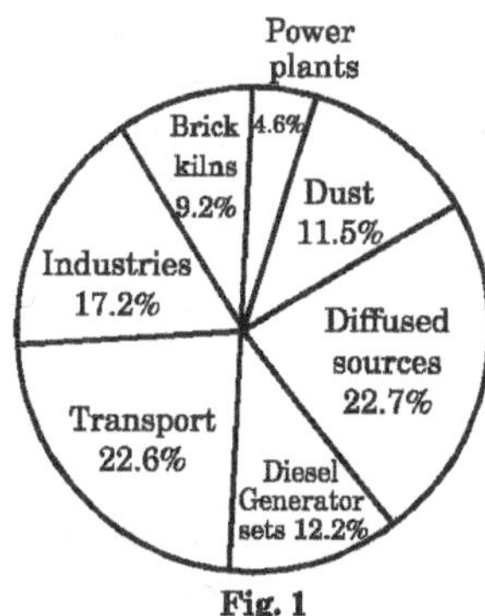

Fig. 1

Based on your understanding of the passage, answer any six out of the eight questions by choosing the correct options :

31. Select the option that highlights the main idea of the passage.
    (a) To educate people about the threat of air pollution
    (b) To warn people of the threat of air pollution and educate them about the safety measures
    (c) To discuss the status of pollution in Kolkata and share the details of the study
    (d) To educate people on Exceedance Factor method and share the results of the study

32. Select the option that displays the correct 'cause and effect' relationship.

Cause	Effect
(a) Traffic and transportation problem	4.6 million deaths
(b) Lack of open spaces	Mega cities
(c) Air pollution	Respiratory diseases
(d) Air quality monitoring stations	Emission of NO_2

33. Read the following statements :
    (i) Air pollution kills 4.6 million people every year in India.
    (ii) Air pollution is causing health hazards to more people than water pollution.
    (a) (i) is true and (ii) is false
    (b) (i) is false and (ii) is true
    (c) (i) is true and is responsible for (ii)
    (d) Both (i) and (ii) are false

34. The author's opinion on the development of Mega cities is
    (a) Cities face transportation problem due to heavy traffic.
    (b) Urbanization leads to deterioration of air quality.
    (c) Mega cities are the right spots to study air pollution.
    (d) Cities face the problem of congestion

35. Select the option that lists the author's recommendation to the people.
    i. He wants people to be aware that air pollution is a major threat.
    ii. He urges people are not to live in mega cities.

iii. He advises people to follow pollution averting activities seriously.

iv. He wants people to reduce vehicular emissions.

(a) i & ii   (b) ii & iii

(c) 1 & iii   (d) iii & iv

36. Select the option that displays the true statement as per fig. 1.

(a) Dust and power plants are the causes for maximum pollution.

(b) Pollution caused by transport is much more than the pollution caused by industries.

(c) The use of diesel generator is responsible for more than 50% of air pollution.

(d) Dust stands fourth in the list that causes air pollution.

37. Read the passage below :   (1 × 6 = 6)

[DELHI Term II, 2022]

1. Our history makes it evident that the Indian Plastics Industry made a vigorous beginning in 1957 but it took more than 30 years for it to pervade Indian lifestyles. In 1979, 'the market for plastics' was just being seeded by the state-owned Indian Petro-Chemicals and it was only in 1994 that plastic soft drink bottles became a visible source of annoyance.

2. In the same year, people in other cities were concerned about the state of public sanitation and also urged regulatory bodies to ban the production, distribution and use of plastic bags. However the challenge was greater than it appeared at first.

3. The massive generation of plastic waste in India is due to rapid urbanisation, spread of retail chains, plastic packaging form grocery to food and vegetable products, to consumer items and cosmetics.) The projected high growth rates of GDP and continuing rapid urbanisation suggest that India's trajectory of plastic consumption and plastic waste is likely to increase.

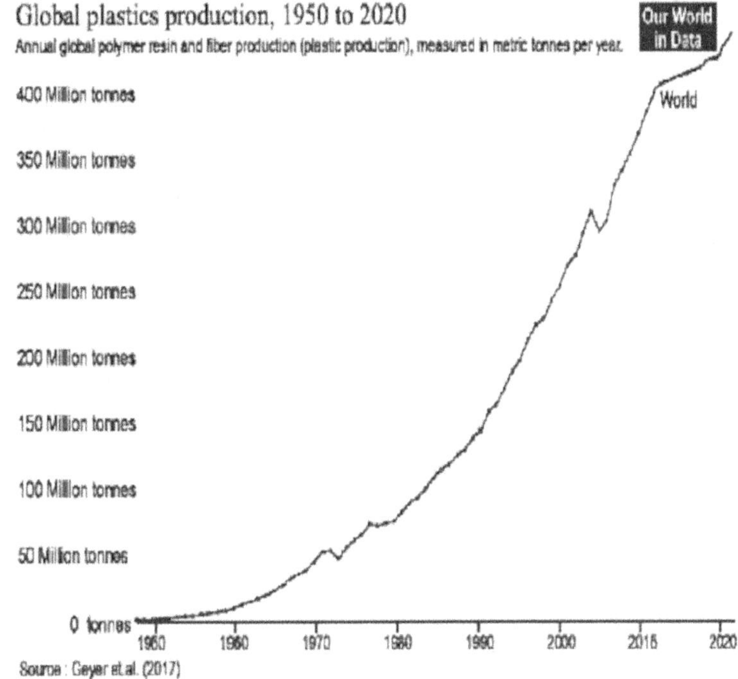

4. According to the United Nations Environment Programme (UNEP) report of 2018, India stands among few other countries like France, Mongolia and several African countries that have initiated total or partial national-level bans on plastics in their jurisdictions. On World Environment Day in 2018, India vowed to phase out single-use plastics by 2022, which gave a much needed impetus to bring this change.

5. In this context, thereafter ten states (Andhra Pradesh, Chhattisgarh, Gujarat, Himachal Pradesh, Karnataka, Madhya Pradesh, Meghalaya, Odisha, Rajasthan and Tamil Nadu) are currently sending their collected waste to cement plants for co-processing, twelve other states/ UTs are using plastic waste for polymer bitumen road construction and still four other states are using the plastic waste for waste-to-energy plants and oil production. A world of greater possibilities has now opened up to initiate appropriate and concrete actions to build up the necessary institutions and systems before oceans turn, irreversibly into a thin soup of plastic.

6. However there is no one single masterstroke to counter the challenges witnessed by the staggering plastic waste management in the country. The time is now to formulate robust and inclusive National Action Plans and while doing so, the country will establish greater transparency to combat the plastic jeopardy in a more sustainable and holistic way.

Based on your understanding of the passage answer ANY SIX out of the seven questions given below :

i.   What does the writer mean by 'visible source of annoyance'?

ii. Why did people demand a ban on plastics ?

iii. What created a demand for plastics in India ?

iv. With reference to the graph write one conclusion that can be drawn about the production of plastics in 2019 (approximately).

v.   What does the upward trend o the graph indicate ?

vi. What does the line, oceans turning 'irreversibly into a thin soup of plastic', suggest ?

vii. What step must be taken to combat the challenges of plastic waste management ? What will be its impact ?

38. Read the following report and answer the questions by choosing the correct/most appropriate option :   [1 × 10 = 10]

[DELHI 2023]

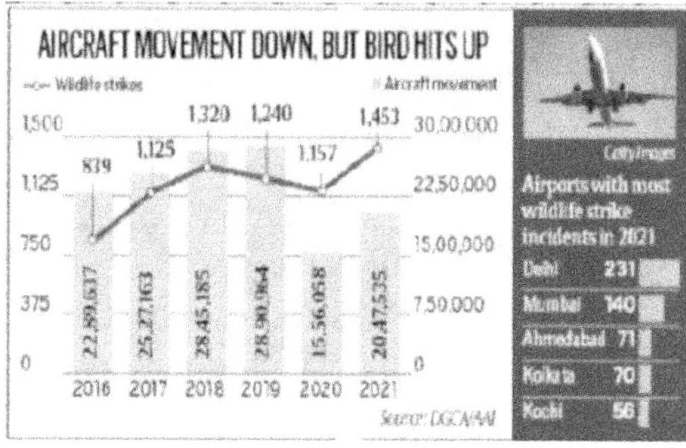

(1) **How bird hits happen, why they are a concern?**

New Delhi June 20

At least two bird strike incidents happened on Sunday. Both aircrafts returned to their airport of origin and were, grounded for maintenance. An ABC aircraft, which took off from Guwahati towards Delhi, suffered damage to its left engine following a bird hit at 1600 feet. The pilots returned to Guwahati. The other strike happened on another flight from Patna to Delhi. The pilots of the aircraft suspected a bird strike during the take-off roll but continued to climb. Following the take off rotation, they were informed by the cabin crew of sparks emanating from the left engine. Subsequently, the pilots were also informed by air traffic control of smoke coming out of one of the engines. The pilots declared an emergency and returned to Patna.

(2) **Why are bird strikes a concern?**

Bird strikes are among the most common threats to aircraft safety, and they typically occur during take-off or landing. Dozens of bird-strikes happen each day but some can be more dangerous than others. Typically, when birds collide with an aircraft's airframe, it is unlikely to cause significant problems for the pilots flying. But there are instances when the aircraft, engine ingests the birds. This can lead to a loss of thrust for the engine and cause maneuverability problems for the crew. In these cases, where a jet engine ingests a bird, procedures would generally call for pilots to land the plane at the closest airport. While most airframe bird strikes are not, considered critical to air safety, if a collision cracks a window or a wind screen. pilots will look to land as early as possible.

(3) **How critical are bird strikes to air safety?**

Smaller planes would generally be more susceptible to the dangers of the dangers of bird strikes than larger ones.

However, given that bird strikes mostly happen driving take-off and landing, these incidents could distract the pilots during what are highly critical phases of flights that demand the complete attention of the crew.

(4) **What causes bird-strikes?**

The presence of birds around an aircraft increases the chances of a bird strike. In the monsoon, as water puddles emerge on open grounds attracting insects to breed, the presence of birds increases. In some cases, bird hits also happen at higher altitudes when a plane is cruising. These are more dangerous than the low-altitude hits, given that they can cause rapid depressurization of cabins. Other reasons for bird activity around the air field could be presence of landfills or waste disposal sites that can attract a large number of birds.

(i) Does the following statement agree with the information give in paragraph 1.

When an airplane is hit by a bird or is suspected to heve been hit, the passengers must be asked to get down at once.

Select from the following :

True :   If the statement agrees with the information.

False :   If the statement contradicts the information.

Not Given :If there is no information on this.

(ii) Select the option that display the most likely reason for Bird hits.

    (a)   when the aircraft in overloaded

    (b)   at the time of landing or taking off

    (c)   when the crew become negligent

    (d)   when the passengers become panicky

(iii) Complete the sentence appropriately with one word.

Smaller planes are generally more__________ than the larger ones.

(iv) Complete the sentence by selecting the most appropriate option :

When the window or the windscreen of the air plane is cracked due to a bird hit ____.

    (a)   the crew must rush to the cockpit.

    (b)   the pilot must land at the earliest airport.

    (c)   the pilot must inform the maintenance engineer.

    (d)   the pilot must get instructions from the aviation wing what should do in emergency.

(v) Based on the reading of the text, state a point to further the statement.

Dozens of bird hits take place every day ____.

    (a)   but only a few are dangerous.

    (b)   all of them are fatal.

    (c)   but after every bird hit it is imperative to land the aircraft.

    (d)   the pilot should ignore them.

(vi) Complete the sentence based on the following statement.

Complete attention of the crew is demanded during take off and landing.

We can say this because__________.

(vii) Complete the sentence appropriately with one/two words.

In cases where the aircraft engine infests the bird, it leads to the loss of thrust and causes problems in________.

(viii) Which are the areas more prone to bird hits ?

(ix) Based on the reading of the text, state a point to challenge the given statement :

The area around air fields should be clear of any waste disposal sites.

(x) Look at the graph. It shows that between 2016 and 2021, whereas air flights have come down, the bird-hits have gone up. This implies that the incidence of bird hits has

   (a) decreased

   (b) increased

   (c) remained constant

   (d) been alarming

🔑 Solutions

1. (a)

   (i) Eradication of child labour and ensuring compulsory primary education for every Indian child, are the goals that no government has achieved so far. [2]

   (ii) (i) Different states have different rules regarding the minimum age of employment.

       (ii) There is no ban on child labour in non-hazardous occupations.

       (iii) The act does not apply to the unorganized sector as it only talks about the organised or factory sector.

       (iv) Lack of effective implementation of the existing laws. [2]

   (iii) Among several reasons for industries preference for child labour, it's their agile fingers, high level of concentration and capacity to work hard for extremely low wages. [2]

   (iv) (i) Prone to incapacitating diseases which can affect them for life.

       (ii) Limbs get affected due to working in cramped and unhygienic places.

       (iii) Mental and physical development is permanently impaired.

       (iv) Stay uneducated and lacking overall growth. (any two). [2]

   (v) The Supreme Court's directive of 1997 allows punitive action against employers of child labour. [1]

   (b) (i) Hazardous [1.5]

       (ii) Hostile [1.5]

2. (a)

   (i) Stress is a reaction of the body to any demands or changes in its internal and external environment. Factors such as the imbalance between demands and resources change in temperature, pollutants, humidity and working conditions lead to stress. [2]

   (ii) The various signs that can be observed are:

       (a) Change in the attitude and behaviour [0.5]

       (b) Muscle tension [0.5]

       (c) Palpitation, high blood pressure, indigestion and hyperacidity. [0.5]

       (d) Depression, lethargy, a weakness for work. [0.5]

   (iii) The different diseases caused by stress are:

       (a) Heart diseases [0.5]

       (b) Ulcers [0.5]

       (c) Insomnia [0.5]

       (d) Neurological depression [0.5]

       (e) Hypertension

       (f) Injuries due to accidents.

   (iv) (a) Relaxation techniques [1]

       (b) Dance movement [1]

   (v) (a) Reaction to stress is peculiar to an individual [0.5]

       (b) It lowers his performance capacity [0.5]

       (c) Leads to Chronic fatigue [0.5]

       (d) Makes Disinterested. [0.5]

   (b) (i) collapse [1]

       (ii) reprimand [1]

       (iii) lethargic [1]

3. (a)

   (i) Air pollutant is a substance which is present in the atmosphere in an amount exceeding its normal concentration. [1]

   (ii) Air pollutant can either be gaseous (carbon monoxide, carbon dioxide, ozone etc.) or it can be in the form of particulate matter (dust of various inorganic or organic origins). [2]

   (iii) A feeling of suffocation occurs in a closed place due to the accumulation of carbon dioxide exhaled. This feeling may be compounded if the room is airtight. [1]

   (iv) A group of symptoms in poorly ventilated homes characterised by a general feeling of sickness, headache, dizziness and irritation of mucous membranes is described as the sick building syndrome. [2]

   The syndrome is getting commoner in big cities with over furnished small houses.

   (v) Indoor smoking is an important source of indoor pollution as there are ore 3000 chemical constituents in tobacco smoke which are harmful to human health. [1]

(*vi*) We can overcome the dangers of indoor air pollution by ensuring proper ventilation in our house. This way we will be able to get rid of increased concentrations of oxides of nitrogen and sulphur, carbon monoxide and other indoor pollutants. Care should also be taken to isolate persons with infective illness. [2]

(*b*) (*i*) nausea [1]

(*ii*) persistent [1]

(*iii*) dampness [1]

4. (*a*) Dietary Fibres- Indigestible Carbohydrates.

1. Importance

1.1 Essential ingredient of bal. diet.

(*i*) Suggested intake-40 gms. /day

1.2 Contains gums & pectin

(*i*) PP Blood sugar levels

1.3 Diet rich in fibres

(*i*) The ↓ incidence of CHD

(*ii*) Controls irritable bowel syndrome

(*iii*) ↓ Dental caries.

2. Source

2.1 Cereals & Grains

2.2 Fruits

(*i*) Citrus fruits

(*ii*) Fruits with seeds

2.3 Green leafy vegetables

3. Physiological outcome

3.1 Not digested by enzymes in the body

3.2 Hold water

(*i*) gets swollen → relives constipation

3.3. Increases transit time in Gut

(*i*) ↓ risk of colon cancer

(*ii*) checks obesity

4. Adverse effects

4.1 Binds trace elements.

(*i*) Hampers absorption-nutritional deficiency.

Abbreviations and symbols used.

1. bal - balance

2. gms - grams

3. & - and

4. P. P. - Post-Prandial

5. CHD. - Coronary Heart Disease

6. ↓ -lower

7. → -lead to

(*b*) Summary

Dietary fibres are indigestible carbohydrates which are essential ingredients of balanced diets with a suggested intake of 40 grams per day. Fibres are rich in gums and pectin that lower Post-Prandial Blood Sugar Levels. Diet rich in fibres lowers incidence of controls leading to irritable bowel syndrome and dental caries. The main source of it are cereals and grains, fruits both citrus and with seeds and green leafy vegetables. It is not digested by the enzymes in the body, holds water and increases transit time in the get there by relieving constipation checking obesity and lowering the risk of colon cancer. It binds trace elements that hamper their absorption leading to a nutritional deficiency which seems to be the only adverse effect.

5. (*a*)

(1) Teachers and parents want children to learn values like hard work, contentment, honesty and compassion. [2]

(2) When children are given too much too soon, they grow up to be adults who have difficulty coping with life's disappointments. Such children may develop a distorted sense of entitlement that hampers their success in the workplace and in relationships. [2]

(3) Today's children want more because nowadays there is so much more to want. Moreover, they consider luxurious items as essential utilities. [1]

(4) In today's world, parents need to strike a balance between the advantages of an affluent society and the critical life lessons that come from waiting, saving and working hard to achieve goals. [2]

(5) There is a need to set limits for children because they feel better and more secure where they live within a secured structure. [2]

(*b*) (1) Contentment [1]

(2) Precious [1]

(3) Essential [1]

6. (*a*) (*iv*) All of the above [1]

(*b*) (*i*) Christianity [1]

(*c*) (*ii*) Entrance to the church is nondescript [1]

(*d*) (*iv*) Both (*i*) and (*ii*) [1]

(*e*) According to the Greek belief, the stone of anointing is a place where Christ was removed from it. [1]

(*f*) Emperor Constantine built Rotunda to safeguard the Holy Sepulchre and the remaining Structure round it. [1]

(*g*) Pilgrims have a very casual attitude and completely unaware about the history and tradition. They are more into capturing pictures and appreciating the novelty of the church. [1]

(*h*) According to the gospels, Jesus' Crucification occurred at a place outside the city walls with graves nearby and as the archaeologists have discovered tombs from the biblical era hence the site is compatible. [1]

(*i*) 'Room of the tomb' is a very small place, hence the pilgrims entered into a single file. [1]

(*j*) The women knelt down to pray to look at the large marble slab, hence became very sentimental to hide her tears. [1]

(*k*) (*i*) Tomb [1]

    (*ii*) Non-descript. [1]

7. (*a*) (*i*) By travelling light [1]

  (*b*) (*iv*) Both (*i*) and (*ii*) [1]

  (*c*) Earlier pilgrimages were a penance to stay near nature and did not require luxury rooms and big cars to travel, now they have become more of a tourism opportunity where people go for a picnic. [1]

  (*d*) When pilgrimages turn into picnics, the entire significance of pilgrimage as a sadhana is lost. It becomes more of a social gathering a life of comfort and a boost to the ego, where pilgrims brag about charity and their special darshan. [1]

  (*e*) Pilgrimages are no more about travelling on foot and living in the ashrams with basic necessities, it has become a picnic with all the comfort ac rooms, travelling by car with a large group to have all the fun and entertainment. Hence, we are complacent in our spiritual efforts. [1]

  (*f*) We are ruining our bodies because of the extra comfort that we are adapting our bodies into. We are not making any efforts to make our body work and adjust in adverse conditions rather making it all the more tender. Nature is just like everyone's mother and would act destructively by affecting our health etc. sooner or later and force us to understand this truth. [1]

(*g*) In olden day's pilgrimages were more of a sadhna to love people, stay close to nature, - understand it, stay healthy and eat healthy. It was also for seeking freedom from attachment' It was not to adhere to materialistic pleasure and live a luxurious life. [1]

(*h*) It conveys that pilgrimages are a religious connotation and undertaken for ritualistic purposes, to understand the realities of life, to stay close to nature and should not be taken as a tourism opportunity where you gather a large group, enjoy amongst all the luxuries and make a life rest upon the only comfort. You shall learn to live in hardships and only basic things needed for survival.

(*i*) (*i*) Evolution [1]

    (*ii*) complacent [1]

8. (*a*) (*ii*) he added a lot of grandeur to Mewar [1]

  (*b*) (*iii*) its small area and small population. [1]

  (*c*) (*i*) the flag of Mewar seemed to be lowered. [1]

  (*d*) (*iii*) most of its rulers were competent. [1]

  (*e*) Bappa Rawal was the earliest King or Mewar as mentioned in the passage. [1]

  (*f*) Rana Kumbha had given a new stature to the kingdom through victories and developmental work. During his reign, literature and art also progressed extraordinarily. [1]

  (*g*) The pleasant, loving and the cheerful nature of the people of Mewar is worthy of admiration according to the writer. [1]

  (*h*) The peaceful and prosperous life of the people of Mewar for a long span of time would have made the art and literature flourish in Mewar. [1]

  (*i*) The rulers were very liberal and allowed people from other communities and kingdoms to come and carry out construction work. [1]

  (*j*) The erection of Vijaya Stambha and Kirti Stambha in the same fort signifies the closeness between the King and the subjects of Mewar. [1]

  (*k*) (*i*) astonishing [1]

    (*ii*) testimony [1]

9. (*a*) (*i*) among rocks. [1]

  (*b*) (*iv*) is impulsive and impatient. [1]

  (*c*) The mother panther rarely delivers five cubs. [1]

(*d*) If the panther cubs are not born blind, they might drift away from the place of safety. [1]

(*e*) The 'Mahout' drives his elephant away as he wants him to be away from the sight of the panther. [1]

(*f*) The tigress spits at its cubs, as they do not make a beeline to the kill and to make them come back to her heels. [1]

(*g*) From the narrator's observation, the nature of the tigress is caring and loving towards her cubs. She even acts like a good teacher to her cubs. [1]

(*h*) The panther does not face the risk of extinction because of the safety provided by the mother panther. It enjoys wider distribution [1]

(*i*) (*a*) = drifting [1]

(*b*) descended. [1]

10. (*a*) (*ii*) no one stared at him. [1]

(*b*) (*ii*) Heaven Lake [1]

(*c*) (*iv*) there were thick quilts on the bed. [1]

(*d*) (*ii*) a shining prism [1]

(*e*) The two things that made the narrator uncomfortable are the overpowering smell of the goat's cheese being eaten by the man sitting behind and the leaking of the bus windows. [1]

(*f*) A few cattle drink at a clear stream flowing past moss-covered stones made the scene look like a Constable Landscape. [1]

(*g*) As the bus climbed higher, the narrator regretted of not bringing anything warm to wear. [1]

(*h*) The narrator liked to buy food from outside as kebabs, cooked on skewers over charcoal braziers were good, highly-spiced and well-done. [1]

(*i*) The pair of trousers lent by Mr Cao are several sizes too large but more than comfortable. [1]

(*j*) Mr Cao did not like the narrator to swim in the lake because many people drowned there. [1]

(*k*) (*i*) vendors [1]

(*ii*) exaggerated [1]

11. (*a*) (*iv*) treasury officer [1]

(*b*) (*iv*) give company to officers [1]

(*c*) Thackeray came to Kittur to terrorise the rulers and people of Kittur so that they would lay down their arms. [1]

(*d*) Kittur officials refused to give the desired assurance to Thackeray as no documents could be signed without sanction from Rani Chennamma. [1]

(*e*) When the Horse Artillery stormed into the fort, Sardar Gurusiddappa, who had kept his men on full alert, commanded his men to chase them away. The British Horse Artillerymen, being completely overrun and routed, had to get out through the escape window. [1]

(*f*) The Kittur soldiers had captured forty persons, including twelve children and a few women. For the women and children, Rani had the only gentleness. She took them inside the palace and gave them food and shelter. [1]

(*g*) The British women were touched by this gentle and noble gesture of the Rani. They would have felt safe and secured. [1]

(*h*) The Rani refused to meet Thackeray because he had come with an army to threaten Kittur into submission to British sovereignty. [1]

(*i*) (*i*) stormed [1]

(*ii*) defiant [1]

12. (*a*) (*iii*) it is believed that the plants bring the rain. [1]

(*b*) (*i*) it tells them when to sow and when to harvest [1]

(*c*) (*i*) it brings mud and sickness with it [1]

(*d*) (*iii*) the crops need the sun and the heat to ripen [1]

(*e*) They want us to understand the rains because they are of various kinds and they are meaningful. They are necessary for the crops to grow. Besides, they serve as an almanac for the farmers. [1]

(*f*) For them, Durga Puja means the end of rain. [1]

(*g*) Sezuo refers to week-long rains when clothes don't dry, mould smells and there forms fungus on the floor. [1]

(*h*) Farming is the occupation of more than half the population. [1]

(*i*) Farmers love rain because they know it gives life to nature and human beings while city people dislike it because they don't want mud and sicknesses. [1]

(*j*) At the end of October and after that, rain becomes a memory for the farmers as it is when it completes its cycle. [1]

(*k*) (*i*) blossoming [1]

(*ii*) Incessantly [1]

13. (*a*) (*iii*) cycling on a stationary bike   [1]

(*b*) (*ii*) the brain is strengthened by multiplying them   [1]

(*c*) Exercise works like a fertilizer in our brain. More capillary beds are formed in our muscles and brain. It makes our body and mind healthier.   [1]

(*d*) It makes him healthier, more energetic and sharper.   [1]

(*e*) Neurotransmitters help the cells to communicate with each other for better, faster functioning.   [1]

(*f*) Cycling also elevates our mood, relieves anxiety, increases stress resistance, and banishes the blues.   [1]

(*g*) It's more important for adults because with every passing year our brain shrinks. Exercise restores and protects the brain cells.   [1]

(*h*) It is itself a stress because it releases a particular hormone to raise our heartbeat, blood pressure and blood glucose.   [1]

(*i*) (*i*) Fertilizer   [1]

(*ii*) sedentary   [1]

14. (*a*) Waste Management & Health

1. Clean Surroundings

(*a*) Personal hygiene not enough

(*b*) Clean surroundings necesry for health

(*c*) Dengue & chikangooniya are results of poor public health   [1]

2. Swachha Bharat

(*a*) Swacha Bharat- working in this dirctn

(*b*) Instd of waste mangmnt, it's focusing on waste for energy

(*c*) Has a long way to go   [1]

3. City Compost

(*a*) Lots of city compost from biodegrdbl waste

(*b*) City compost- an altrntive to farmyard manure

(*c*) Will clean cities

(*d*) A powrfl altrntive to chemical fertilizrs

(*e*) Makes soil porous, roots stronger

(*f*) Unlike farmyard manure, it's free from weed seeds   [1]

4. Efforts of some States

(*a*) States laying plastic roads

(*b*) Plastic roads- more enduring

(*c*) Plstic roads rid city of plastic waste   [1]

ABBREVIATIONS

1. necesry- necessary

2. dirctn- direction

3. Instd- instead

4. mangmnt- management

5. biodegrdbl- biodegradable

6. altrntive- alternative

7. powrfl- powerful

8. fertilizrs- fertilizers

9. Plstic- plastic   [1]

(*b*) Personal hygiene is not sufficient. To be truly healthy, we will have to keep the surroundings healthy. Epidemics like chikangooniya spread because of poor public health conditions. But it is pleasant to know that swachh Bharat campaign is working towards it. However, it has a long way to go. It should focus on waste management before it zeroes in on waste for energy.

City compost is a great and more effective alternative to farmyard manure. It is free from the seeds of weeds. It helps the crops more. Doing this will rid our cities of waste material.

Some states are laying plastic roads which are a welcome step as it rids the cities of plastic waste and the plastic roads are more enduring.   [3]

15. (a) (i) (c) 80%.   [1]

(ii) (b) 2015   [1]

(iii) (d) large molecule polymers.   [1]

(iv) (b) plastic bags and soda-can rings. [1]

(v) (c) California and Indonesia.   [1]

(b) (i) Discarded plastic bags, cups and bottles are the plastic articles that generally cause pollution in the sea.   [1]

(ii) Plastics in oceans last for a longer duration and hence introduce dangerous chemicals into marine ecosystem that results in harming the marine lives.   [1]

(iii) Plastic doesn't biodegrade or break down naturally. Instead, it just fragments, or breaks into tiny pieces over time. This way microplastic is formed which can potentially stick around for hundreds or even thousands of years.   [1]

(iv) Plastic is compared to sponge because a sponge has absorbing qualities. Similarly, plastic tends to absorb harmful chemicals from its surroundings.   [1]

(v) The biggest impact of plastic pollution on sea life is that it can make seals, turtles and even whales entangle in plastic netting. As a result, these animals can starve to death moreover, the plastic can cut into the animals' skin causing wounds that develop severe infections. **[1]**

(vi) Scientists are trying on working towards new materials that are safer for the environment. They are testing a new polymer that breaks down more easily in seawater. **[1]**

(c) (i) When people litter, or when trash is not properly disposed off, things like plastic bags, bottles, straws, foam beverage cups get carried away to the sea by winds and waterways. This is how plastic waste enters the ocean. **[2]**

(ii) It is really true to say that plastic is everywhere in the world today as it can be found in basic accessories of life such as shoes, clothing, household items, electronics, etc. **[2]**

(iii) The property of plastic which makes it a problem pollutant is that it doesn't biodegrade or break down naturally. Instead, it just fragments, or breaks into tiny pieces over time. These tiny pieces, known as microplastic, can potentially stick around for hundreds or perhaps even thousands of years. **[2]**

(iv) Scientist Jambeck said that 'Individuals actions make a big difference'. She suggested that disposing off plastic properly for recycling or trash collection is a key step. And, simple things like reusable water bottles, mugs and bags, and banning the use of straws really cuts down on waste. These are the things suggested for having healthier oceans. **[2]**

(d). (i) dumped **[1]**

(ii) unfortunately **[1]**

(iii) resemble **[1]**

16. (a) SLEEP AND ITS IMPORTANCE

1. NEED OF ENOUGH SLEEP

1.1 Good Night's Sleep Ess.

1.1.1 Preserves brain health

1.1.2 meet the nxt day with positive attitude

1.2 Six to eight hours sleep a night

1.3 Less than six to eight in older age

1.4 Sleep depr. causes stress

2. SLEEP DEPRIVATION

2.1 Perf. of memory is affected

2.2 causes stress

2.3 lay in bed 30-60 min. than normal time

2.4 relax with no thoughts in mind

3. INSOMNIA

3.1 Cnslt. a doctor

3.2 Affects ability to remember

3.3 Depletes immune system, makes accident prone

3.4 depression, neg. outlook towards life.

4. STRESS MANAGEMENT

4.1 Essential for maximizing brain pow.

4.2 Make it priority to relax

4.3 minute or two of deep breathing

4.4 Best ideas and memories come during relaxation time.

5. MEDITATION

5.1 Meditation - A part of rel. and spiritual life.

5.2 Adopted in Western Countries

5.2.1 develops peace of mind, lowers stress

5.3 Evid. reg. meditation restores sleeping problems

5.4 protects brain against aging

Abbreviations:

Ess.	-	Essential
nxt	-	Next
pos.	-	positive
depr.	-	deprivation
Perf.	-	Performance
cnslt.	-	Consult
pow.	-	power
rel.	-	religious
Evid.	-	Evidence
reg.	-	regular

[5]

(b) Summary

There is a need for enough sleep. A good night's sleep is important as it preserves brain health and helps to meet the next day with a positive attitude. Six to eight hours of sleep is required for an adult and, slightly less as one grows older. Sleep deprivation affects memory and causes stress. to get enough sleep, try to go to bed thirty to sixty minutes earlier than normal time, relax with no thoughts in mind. If suffering from insomnia, consult a doctor; it affects the ability to remember, depletes immune system, makes accident prone, causes depression and negative attitude towards life. Stress management is essential for maximising brain power, make it a priority to relax and practice deep breathing. The best ideas and memories come during relaxation time. Meditation is a part of religious and spiritual life. Western countries are adopting it as it develops peace of mind and reduces stress. There is evidence that regular meditation lowers sleep problems and protects brain against aging. [5]

17. (a) Title – Pros and Cons of a Television

Note Making —

Introduction

- Good for those who carefully choose the shows that they watch.
- Television has its own pros and cons.

Advantages of Television

- Increases knowledge about the world.
- benefits the elderly or patients to consume their time
- Shows diff. programmes based on study, medicine.
- offers non-native speakers the advantage of daily informal language practice.
- Enhances vocab.

Disadvantages of Television

- children watch TV for more than 6 hours
- Weakens concer.
- causes dissatisfaction in people's lives.
- kids only pay attention during commer.
- Children tend to believe that violence is common in society.
- Children become violent

Abbreviations

- vocab. – vocabulary
- diff. – difference
- concer – concentration
- comm. – commercial   [4]

(b) Summary —

Television has a two way impact in one's life. On one hand it is good for those who are careful enough to watch only what is productive. It also helps people to do their daily informal practice of language and increases vocabulary. On the other hand it also has a set of disadvantages. Children tend to watch television for long hours that impacts their concentration levels. Most of the time, the kids pay attention only during commercials. Looking at crime stories, children tend to believe that violence is a part of the society and this at times is reflected in their behaviour. [4]

18. (c) Lines from the passage: "What's the one thing that you associate with your college days? For me, it was consuming copious amounts of chai. A cup of tea was a panacea to all troubles and the companion to all joys." [1]

19. (a) "In those days, there was a huge liking for Chinese food and hence, the name and the choice of cuisine," he says. This line proves the answer. [1]

20. (b) "The business did so well that soon he had installed more than ten telephones....." [1]

21. (c) "Since it was the OTs that gave us our identity,......" [1]

22. (c) "...because some officer came in and decided to teach us how to make them." This shows feeling of acceptance and closeness. [1]

23. (d) "....While the money we make is not great, the respect and the love we have accumulated over the years is what keeps us going." [1]

24. (d) Patronized means supported. [1]

25. (a) The willingness to work hard made him successful. [1]

26. (b) Humilities means being humble and unpretentious, that is the reason, haw he and his family learnt new dishes from the officers and he appreciate them. [1]

27. (c) Trust was built with the passage of time (serving two generations). [1]

28. **Any eight to be attempted.**   [1 × 8 = 8]

(i) We don't take the first step towards a good cause because we underestimate ourselves and think that such a big task cannot be done by us in isolation. [1]

(ii) A two-uses-attitude is a technique in which an article is reused twice to give it a longer lease of life which ends up extracting less raw material from the nature. [1]

(iii) To avoid abuse of paper, the clean side of envelopes can be used to write small notes, lists and reminders around the house. We should avoid the use of paper napkins or paper plates. [1]

(iv) The result of an effective way of garbage disposal is clean and beautiful neighbourhoods. [1]

(v) All the kitchen waste should be collected separately and then compost it to convert it into good garden manure. [1]

(vi) The making of garden manure can be done as community project by digging a large pit in the colony where everyone can contribute to their share of kitchen waste. [1]

(vii) It takes approximately three to six months to make good garden manure. [1]

(viii) Conscious in Para 3 means being concerned or interested. [1]

(ix) Imperative in Para 4 means completely necessary. [1]

29. (i) The correct option is (c) i.e. it includes physical activity. [1]

(ii) In the text the author wants to convey that Cricket is a game bound within rules and usually does not go out of those rules. So, it does not carry any secrets. [1]

(iii) Watching the game of Cricket gives rise to:
(a) Make us experience the thrill of war. [½]
(b) Calms our impatience without creating any conflict. [½]

(iv) The correct option is (c) i.e. generate. [1]

(v) The correct option is (b) i.e. watching a cricket match makes the viewer believe that he is fighting a battle. [1]

(vi) The correct option is (c) i.e. a spectator who enjoys the match as an armchair soldier. [1]

(vii) The writer aptly compares games to a morality play as the rules are made by us and thus can easily be tested for fair and foul conduct, principles of reward and punishment, and emotions of joy and disappointment by the people who are involved or engaged in them also show morality. [1]

(viii) morality play [1]

(ix) then they lose the purpose of providing entertainment and purging of aggressiveness. [1]

(x) The correct option is (b) i.e. The Benefits of Playing Cricket. [1]

30. A. (a) (ii) Chennai [1]
(b) (iii) National Organ and Tissue Transplant Organisation [1]
(c) (iii) to carry the harvested organs in the shortest possible time. [1]
(d) (iv) the cost is prohibitive [1]
(e) (i) they don't have well trained experts [1]
(f) (iii) four hours [1]

B. (a) The traditional method of transporting organs by road is referred to as green corridor. [1]
(b) Smooth transportation of the retrieved organ is necessary so as to help those who are awaiting a life saving transplant of an organ. Moreover, organs tend to have a very short preservation time. [1]
(c) The Chennai Traffic Police reached destination within 11 minutes during peak hours of traffic and save the life of a 9 year old girl. This reflects the dedicated attitude that the Chennai Traffic Police possess towards their duty. [1]
(d) Cadaver Organs have a short span of life and hence transplant should be done in a few golden hours only. Few golden hours refer to the limited time span that is taken to transport the organs. [1]
(e) The heart transplant costs about 15-20 lakh per operation and the post operative treatment and medicines costs Rs. 30,000 per month lifelong. [1]

C. (a) Preserve [1]
(b) Accomplished [1]

31. (a) The passage deals with the issue of Air Pollution at the global level. [1]

32. (c) Air pollution leads to respiratory diseases. [1]

33. (b) (i) Air pollution kills 4.6 million people around the globe and not India. (ii) Para 4 clearly indicates that the respondents with respiratory diseases have outnumbered water borne diseases. [1]

34. (b) "Urban air quality in most mega cities has been found to be critical." [1]

35. (c) Information in Para 5. [1]

36. (b) Transport- 22.5% ; Industries17.2% [1]

37. **Any six to be attempted.** [1 × 6 = 6]

(i) Visible source of annoyance means that it was in 1994 that the plastic bottles emerged in such huge numbers that it became irritating for the common man. It was not much of botheration earlier. [1]

(ii) People demanded a ban on plastics because they could understand the adverse effect of plastic on hygiene. So being concerned about the state of public sanitation, people urged the regulatory bodies to"ban the production, distribution and use of plastic bags. [1]

(iii) Rapid urbanisation, spread of retail chains, plastic packaging from grocery to food and products, to consumer items and cosmetics etc. created a demand for plastics in India. [1]

(iv) It suggests that there is a steady rise in the production of plastic in 2019. [1]

(v) The upward trend of the graph indicates that India's trajectory of plastic consumption and plastic waste is likely to increase. [1]

(vi) The line, oceans turning 'irreversibly into a thin soup of plastic', suggests the dark future with all the plastic waste floating on the surface of the ocean water. It is termed as irreversible as it is almost an impossible task to clean the ocean water. [1]

(vii) To combat the challenges of plastic waste management, the country must formulate robust and inclusive National Action Plans to regulate plastic waste.

As a result, the oceans will be free from plastic and country will establish greater transparency to combat the plastic jeopardy in a more sustainable and holistic way. [1]

38. (i) Not Given [1]

(ii) The correct option is (b) i.e. at the time of landing or taking off. [1]

(iii) susceptible [1]

(iv) The correct option is (b) i.e. the pilot must land at the earliest airport. [1]

(v) The correct option is (a) i.e. but only few are dangerous. [1]

(vi) these are highly critical phases of flying [1]

(vii) maneuverability [1]

(viii) Areas with presence of more bird activity [1]

(ix) The presence of waste disposal sites around air field can attract a large number of birds. [1]

(x) The correct option is (b) i.e. increased. [1]

Summary

Introduction:

Note-making is basically writing down the important points which are used further.

Given below are the purpose of Note-Making:

(*i*) To make a presentation on a particular topic.

(*ii*) To plan any speech or any lecture.

(*iii*) To write any report or any composition.

(*iv*) To make a summary of any text.

(*v*) To convey any message by mentioning important points.

(*vi*) To revise any lesson before examination.

Steps to make Notes:

(*i*) The first and the important step is to read the lesson or any given article carefully with proper concentration to get the answer to the following questions:

(*a*) What is the objective of the passage?

(*b*) How is the theme of the passage developed?

(*ii*) To find out the main points and supporting details in the text. The notes should be brief and contain all the necessary information.

(*iii*) Appropriate heading should be given and if required, the heading can be further divided into sub headings.

(*iv*) The last step is to organize the information in a systematic order.

Characteristics of Note-Making:

(*i*) Notes are shorter than the original text and are not written in grammatically correct sentences.

(*ii*) Helping words are usually avoided in the notes. The main points and the supporting points are different.

(*iv*) Information is made brief using symbols, abbreviations etc.

(*v*) Every heading and supporting points should not exceed 5 words and should be numbered. Try making the notes within 4 to 5 headings.

(*vi*) Summary is prepared on the bases of the notes prepared in a systematic manner that contains the structure of the original text. The summary should not exceed the word limit of 80 words.

Format:

Heading/Title

1. Heading

   1.1

   1.2

   1.3 Supporting points

   1.4

2. Heading

   2.1

   2.2

   2.3 Supporting points

   2.4

3. Heading

   3.1

   3.2

   3.3 Supporting points

   3.4

4. Heading

   4.1

   4.2

   4.3 Supporting points

   4.4

Key To Abbreviations			
1.	E.g.	–	example
2.	Etc.	–	et cetera
3.	&	--	and

PREVIOUS YEARS'
EXAMINATION QUESTIONS

1. Read the passage given below and answer the questions that follow: [8 marks]

[DELHI 2011]

There is nothing more frustrating than when you sit down at your table to study with the sincerest of intentions and instead of being able to finish the task at hand, you find your thoughts wandering. However, there are certain techniques that you can use to enhance your concentration. "Your concentration level depends on several factors," says Samuel Ghosh, a social counsellor. "To develop your concentration span, it is necessary to examine various facts of your physical and internal self" she adds.

To begin with, one should attempt to create the physical environment that is conducive to focused thought. Whether it is the radio, TV or your noisy neighbours, identify the factors that make it difficult for you to focus. For instance, if you live in a very noisy neighbourhood, you could try to plan your study hours in a nearby library.

She disagrees with the notion that people can concentrate or study in an environment with distractions like a loud television, blaring music etc. "if you are distracted when you are attempting to focus, your attention and retention powers do not -work at optimum levels," cautions Ghosh. "Not more than two of your senses should be activated at the same time," she adds. What that means is that music that sets your feet tapping is not the ideal accompaniment to your books.

Also, do not place your study table or desk in front of a window. "While there is no cure for a mind that wants to wander, one should try and provide as little stimulus as possible. Looking out of a window when you are trying to concentrate will invariably send your mind on a tangent," says Ghosh.

The second important thing, she says, is to establish goals for oneself instead of setting a general target and then trying to accomplish what you can in a haphazard fashion. It is very important to decide what you must finish in each span of time. The human mind recognizes fixed goals and targets and appreciates schedules more than random thoughts. Once your thoughts and goals are in line, a focused system will follow.

She recommends that you divide your schedule into study and recreation hours. When you study, choose a mix of subjects that you enjoy and dislike and save the former for the last so that you have something to look forward to. For instance, if you enjoy verbal skill tests more than mathematical problems, then finish Maths first. Not only will you find yourself working harder, you will have a sense of achievement when you wind up.

Try not to sit for more than 40 minutes at a stretch. Take a very short break to make a cup of tea or listen to a song and sit down again. Under no circumstances, should one sit for more than one and a half hours. Short breaks build your concentration and refresh your mind. However, be careful not to overdo the relaxation. It may have undesired effects.

More than anything else, do not get disheartened. Concentration is merely a matter of disciplining the mind. It comes with practice and patience and does not take very long to become a habit for life.

(a) Based on your reading of the above passage make notes on it in points only, using abbreviations wherever necessary. Supply a suitable title.   [5 marks]

(b) Write a summary of the above in 80 words   [3 marks]

2. Read the passage given below and answer the questions that follow: [8 marks]

[DELHI & ALL INDIA 2012]

Research has shown that the human mind can process words at the rate of about 500 per minute, whereas a speaker speaks at the rate of about 150 words a minute. The difference between the two at 350 is quite large.

So, a speaker must make every effort to retain the attention of the audience and the listener should also be careful not to let his mind wander. Good communication calls for good listening skills. A good speaker must necessarily be a good listener. Listening starts with hearing but goes beyond. Hearing, in other words, is necessary but is not a sufficient condition for listening. Listening involves hearing with attention. Listening is a process that calls for concentration. While listening, one should also be observant. In other words, listening has to do with the ears, as well as with the eyes and the mind. Listening is to be understood as the total process that involves hearing with attention, being observant and making interpretations. Good communication is essentially an interactive process. It calls for participation and involvement. It is quite often a dialogue rather than a monologue. It is necessary to be interested and also show or make it abundantly clear that one is interested in knowing what the other person has to say.

Good listening is an art that can be cultivated. It relates to skills that can be developed. A good listener knows the art of getting much more than what the speaker is trying to convey. He knows how to prompt, persuade but not to cut off or interrupt what the other persons must say. At times the speaker may or may not be coherent, articulate and well organised in his thoughts and expressions. He may have it in his mind and yet he may fail to marshal the right words while communicating his thought. Nevertheless, a good listener puts him at ease, helps him articulate and facilitates him to get across the message that he wants to convey. For listening to be effective, it is also necessary that barriers to listening are removed. Such barriers can be both physical and psychological. Physical barriers generally relate to hindrances to proper hearing whereas psychological barriers are more fundamental and relate to the interpretation and evaluation of the speaker and the message.

(*a*) On the basis of your reading of the above passage, make notes in points only, using abbreviations wherever necessary. Supply a suitable title. [5 marks]

(*b*) Write a summary of the above passage in 80 words. [3 marks]

3. Read the passage carefully.

[DELHI & ALL INDIA 2014]

1. I remember my childhood as being generally happy and can recall experiencing some of the most carefree times of my life. But I can also remember, even more vividly, moments of being deeply frightened. As a child, I was truly terrified of the dark and getting lost. These fears were very real and caused me some extremely uncomfortable moments.

2. May be it was the strange way things looked and sounded in my familiar room at night that scared me so much. There was never total darkness, but a street light or passing car lights made clothes hung over a chair take on the shape of an unknown beast. Out of the corner of my eye, I saw curtains move when there was no breeze. A tiny creak in the floor would sound a hundred times louder than in the daylight and my imagination would take over, creating burglars and monsters. Darkness always made me feel helpless. My heart would pound and I would lie very still so that 'the enemy', wouldn't discover me.

3. Another childhood fear of mine was that I would get lost, especially on the way home from school. Every morning, I got on the school bus right near my home that was no problem. After school, though, when all the buses were lined up along the curve, I was terrified that I would get on the wrong one and be taken to some unfamiliar neighbourhood. I would scan the bus for the faces of my friends, make sure that the bus driver was the same one that had been there in the morning, and even then, ask the others repeatedly to be sure, I was in the right bus. On school or family trips to an amusement park or a museum, I wouldn't let the leaders out of my sight. And of course, I was never very adventurous when it came to taking walks or hikes because I would go only where I was sure I would never get lost.

4. Perhaps one of the worst fears I had as a child was that of not being liked or accepted by others. First, I was quite shy. Secondly, I worried constantly about my looks, thinking people wouldn't like me because I was too fat or wore braces. I tried to wear, the right

clothes' and had intense arguments with my mother over the importance of we airing flats instead of saddled shoes to school. Being popular was very important to me then and the fear of not being liked was a powerful one.

5. One of the processes of evolving from a child to an adult is being able to recognise and overcome our fears. I have learnt that darkness does not have to take on a life of its own, that others can help me when I am lost and that friendliness and sincerity will encourage people to like me. Understanding the things that scared us as children helps to cope with our lives as adults.

(a) Based on your reading of the above passage, make notes using headings and subheadings. Use recognizable abbreviations wherever necessary.

(b) Make a summary of the passage in not more than 80 words using the notes made and suggest a suitable title.

Title: Recalling Childhood Fears as an Adult

[3 marks]

4. Read the passage given below: [8 marks]

[DELHI & ALL INDIA 2015]

It is surprising that sometimes we don't listen to what people say to us. We hear them, but we don't listen to them. I was curious to know how hearing is different from listening. I had thought both were synonyms, but gradually, I realised there is a big difference between the two words.

Hearing is a physical phenomenon. Whenever somebody speaks, the sound waves generated reach you, and you definitely hear whatever is said to you. However, even if you hear something; it doesn't always mean that you actually understand whatever is being said. Paying attention to whatever you hear means you are really listening. Consciously using your mind to understand whatever is being said is listening.

Diving deeper, I found that listening is not only hearing with attention but is much more than that. Listening is hearing with full attention, and applying our mind. Most of the time, we listen to someone, but our minds are full of needless chatter and there doesn't seem to be enough space to accommodate what is being spoken.

We come with /a lot of prejudices and preconceived notions about the speaker or the subject on which he is talking. We pretend to listen to the speaker, but deep inside, we sit in judgement and are dying to pronounce right or wrong, true or false, yes or no. Sometimes, we even come prepared with a negative mindset of proving the speaker wrong. Even if the speaker says nothing harmful, we are ready to pounce on him with our own version of things.

What we should ideally do is listen first with full awareness. Once, we have done that we can decide whether we want to make a judgement or not' Once we do that, communication will be perfect and our interpersonal relationship will become so much better' Listening well doesn't mean one has to say the right thing at the right moment. In fact, sometimes if words are left unspoken, there is a feeling of tension and negativity. Therefore, it is better to speak out your mind but do so with awareness after listening to the speaker with full concentration.

Let's look at this in another way. When you really listen, you imbibe not only what is being spoken, but you also understand what is not spoken as well. Most of the time we don't really listen even to people who really matter to us. That's how misunderstandings grow among families, husbands and wives, brothers and sisters.

(a) On the basis of your reading of the above passage, make notes on it using headings and sub-headings. Use recognizable abbreviations (wherever necessary – minimum four) and a format you consider suitable. Also, supply an appropriate title to it.   [5 marks]

(b) Write a summary of the passage in about 80 words.   [3 marks]

Title - Listening Verses Hearing

5. Read the passage given below: [8 marks]

[DELHI & ALL INDIA 2016]

People tend to amass possessions, sometimes without being aware of doing so. They can have a delightful surprise when they find something useful which they did not know they owned. Those who never must change house become indiscriminate collectors of what can only be described as clutter. They leave unwanted objects in drawers, cupboards and attics for years to believe that they may one day need them. Old people also accumulate belongings for two other reasons, lack of physical and mental energy, and sentiment. Things owned or a long time are full of associations with the past, perhaps with the relatives who are dead, and so they gradually acquire a sentimental value.

Something are collected deliberately in an attempt to avoid wastage. Among these are string and brown Paper kept bv thrifty people when a parcel has been opened. Collecting small items can be a mania. A lady cuts out from newspaper sketches of model clothes that she would like to buy if she had money. As she is not rich the chances are that she will never be able to afford such purchases. It is a harmless habit, but it litters up her desk.

Collecting as a serious hobby is quite different and has many advantages. It provides relaxation for leisure hours, as just looking at one's treasure is always a joy. One doesn't have to go out for amusement as the collection is housed at home. Whatever it consists of stamps, records, first editions of books, China-there is always something to do in connection with it, from finding the right place for the latest addition to verifying facts in reference books. This hobby educates one not only in the chosen subject, but also in general matters which have some bearing on it.

There are other benefits also. One gets to meet like-minded collectors to get advice, compare notes, exchanges articles, to show off one's latest find etc. So, one's circle of friends grows. Soon the hobby leads to travelling, perhaps a meeting in another town, possibly a trip abroad in search of a rare specimen, for collectors are not confined to one country. Over the years one may well become an authority on one's hobby and will probably be asked to give informal talks to little gatherings and then, if successful, to larger audiences.

(a) On the basis of your understanding of the above passage make notes on it, using headings and subheadings. Use recognisable abbreviations (Wherever necessary -minimum four) and a format you consider suitable. Also, supply an appropriate title to it.   [5 marks]

(b) Write a summary of the passage in about 80 words.   [3 marks]

6. Read the passage given below and answer the questions that follow:

[DELHI & ALL INDIA 2017]

The most alarming of man's assaults upon the environment is the contamination of air, earth, rivers, and sea with lethal materials. This pollution is for the most part irrevocable; the chain of evil it initiates is for the most part irreversible. In this contamination of the environment, chemicals are the sinister partners of radiation in changing the very nature of the world; radiation released through nuclear explosions into the air, comes to the earth in rain, lodges into the soil, enters the grass or corn, or wheat grown there and reaches the bones of a human being, there to remain until his death. Similarly, chemicals sprayed on crops lie long in soil, entering living organisms, passing from one to another in a chain of poisoning and death. Or they pass by underground streams until they emerge and combine into new forms that kill vegetation, sicken cattle, and harm those who drink from once pure wells.

It took hundreds of millions of years to produce the life that now inhabits the earth and reached a stage of adjustment and balance with its surroundings. The environment contained elements that were hostile as well as supporting. Even within the light of the sun, there were shortwave radiations with power to injure. Given time, life has adjusted and a balance reached. For time is the essential ingredient, but in the modern world there is no time.

The rapidity of change and the speed with which new situations are created follow the heedless pace of man rather than the deliberate pace of nature. Radiation is no longer the bombardment of cosmic rays; it is now the unnatural creation of man's tampering with the atom. The chemicals to which life is asked to make adjustments are no longer merely calcium and silica and copper and all the rest of the minerals washed out of the rocks and carried in the rivers to the sea; they are the synthetic creations of man's inventive mind, brewed in his laboratories, and having no counterparts in nature.

(a) On the basis of your understanding of the above passage make notes on it using headings and sub-headings. Use recognizable abbreviations (wherever necessary-minimum four) and a format you consider suitable. Also supply a title to it.

(b) Write a summary of the passage in about 80 words.

🔑 Solutions

1. (a) Title: Concentration/Developing Concentration

   Note-making

   1. Hurdles to Concentration
      (a) Radio, TV
      (b) Wandering thoughts
      (c) Noisy environment
   2. Technique of Enhancement
      (a) Avoid distractor
      (b) Study table should be kept away from the window
      (c) Set specific goals; time management
   3. Ultimate Help
      (a) Balance study & leisure hrs.
      (b) Don't be disheartened
      (c) Discipline the mind.

   (b) Summary

   Mostly our thoughts start wandering because of radio, TV and noisy environment. We need to identify the reasons in our physical and internal environment which affect our concentration. We can concentrate or study only when distractions are avoided. We should set our goals and try to achieve them. Time should be well managed for study and recreation. A disciplined mind and not getting disheartened attitude is a must. Concentration is the key to study and in meeting our goals in life.

2. (a) Title: Human Mind

   Notes-

   (a) Words Process
       (i) Processing 500 wpm
       (ii) Speaking 150 wpm
   (b) Retain the Attn.
       (i) Audience
       (ii) Listener
   (c) Good Comm.
       (i) Hearing or listening
       (ii) Concentration
       (iii) Attention
       (iv) Interpretation
   (d) Listening barriers
       (i) Physical
           Hindrance
       (ii) Psychological
           (i) Interpretation
           (ii) Evaluation

   (b) Summary

   Research has proved that the difference between processing and speaking rate is 350 w.p.m. which is quite large. The attention of the audience and listener should not wander. A good speaker must necessarily be a good listener. Good listening is an art that can be developed. For effective listening physical and psychological barriers, must be removed. In short, good communication is necessary for an interactive process.

3. (a)

   1. Recalling childhood moments
      1.1 happy & carefree
      1.2 terrified of darkness & getting lost
   2. Childhood Fears
      2.1 Feeling helpless in the dark
          2.1.1 Strange shadows - an unknown beast
          2.1.2 Moving curtains
          2.1.3 Creaking sounds
          2.1.4 Imagining burglars & monsters
          2.1.5 Lying still, with a pounding heart
      2.2. Fear of getting lost (on the way home)
          2.2.1 Scanning school buses-familiar faces, same driver
          2.2.2 Re-confirming the bus
          2.2.3 Not letting leaders out of sight
          2.2.4 Avoiding adventurous act.
          2.2.5 Going with the surety of not being lost
      2.3. Fear of not being liked
          2.3.1 Quite shy
          2.3.2 Worried about looks - fat, wore braces, clothes
          2.3.3 Wearing right clothes
          2.3.4 Flat vs. saddled shoes for school
          2.3.5 Imp. of popularity
   3. Coping with childhood fears as an adult
      3.1 Undg. evolution process - child to adult
      3.2 Recognising & overcoming fears
      3.3 Accepting help from others
      3.4 Role of friendliness & sincerity
      3.5 Undg. things that scared

Abbreviations used

1. & - and
2. act. - activities
3. vs. – versus
4. imp. - importance
5. undg. – understanding

(b) Summary

My childhood was generally happy and had carefree moments. However, darkness scared me with its shadows, unexpected movement of curtains and creaking sounds. It made me feel helpless and I used to lie still, with a pounding heart. I was scared of getting lost. Before boarding my school bus, I scanned it for familiar faces. I was shy and afraid of not being liked by others. As I developed from a child to an adult, I realised that understanding thing that scared us as a child help in coping with life.

4. (a) NOTES:

1. Listening vs. Hearing
    1.1 Difference between the two synonyms
    1.2 Hearing but not listening
    1.3 Paying attention
    1.4 Hearing as a physical phenomenon
    1.5 Consciously using your mind
    1.6 Mind full of needless chatter
    1.7 Accommodating what is said

2. Judgement about the speaker
    2.1 Prejudiced & preconceived notions
    2.2 Dying to pronounce right or wrong
    2.3 Neg. mindset
    2.4 Proving our ver. of things right

3. The ideal way of listening
    3.1 Listen first
    3.2 Listen with awareness
    3.3 Think before you judge
    3.4 Words unspoken leave a feeling of tension and negativity
    3.5 Speak your mind out

4. Listening to understand people
    4.1 Imbibe what is not spoken
    4.2 Times when we don't listen to people who matter
    4.3 Triggers misunderstanding

Abbreviations used:

1. Vs. - verses
2. Neg. - negative
3. Ver. - version
4. Don't - Do not
5. Conc. - concentration
6. Comm. - communication

(b) Summary

Sometimes, we hear people but do not listen to them attentively. The difference between the two synonyms is that one is a physical phenomenon while the other is a conscious use of the mind. We, as listeners often have preconceived notions about the speaker. We come prepared with a negative mindset, tend to prove them wrong and pounce our own version of things. Ideally, we should listen to them, understand their perception and stop judging them in order to avoid misunderstandings.

5. (a) Collecting-A Hobby

1. Reasons why old people accu. belongings
    1.1 lack of phy. & mental energy
    1.2 Sentiment

2. Colleng. Things
    2.1 Avoid wastage
    2.2 Mania

3. Colleng. as a serious hobby
    3.1 relxn. for leisure hours.
    3.2 amusnt.
    3.3 source of edu.

4. Other benefits of colleng.
    4.1 growth of frnd circle.
    4.2 travelling.
    4.3 meeting in another town.
    4.4 able to address audience.

Key to abbreviations

accu. = accumulating

phy = physical

colleng. =collecting

relxn. =relaxation

amusnt. =amusement

edu. = education

frnd. = friend

(*b*) Summary

People have a habit of collecting different kinds of things and they do it unknowingly. They leave unwanted objects in drawers, cupboards for years believing that they may use them in the future. The two reasons why older people gather stuff are due to the want of physical and mental energy and sentiment. Collecting small items can be done to avoid wastage or it can be an obsession. There are many advantages for those who have collecting as a serious hobby. It gives relaxation for leisure hours, amusement and it is a source of education. The other benefits of collecting are: there would be a growth of friend circle, it leads to travelling, meetings in another town and even one can become an authority on one's hobby and will be able to address gatherings and audiences.

6. (*a*) PATH TO ANNIHILATION

   1. Humans Exploiting Nature

      A. contamination of the environment

      B. I. Rd, ch

      C. irrevocable damage

   2. Self-Destruction

      A. ch causing poisoning

      B. rd causing deaths

   3. What are humans Missing Out?

      A. bal with nature

      B. humans progressing swiftly

      C. nature unable to cope

   4. Worsening Situation

      A. mutilation

      B. atomic bomb destruction

      C. synthetic malts

(*b*) Summary

Our Environment is slowly being destroyed by human, and the main culprit being the chemicals along with the harmful nuclear radiations. We are exposed to them through a 'poison and death chain'. The chemicals enter the soil through rain or repeated sprinkling on crops and enter our body. The environment has always been exposed to these difficulties. Everyone has fought and evolved to adjust with nature, as these atrocities came from nature itself. But the manmade challenges are difficult to deal with.

Writing Skills
&
Short Composition

SHORT COMPOSITIONS

1. Notice

Summary

Introduction:

Notices are written to convey some information or make a formal announcement about a particular event. They are short composition. The notices are either given in newspapers or are displayed on the notice board. They are simple and lucid in style.

Some Useful Tips:

- The beginning of notice is usually "This is to in form" or "It is hereby informed that".
- The word notice along with a particular title and the name of the institute/organization should be written.
- The answers to the question 'What', 'Where' and 'When' should be answered.
- The signing of the notice should have a signature, name and designation of the person who is incharge.

Notices can be Categorized Under the Following Heads:

S. No.	Type of notice	Content of the notice	Important information
1	Meeting	Date, time, place, Agenda, purpose, objective Chief Presiding person (if any) Additional information (if any) Contact Address	The notice should contain the date of issuing the notice.
2	Events	Name, Objective, occasion Date, time, duration, venue Who can participate Additional information (if any) Contact address	The notice should contain the name and designation of the person who is writing the notice. The sign of the person should also be there.
3	Lost and found	Name of the article lost or found Date, time and place Specific marks for identification Contents Whom, when, where to contact	It should be written in a box.
4	Tours and Camps	Name of the club/Association Objective Name of the destination Duration Occasion Expenditure Additional information (if any) Contact address	The language of this type of notice should be formal and simple. It is written in third person.

Format:

Name of the Institute/Organization
NOTICE

Date (On which the notice is issued)

Heading (What is the motive of the notice)

(Body of the notice) This is to inform ....

....

....

....

....

Date:

Time:

Venue:

For further details contact undersigned

Sign (Person who is writing the notice)

Name

Designation (The post or position of the person who is writing the notice)

PREVIOUS YEARS'
EXAMINATION QUESTIONS

1. You are Secretary of Gymkhana Club, Madurai. Write a notice in not more than 50 words informing the members to attend an extraordinary meeting of the governing body. Include details like date, time, venue etc. Sign as a Prabhu/Pratibha.   [ALL INDIA 2011]

2. Due to a sudden landslide and inclement weather, St. Francis School, Vasco must be closed for a week. As Principal of that school, draft a notice in not more than 50 words to be displayed at the school main gate notice board.

         [ALL INDIA 2011]

3. You are Srinivas/Srinidhi of D.P. Public School, Nagpur. As Student Editor of your school magazine, draft a notice in not more than 50 words for your school notice board inviting articles/sketches from students of all classes.   [DELHI 2011]

4. You lost your Titan wrist-watch in your school. Draft a notice, in not more than 50 words, to be placed on your school notice board. You are a student of Class XII of Rani Ahalya Devi Senior Secondary School, Gwalior. Sign as Rani/Ram.   [ALL INDIA 2012]

5. Your school has planned an excursion to Lonavala near Mumbai during the autumn holidays. Write a notice in not more than 50 words for your school notice board, giving detailed information and inviting the names of those who desirous to join. Sign as Naresh/Namita, Head Boy/Head Girl, D. V. English School, Thane, Mumbai.   [DELHI 2012]

6. You are Smitha/Sunil, Secretary AVM Housing Society. You are going to organise a blood donation camp. Write a notice is not more than 50 words, urging the members of your society to come in large numbers for this noble cause. Invent all the necessary details.

         [DELHI 2013]

7. You are Vineeta/Vikram, School pupil Leader of Rani Laxmi Bai Senior Secondary School, Gwalior. Draft a notice for your school notice board in not more than 50 words inviting the names of the students who want to participate in the cultural programme organised in aid of the victims of the recent Assam floods.

         [ALL INDIA 2013]

8. An interschool Kabaddi Competition is organized by your school. Write a notice, in not more than 50 words, requesting the students to be present at the venue to encourage the players. Invent all the necessary details. You are Arjun the sports captain of your school.   [DELHI 2014]

9. Every year-in the central park of the city a flower show is held in the month of February. Your school has received a circular from the District Collector inviting your students to visit it. Write a notice in about 50 words informing the students about the show and advising them to go and enjoy it. You are Navtej/Navita, Head Boy/Head Girl Sunrise Public School, Surat.

[DELHI 2015]

10. Sarvodaya Education Society, a charitable organisation is coming to your school to distribute books among the needy students. As Head Boy/Head Girl, Sunrise Public School, Surat, write a notice in about 50 words asking such students to drop the lists of books they need in the box kept outside the Principal's office. You are Navtej/Navita.

[DELHI 2015]

11. Your club is going to organise an interclass singing competition' Write a notice in about 50 words inviting names of the students who want to participate in it. Give all the necessary details. You are Navtej/Navita, Secretary, Music Club, Akash Public School, Agra.

[ALL INDIA 2015]

12. Water supply will be suspended for eight hours (10 am to 6 pm) on 6th of March for cleaning of the water tank. Write a notice in about 50 words advising the residents to store for a day. You are Karan Kumar/Karuna Bajaj, Secretary Janata Group Housing Society, Palam Vihar, Kurnool.

[DELHI 2016]

13. While walking in a park in your neighbourhood you found a small plastic bag containing some documents and some cash. Write a notice in about 50 words to be put on the park notice board asking the owner to identify and collect it from you. You are Amar/Amrita 9399123456.

[DELHI 2017]

14. Arts Club of your school is going to organize a drawing and painting competition. Write a notice in not more than 50 words, to be displayed on the school notice board, inviting students to participate in it. Give all the necessary details.

You are Rishabh/Ridhima, Secretary, Arts Club, Sunrise Public School, Gurugram, Haryana.

[DELHI 2019]

Directions (15-17) : Vineeta is the Head girl of Gandhi Memorial School, Nagpur. She is asked to draft a notice informing students of class XII about a workshop on stress management.

[DELHI Term I, 2022]

15. Select the option that best justifies the title for the notice.

(a) Workshop for class XII students

(b) How to manage stress

(c) Stress management workshop for class XII students

(d) Attention ! class XII students

16. Select the appropriate option that lists important details that Vineeta should include in her notice.

(a) Time to reach the venue, dress code for students, data, name of the resource person

(b) Date, venue, time, name of the resource person

(c) Date, duration, reason to attend, name of the resource person

(d) Date, venue, time, dress code for students

17. Help Vineeta by choosing the right option to complete the statement in her notice.

The workshop will be ______ and will teach some ______ to effectively manage stress

(a) conducted, time

(b) effective, tipe

(c) interesting, students

(d) beneficial, techniques

18. Attempt any ONE from (a) and (b) given below :

You are Neelam/Nitesh, Secretary of the school Library Club. The club is organizing an inter school "Let's Read a Book" week to help develop and encourage the habit of reading among children. Draft a notice in about 50 words, for the school notice board inviting club members from classes X-XII to be student volunteers for the event. Mention day, date, time and venue.

OR

Draft a notice in about, 50 words, urging students of classes IX and XI to be volunteer teachers for a three-week literacy camp to be held in your school from Monday 15th May to Friday 2nd June as part of the community service internship. Children from the neighborhood slums would be taught basic reading, writing, listening, speaking, and numerical skills. Mention the timings and the venue of the camp. You are Rita/Kailash Teacher – in – charge of community service.   [DELHI 2023]

🔑 Solutions

1.   **Gymkhana Club, Madurai**

Notice

18th March 2011

Governing Body Meeting

This is to inform to all the esteemed members of the club that an extraordinary meeting of the governing body is going to be held on coming Sunday. It is mandatory for all members to attend this meeting.

Date: 22/03/2001.

Time: 7 p.m. onwards

Venue. Conference Hall, Gymkhana Club

Thanks

Prabhu (Secretary)

Gymkhana Club

Madurai

2.   **St. Francis School Vasco**

Notice

11th April, 2011

School Closed

(Sudden Landslide and Inclement Weather)

It is to inform to all the students of St. Francis School, Vasco that due to a sudden landslide and inclement weather, the school has been closed for a week from 19.03.2011 to 24.03.2011.

School will reopen on 26.03.2011, Monday at its usual time.

Thanks

Principal

St. Francis School

Vasco

3.   **D.P. Public School Nagpur**

Notice

Feb. 5, 2011

Articles for School Magazine

This is to inform to all of you that our school magazine 'Developer' is going to be published next month. Students are requested to submit articles and sketches for the magazine. Topics of the article are Environment pollution, conservation of wildlife or any social issue. Articles should not exceed 500 words. Good and attractive sketches on A4 sheet need to be submitted. All these are to be submitted to the editorial board of the magazine within fifteen days.

Srinivas

Student Editor

4. **Rani Ahalya Devi Sr. Sec. School, Gwalior**

Notice

15th Oct, 2012

Watch Lost

Lost a Titan Wrist Watch in the school Premises during recess today. My name Rani is engraved on its back cover. The finder is requested to return the same to the undersigned.

A treat is promised.

Rani

XII-B

5.   **D. N. English School, Thane, Mumbai**

Notice

3rd March, 2012

Excursion to Lonavala

This is to inform all the students of class XII that our school's Excursion Club is planning for an excursion to Lonavala near Mumbai during the autumn holidays. The tour will be for 10 days from 1st June to 10th June. The lodging and boarding charges will be Rs. 3000 per head. Those, who are interested, can give their names with full payment in the school office. For further information, contact undersigned

Naresh

(Head Boy)

6.   **AVM Housing Society (Welfare Club)**

Notice

19th March, 2013

Blood Donation

This is to inform all the students and staff members that Lion's Club has been going to organise a Blood Donation Camp on the eve of school foundation day. All the students are requested to persuade their parents and neighbours to donate blood for noble cause of the humanity.

Date: 20th March

Time: 9 A.M. to 2 P.M.

Venue: Cricket ground in school Campus.

Donate the blood generously. A drop of blood can save the precious life. Donors will be provided a donor certificate with light refreshment. For registration or further query, please contact undersigned.

Smitha

(Secretary)

7. Rani Laxmi Bai Sr. Sec. School, Gwalior

Notice

2nd March, 2013

Cultural Evening

Our school is organising a cultural evening to collect funds for the victims of the recent Assam floods on 10th March, 2013 at 4 p.m. in the auditorium. Those students are interested to participate in the programme may contact from the leader. All the students are requested to make it a success. The Hon'ble education minister will be the Chief Guest. Students are allowed to bring their friends and relatives.

Ticket: Rs. 50

Vineeta

Sch. Pupil Leader

8. NCR School, Delhi

Notice

March 23, 2014

Inter-School Kabaddi Competition

An inter-school kabaddi competition will be held on Saturday, February 20, from 9am. in our school playground. All the students are requested to be present at the venue to cheer and encourage the participants. Please note that cameras and eatables will not be allowed. For any query, contact the undersigned.

Arjun

Sports Captain

9. Sunrise Public School, Surat

Notice

10 February, 2015

Flower Show

All the students of the school are invited by the District Collector to the Flower Show that is being organised in the Central Park on 20 February, 2015. The event will showcase different varieties of flowers and would be very informative and interesting. The students may take their passes from the undersigned before 19th February, 2015.

Navita

(Head Girl)

10. Sunrise Public School, Surat

Notice

12 February, 2015

Book Distribution

This is to inform all those students who are in need of books that Sarvodaya Education Society, a charitable organisation, is coming to our school for distribution of books. Interested students should drop the lists of books they need in the box outside the principal's office by 16 February, 2015.

Navtej

(Head Boy)

11. Akash Public School, Agra

Notice

12 March, 2015

Inter-class Singing Competition

An Interclass Singing Competition will be organised on 20 March, 2015 for the students of Akash Public School. Each class will be represented by one student. The class monitor is required to get the name of the representative registered with the undersigned before 15th March, 2015. The winning class will be rewarded suitably.

Navtej

Secretary (Music Club)

12. **Residents Welfare Association Janata Group Housing Society, Palam Vihar, Kurnool**

Notice

4th March, 2016.

Water Supply to be Suspended

This is to inform all the residents of Janta Group Housing Society, Palam Vihar, that there would be suspension of water supply for 8 hours on 6th March, from 10 am to 6 pm in the society. This is due to cleaning of water tank. So, you are requested to store enough water to avoid the scarcity.

Karan Kumar

Secretary

Janta Group Housing Society

13. **Lodhi Garden, New Delhi**

Notice

March 09, 2017

Lost And Found

A small plastic bag containing some documents and some cash has been found near the gate no. 2 of Lodhi Garden. The documents consist of some balance sheets and images. If anyone has lost such a bag, please collect the same from me. My contact no. is 9399123456.

Amar

D-18, Lodhi Colony

14. **Sunrise Public School, Gurugram**

Notice

1st March 2019

Drawing And Painting Competition

This is to inform all the students that the school is going to organise a Drawing & Painting Competition. Arts club requests all the budding artists and creative students to participate and enjoy a fun afternoon with colours. The details of the competition are as follows:

Date & Day: 8th March, 2019, Friday

Time: 11:00 am to 1:00 pm

Venue: **School Auditorium**

Interested students are requested to give their names to their respective class teacher latest by 6th March 2019. For further details, please contact the undersigned.

Sd/-

Ridhima

(Secretary, Arts Club)   [4]

15. (c) Precise information conveyed by the title.

[1]

16. (b) Dress code for students in the school is school uniform and so need not be mentioned separately.   [1]

17. (d) Workshop would benefit the students and techniques not tips are imparted to effectively manage stress.   [1]

18. **XYZ School**

Notice

26 February, 2023

Let's Read a Book : The school Library Club is organising an inter-school "Let's Read a Book" event for one week starting from March 1 between 10 am to 4 pm till March 7 everyday at the school campus. The aim of the event is to encourage students to inculcate the habit of reading books. Moreover, reading would help students gain knowledge and get their brains activated. Students of grades XI and XII are welcome to volunteer for the event and give their names to the undersigned at the library.

Neelam

Secretary   [5]

OR

XYZ School

Notice

26 February, 2023

Literacy Camp : The school is organising a literacy camp for three weeks from 15th May to 2nd June at the school campus between 9 am and 12 pm. The camp is aimed at teaching the children from neighbourhood slums the basic reading, listening, speaking and numeracy skills. This literacy camp is being organised as a part of community service internship and students fo classes IX and XI are welcome to volunteer to give back to the community. Those interested can provide their information to the undersigned during school hours at the Literacy Club.

Rita

Teacher-in-charge (Community Service)   [5]

2. Drafting Posters

Summary

Introduction:

A poster is an information to make an announcement or appeal or to spread awareness among the public. Posters are usually made attractive to attract the people.

Purpose:

(i) To create awareness among people.

(ii) To warn against some danger.

(iii) To promote some product.

(iv) To make an announcement of a cultural show/ exhibition etc.

Layout:

(i) It should be made attractive using some sketches.

(ii) Different fonts can be used.

(iii) Some slogans and quotations can be used.

Content:

(i) The theme of the poster should be clear and appropriate.

(ii) The name of the issuing authority should be clearly mentioned.

(iii) Some contact details should be mentioned.

(iv) The content of the poster should be arranged in a systematic manner.

Format:

Format of Poster

DESIGNING IN ARTISTIC WAY Use eye catching slogans • No fixed pattern • Any shape or font size • Broad ideas no details Issued by –XYZ Authority

PREVIOUS YEARS' EXAMINATION QUESTIONS

1. You were very upset about the reports on communal riots in various parts of the country As a concerned social worker, design a poster in not more than 50 words, highlighting the importance of communal harmony. You are Vinay / Vinita.   [ALL INDIA 2014]

2. You are Secretary, Social Service League of your school. Design a poster to be displayed in your colony and in a local hospital premises inspiring people to make a pledge to donate eyes and other organs of their bodies.   [Delhi 2020]

Solutions

1. Peace, Harmony, Love and Brotherhood are the pillars of a strong nation.

Let's make our nation stronger by strengthening these pillars.

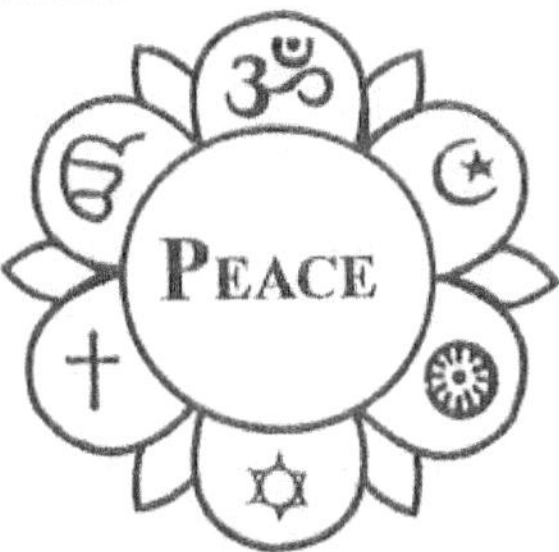

Issued in public interest by Vinay

2.

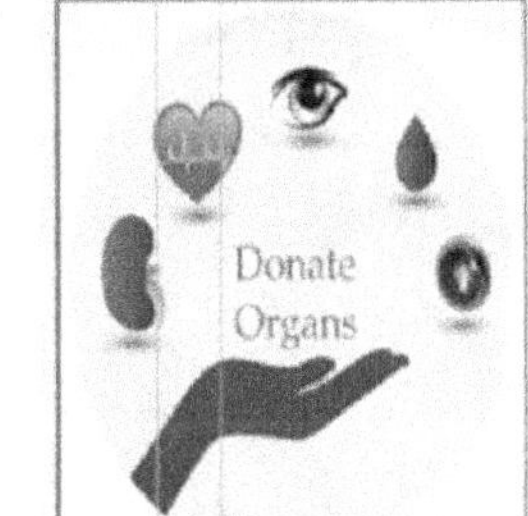

Not All Superheros Are Found In Movies Donate Your Organs And Be Someone's Superhero   [4]

3. Advertisements

Summary

Introduction:

It is a type of public announcement which is made through a popular medium that focuses on a large number of people.

Advertisements are usually written for the promotion of goods, services etc. It can also be written to give information about missing persons etc.

Advertisements can be made through newspaper, magazines, TV and radio. They are made brief containing the required information.

In newspaper or magazines the advertisements are basically of two types:

(*i*) Classified advertisements: These are placed by individuals to promote their services or because of the need for goods and services. These ads are chargable according to the space they occupy in the newspaper or magazines. They are usually short and contain complete information.

(*ii*) Display/commercial advertisement: These advertisements are made attractive and are usually included under the category of posters. They convey the complete message.

Categories of classified Advertisements:

(*i*) Situation vacant: Title/Heading
  - Wanted/Required/Situation vacant
  - Name of the post
  - Number of posts
  - Qualification
  - Preferences
  - Salary
  - To whom and how to apply

(*ii*) To Let:
  - Type of accommodation
  - Size
  - Facilities
  - Preferences
  - Contact address and phone number

(*iii*) Sale/Purchase of property or vehicle:
  - Available/Sale/Purchase
  - Type of accommodation/vehicle
  - Description of accommodation-Size, facilities, location etc.
  - Description of vehicle-vehicle model, colour, accessories, condition, etc.

(*iv*) Tours and travels:
  - Destination and duration
  - Details of facilities-stay, boarding, food, etc.
  - Cost and discount
  - Package if any
  - Travel agency: Agency and phone number

Format:

Situation Wanted
Electronic Engineer. Graduate from IIT Gandhinagar, fluent in English, 6 year work experience in IT field, seeking job in Ahemdabad.
Expected Salary-40,000
Email ID: abc@gmail.com Ph. No.: 9345201875
Name

PREVIOUS YEARS' EXAMINATION QUESTIONS

1. You want to rent out your newly constructed flat in the heart of the city. Draft an advertisement in not more than 50 words to be published in 'The Deccan Herald', Bangalore under classified columns. Give all the necessary details. You are Mohan/Mahima of Jayanagar, Bangalore.

[DELHI 2011]

2. C.P.R. Senior Secondary School, Meerut is looking for a receptionist for the school. Draft an advertisement in not more than 50 words to be published in classified columns of Hindustan Times. You are Romola Vij, Principal of the school.   [DELHI 2012]

3. You are Mohan / Mohini, General Manager of P.K. Industries, Hyderabad. You need in accountant for your company. Draft, in not more than 50 words, an advertisement to be published in 'The Hindu' in classified columns.   [ALL INDIA 2012]

4. You are General Manager, Hotel Dosa, Gurgaon. You need a lady Front Office Assistant with sound knowledge of computers. She must be a graduate and good in communication skills with pleasing manners. Draft an advertisement in not more than 50 words to be published in Gurgaon Times.   [DELHI 2013]

5. You have a three bedroom flat in Dwarka, which you want to let out on rent. Draft an advertisement in not more than 50 words to be published in "The Times of India', under classified columns. Contact 2758902.   [ALL INDIA 2013]

6. You possess an acre of land in the heart of the city. You want to dispose of this property since you have decided to buy a flat. Write an advertisement to be published in a national daily, giving all the necessary details. You are Krishan of Moti Nagar, Delhi.   [DELHI 2014]

7. Your school, Akash Public School, Agra needs a canteen manager. On behalf of the Principal, write an advertisement in about 50 words to be published in the classified columns of a local daily. Mention the educational and professional qualifications, other qualities required in the management who to apply to and the last date for the receipt of applications.   [ALL INDIA 2015]

8. Principal, Sunrise Global School, Agra requires a receptionist for her school. Draft a suitable advertisement in about 50 words to be published in the classified columns of a national newspaper giving all the necessary details of qualifications and experience required in the receptionist   [DELHI 2016]

9. You are Karan Kumar/Karuna Bajaj a leading lawyer practising in Surat. You want to buy an independent house at City Light Road to be used as office-cum-residence. Draft an advertisement in about 50 words for the classified columns of a local newspaper. You can be contacted at 45645678.   [ALL INDIA 2016]

10. You are Vikram/Sonia, an Hon's graduate in history with specialization in Medieval India. You are well acquainted with places of historical interest in Delhi, Agra and Jaipur, You are looking for the job of a tourist guide. Write an advertisement in about 50 words for the situations wanted column of a local newspaper. Your contact no. 999751234.   [Delhi 2017]

11. You are Vikram/Sonia, an electronics engineer who has recently returned from the U.S. and looking for a suitable job in the IT industry. Draft an advertisement in about 50 words for the Situations Wanted column of a national newspaper. Your contact number is 9193010203.   [AI 2017]

12. You are Harish / Harshita of 12, Seva Nagar, Pune. You want to sell your flat as you are shifting to another city for work. Draft a suitable advertisement in not more than 50 words to be published in The Pune Times under the classified columns.   [Delhi 2018]

13. You are Principal of National Public School, Jaipur. You require a TGT (Maths) for your school. Draft a suitable advertisement in not more than 50 words for the Situations Vacant' column of "The National Times' stating essential and desirable qualifications, experience etc of the candidates.   [Delhi 2019]

14. At Rohini, in Delhi you have a three-bedroom flat with all modern amenities. It is fully air-conditioned and has power backup. For the sale of this flat draft a suitable advertisement in not more than 50 words to be published in a local daily. Give all the necessary details. Your contact number is 9911223344.   [Delhi 2020]

 Answer any four out of the five questions given below with reference to the context. **[Delhi Term I, 2022]**

15. Mrs. Sujatha wants to rent out the first floor of her house. She decides to draft an advertisement to be published in a national daily. Choose the correct option under which heading she can publish her advertisement.

    (a) For Sale

    (b) Accommodation Wanted

    (c) Situation Vacant

    (d) To let

16. Select the option that lists the important information that Sujata needs to include in her advertisement.

    i.   Size of the house

    ii. People in the neighbourhood

    iii. Location

    iv. Amenities and facilities

    v.   Distance from Metro Rail Station

    vi. Contact address

    (a) i, iii, v & vi

    (b) i, iii, iv & vi

    (c) ii, iii, v & vi

    (d) i, ii, iv & v

Solutions

1. **For Rent**

Available for rent at 44 Jayanagar, Bangalore a newly constructed flat with three bedrooms, dining hall, first floor spacious balcony, two side open car parking, independent and modern amenities for a small family. Lease is preferred. Contact Mohan: 9717544544

2. **Situation Vacant**

Required a convent educated smart and young lady in the age group of 21-25 with pleasing personality and fluency in communication to work as receptionist for a reputed public School in Meerut. Knowledge of computer besides English will be preferred. Handsome salary and perks. Apply till 19th March with latest resume and recent passport size photograph to the Principal, Romola Vij, C. P. R. Sr. Sec. School, Meerut.

3. **Situation Vacant**

Required competent and experienced accountant capable of handling accounts independently, commerce graduate having at least two years experience in any reputed firm will be preferred. Salary and perk, as per the efficiency and performance of the candidates. Apply in confidence to General Manager, P. K. Industries, Hyderabad up to 15th April.

4. **Situations Vacant**

Wanted a graduate female front office assistance with sound knowledge of computers. The candidate must have sound knowledge of computers. Fluency in communication skills and a pleasing personality is mandatory criteria for this job. Interested candidate should walk in on 16th of April, 2013 along with all relevant documents.

General Manager,

Hotel Dosa

Gurgaon

5. **To Let**

Available on rent Dwarka, DDA MIG Flats, 1st floor, three B/Rs. lobby, balcony fully furnished, well ventilated, walking distance from main market and Metro Station. Rent expected Rs. 22,000 (fixed). Company lease preferred. Contact Mitesh, DDA MIG, Dwarka, Ph. 011-2758902.

6. **For Sale**

Available for sale a 1-acre plot in the heart of the city. Plush green surroundings and posh colony make it most suitable for building residential flats. 200 meters from the nearest metro station. Government approved. Price negotiable. Contact: Krishan, D 44, Moti Nagar, Delhi, Mobile: 9744444544

7. Situation Vacant

Akash Public School, Agra, requires a canteen manager for the school canteen. The candidate should have Dip. in Hotel Management with at least 3 years of managerial experience in the relevant field and willing to work extra hours on special occasions. Interested candidates may apply to the principal of the school latest by 4th April, 2015

8. Situation Vacant

Sunrise Global School, Agra is looking for a young qualified and dynamic female candidate for the position of receptionist with a minimum of two years experience with sound computer knowledge. She should also be fluent in both English. Salary is negotiable Contact 9844544544.

9. Property

For immediate purchase, an independent house at City Light Road for office-cum-residence. Exquisitely designed, 3/4-bedroom house with ultra-modem amenities, along with spacious hall for office set up. Car parking space is a must. Owners or bonafide dealers contact Karan at 45645678.

10. Job Hunt

I am Vikram, an Hon's graduate in History with specialisation in Medieval India. I am currently looking for a job of a tourist guide. I am always driven by a passion of visiting historical places. This passion has made me well acquainted with places of historical interest in Delhi, Agra and Jaipur. If you are looking for candidates with such profile please contact me on 999751234

11. Situation Wanted

I, Vikram, am looking for a job as an electronics engineer in Delhi-NCR region. As I have 2 years experience of working in the US, I would be happy to be associated with any multinational company of repute. Salary is negotiable. Contact Number: 9193010203

12. For Sale

Available for sale Newly Constructed flat in Seva Nagar, 3 B.H.K., attached bathrooms, complete maple woodwork, store room, prime location, near city mall, park facing. Price- 22 lakhs (negotiable). Brokers excuse. Interested contact: Harish – 9744544544.

13. Situations Vacant

WANTED a smart, confident candidate with a Masters/ Ph. D degree in Mathematics, fluent in English as well as Hindi, amicable nature and at least 4 years of experience of teaching in a school affiliated to the CBSE Board for the post of TGT (maths) at National Public school, Jaipur. Remuneration commensurate with performance. Interested candidates to mail their biodata to nps@gmail.com. Selected candidates would be informed via a telephone call. Further interview to be held on th and 5th February, 2019 between 9:00 am and 3:00 pm. For further details, contact the reception : 45600000   [4]

14. TO LET

Available a newly built flat for Bachelors and Family on I floor, GGI Block, Rohini

3BHK, centralized A.C, 24 × 7 power backup with a picturesque Landscaped

Walking distance from Metro station and Ambience Mall

Contact- XYZ

9911223344   [4]

15. (d) To Let means to give property for rental purpose.   [1]

16. (b) Amenities & facilities, contact address are the most important inclusions. Site and address will confirm location also.   [1]

4. Invitations and Replies

Summary

Introduction:

It is basically a verbal or written request asking someone to be somewhere at a particular date or time. They are mainly given to relatives, family, friends etc. on wedding occasions, dinner, functions or parties.

Types of Invitation

1. **Formal Invitation**

   - A printed message in a box with a formal or a respectful tone is suited.
   - Always addressed in third person
   - Avoid short forms or nick names or abbreviations of some words. Only RSVP is written at the end of the invitation at bottom. It means 'Reply if you Please'. It is followed by sender's name, address and phone number.
   - The content of the message is written in the middle mentioning name of the host, date, time, venue, occasion or function.

2. **Informal Invitation**

   - It can either be printed or be a written message.
   - Always addressed to the first person.
   - Since informal, short forms or nick names or abbreviations can be used.
   - It should clearly mention all the details of the host, date, time, venue, function etc.

Tips to Know

- There should be a separate line for each information provided.
- The name of the host should be mentioned clearly.
- It should clearly mention all the details such as date, time, venue, function or occassion.
- In case of inviting a VIP, mention the person's name and designation/post in a dignified and respectful manner.
- Expressions that are used are:

  'request your benign presence' OR 'request the pleasure of your company'
- Always write a formal invitation in third person in simple present tense.

Format

Format for Formal Invitation

<table>
<tr><td>

Host/ Organizer (Springwell Secondary School)

Request the benign presence of your company on the inauguration of their

ANNUAL FUNCTION 'ZEST'

Date : 28th September 2018

Time: 7 p.m. onwards

Venue: School Auditorium

Schedule

Chief Guest Welcome	7:30 p.m.
Principal Speech	7:45 p.m.
Dance performances	8:00 p.m.
Play by Middle Wing	9:00 p.m.
Thanking speech by Chief Guest	9:30 p.m.
Snacks	9:45 p.m.

RSVP   Best Wishes

XYZ   Springwells

Secondary School

813*******

Map Overleaf

</td></tr>
</table>

Format for Formal/Informal Invitation

Sender's Address

....

Date: ....

Dear ABC,

....

Body of the Invitation ....

Date:

Time:

Venue:

Your Truly/ Lovingly,

XYZ

Reply to a Formal Invitation

1. Refusal: Mr. Kashyap is thankful to Mr. Tyagi for the kind invitation extended and would have been very pleased to attend his house warming party but will not be able to attend it due to ill health.

2. Acceptance: Mr. Verma is thankful to Mrs. Gaur for their beloved invitation for the wedding of their daughter and as much delighted in accepting it.

PREVIOUS YEARS'
EXAMINATION QUESTIONS

1. The literary club of your school is putting up the play 'Waiting for Godot'. As secretary of the club, draft an invitation inviting the famous writer Sudeesh Gupta to be the guest of honour at the function. Write the invitation in not more than 50 words. You are Govind/Gauri. [ALL INDIA 2014]

2. As secretary of the Literary Club of st. Anne's school, Ahmedabad, draft a formal invitation in not more than 50 words for the inauguration of the club in your school. [DELHI 2014]

3. On 30th November your school is going to hold its annual sports day. You want Mr Dhanraj Pillai, a noted hockey player to give away the prizes to the budding sportspersons of the school. Write a formal invitation in about 50 wards requesting him to grace the occasion.

   You are Karuna/Karan, Sports Secretary, Sunrise Global School, Agra.

   [ALL INDIA 2016]

4. Your friend, P.V. Sathish, has invited you to attend the wedding of his sister, Jaya. You find that you have an important paper of pre-board examination on the day of the wedding. Thus you cannot attend the event. Write in about 50 words a formal reply to the invitation expressing your regret. You are Puneet/Puneeta Vij, M-114, Fort Road, Chennai.   [ALL INDIA 2017]

5. You are Faiz/Falak Mazumdar living at 39, Udampur Colony, Shimla. You decide to hold a dinner party to congratulate your grandparents on their golden wedding anniversary. Draft a formal invitation in not more than 50 words to all family members to attend a grand dinner at home.   [DELHI 2018]

6. Mr. and Mrs. Agarwal of Pushp Farms, Kolkata, are hosting a party on the occasion of the twenty-first birthday of their daughter, Vinita. Write a letter of invitation to Sonakshi, their niece, giving details of the date, time and venue in about 50 words.   [Delhi Term II, 2022]

7. You are Sarla Dutta, proprietor of Child's Planet, a showroom of children's educational toys. Draft a formal printed invitation in 50 words to be sent to your patrons, friends and relatives inviting them to the opening of the new showroom. Give details such as day, date, time and venue.
[DELHI 2023]

Solutions

1.   The Literary Club of NCR School

Takes enormous pleasure to invite you as the guest of honour for the occasion of ANNUAL THEATRE FESTIVAL. The play is to be held on Saturday 20 December at 6:00 pm. at the school auditorium. Members of the cultural club are putting up the play 'Waiting for Godot.' Your presence will give confidence to the students and make the occasion more significant.

Govind (Secretary)

Literary club, NCR School

2.   St. Anne's School, Ahmedabad

Cordially invites all the students, staff members, parents and PTA members for the inauguration of Literary Club in the school on Monday, 18 March, 2009 between 9:30 am-10:30 pm. The inauguration ceremony will be followed by a snacks party. Everyone is warmly invited to join the same.

Secretary

3. Sunrise Global School

4 April 2016

Mr. Dhanraj Pllai

544, Purvasha Complex

Ranchi,

Subject: Invitation to preside over Annual Sports Day.

Respected Sir,

Our school is going to hold its annual day on 14th of April 2026. The entire school family would feel highly blessed if you give your consent to preside over the function and facilitate the budding sportspersons. For most of the sportspersons, it would be a dream come true to receive awards from you in person.

Scores of students, teachers, parents and prominent personalities of our society would be participating in the function.

With warm regards,

Karan

Sports secretary,

Sunrise Global School, Agra

4. M-114

Fort Road, Chennai

12-05-18

Dear P.V.

I am overwhelmed to hear that Jaya is getting married. I would love to join you on wedding day but unfortunately I have an important pre-board exam on the same day. I regret that I will not be able to attend the wedding.

Yours

Puneet

5. Dear members of The Majumdar Family,

Your kind presence is requested on the auspicious occasion of the GOLDEN WEDDING ANNIVERSARY of our Grandparents Mr Jitendra Mazumdar & Mrs Ekta Mazumdar on 24th April 2018. We are planning a family dinner party on the auspicious day at our house.

R.S.V.P.

Falak

39, Udampur Colony, Shimla

9844544544

6. 51, Pushp Farms

Kolkata.

13th May, 20XX

Dear Sonakshi,

You will be pleased to know that your cousin, Vinita, is celebrating her twenty-first birthday on 15 May 20XX. To celebrate the same we are hosting a grand party on 15 May at Hotel Lake View from 6.30 pm onwards.

With immense pleasure we invite you to be a part of this special occasion. Do come with a plan to stay over for a couple of days so that we can enjoy extended celebrations.

Waiting to share a few happy moments together.

Yours lovingly,

Sunita Agarwal   [3]

7.   Child's Planet

Announces the opening of a

New Showroom

of Children's Educational Toys in

ABC Mall XYZ City

on

5 March, 2023

At 11 a.m.

All are cordially invited.

Visit for the best and latest range of educational toys for children to supplement their education.

Avail an inaugural offer of

10% discount

on all toys.

R.S.V.P.

Sarla Dutta

Proprietor-Child's planet   [5]

1. Letter Writing

Summary

Introduction:

A letter should be written keeping in mind to whom it is written. A letter should contain useful information. It should not suggest discourtesy and indifference to the person addressed.

Classification of Letters:

Letters may be divided into following classes:

(*i*) Business or Official Letters: It is written for registering complaints, for making enquiries, asking for and giving information, placing orders and sending replies.

(*ii*) Letter to the Editor: It is written for giving suggestions or opinions on the issues which are related to public interest.

(*iii*) Application for a job: It is written while forwarding the resume for a job opportunity.

Salutations and Subscriptions:

Family and friends---	Dear...	Yours affectionately/lovingly Or Your loving friend/son etc
Strangers---	Dear Sir/Madam	Yours truly
Business Persons/officials--	Sir	Yours truly/sincerely
Principal/Teachers--	Respected Sir/Madam	Yours obediently Or Yours faithfully
Editors--	Sir	Yours truly/sincerely

Useful Expressions

Enquiry-	I am writing to enquire about Please let us know We will be glad if you
Complaint-	It is a matter of great regret that.... This is to bring to your notice that... This is to complain....
Request-	I would be grateful if..... Kindly oblige me by.....
For job application-	With reference to your advertisement dated X/X/XXXX, I offer myself as a candidate Through some reliable sources, I have come to know that.....

Conclusion:

- Looking forward to your reply
- Thanking you in anticipation for a positive reply.
- With warm regards

Format of a Formal Letter:

Sender's Address

....

....

Date

Receiver's Address

Subject: <u>Underline the subject</u>

Dear Sir,..

....Body......................

....

....Yours Sincerely

Signature

(NAME)

Format for Application for a Job:

Resume

(To be attached with job application RESUME/BIO DATA/CV)

Name	-	....
Father's Name	-	....
Date of Birth	-	....
Educational Qualification	-	....
Experience	-	....
Marital Status	-	....
Corresponding Address	-	....
Phone No.	-	....
E-mail ID	-	....
Language Known	-	....
Hobbies	-	....

PREVIOUS YEARS'
EXAMINATION QUESTIONS

1. Write a letter to the Dean, D.P.I. School of Management, Mumbai, requesting him to apprise you of the details such as eligibility criteria, fees, hostel facility, prospects of placement etc. for admission to P.G. Diploma in HRM. You are Ram /Romola of 21Civil Lines, Bareily **[DELHI 2011]**

2. Write a letter to the Editor, 'Deccan Times', Bangalore about the inadequate parking facilities in the Commercial Street, M.G. Road, which is causing a lot of inconvenience to the people. Offer your suggestions. You are Anoop / Ritu, 24 Hennus Road, Bangalore.

   [DELHI 2011]

3. You are Raman/Rama, a member of Parent-Teacher Association of Little Valley Senior Secondary School, Hyderabad. Write a letter to the Principal of the school asking him to introduce vocational, stream in the school providing facility of teaching such subjects as computers, insurance etc. so that the students may not needlessly continue academic studies. You are residing at 15, Anand Colony, Hyderabad. **[ALL INDIA 2011]**

4. Write a letter to the Manager (Publication) of Little Flower Company, Hyderabad, placing an order for 4 books on Management and Administration recently published by them. You are Ronit/ Rohini, Librarian, H.P. Engineering College, Tirupati. **[ALL INDIA 2011]**

5. You are Pritam/Priti, 27, W. E. A. Karol Bagh, Delhi. You have decided to shift your residence to Faridabad and hence decided to discontinue your membership of Brain Trust Library, Karol Bagh. Write a letter to the Librarian, requesting him to cancel your membership and refund your security deposit of five thousand explaining your inability to continue your membership.

   [DELHI 2012]

6. You are Anu/Arun,13 W. E. A. Karol Bagh, New Delhi. You feel very strongly about the ill-treatment meted out to stray dogs at the hands of callous and indifferent people. Write a letter to the editor of a national daily giving your views on why some people behave in such a manner and how these dogs should be treated.

   [DELHI 2012]

7. Write a letter to the Station Master, Anand, informing him about the loss of your suitcase which you realized only on alighting at Anand. You travelled by Navjivan Express from Chennai to Anand. You are Priya/Prasad of 12, Kasturi Bai Street, Chennai **[ALL INDIA 2012]**

8. As a parent, write a letter to the Principal, ABC School Delhi, requesting him/her to grant your ward Akhil/Asha Arora, permission to attend the school two hours late for a month as he/she has to attend the coaching classes arranged by Sports Authority of India, on being selected for participation in National Swimming Championship. **[ALL INDIA 2012]**

9. As a regular commuter by bus from Noida to Delhi, you. have been witnessing rash driving by the bus drivers daily without an exception. Write a letter to the Editor. 'The Times of India' drawing the attention of the General Manager, Delhi Transport Corporation to this problem. You are Priti / Prakash, 15 Udyog Vihar, Noida.

   [DELHI 2013]

10. You are Amit/Amita living at F-25, Shalimar Colony, New Delhi. You have observed that many school-going children drive around on bikes without a valid driving licence, thereby endangering their own lives as well as those of others. Write a letter to the editor of a national daily with a view to sensitizing students about the risks involved in underage driving. Also, give suggestions. **[DELHI 2011]**

11. Write a letter to your cousin, Raj Prakash who is currently staying at Dubai explaining the process of CCE being used by the CBSE for the Secondary School Examination in its affiliated schools. Also, mention how you and your classmates have reacted to this scheme. You are Narain/ Nisha,20 Fort Road, Mumbai.

    [ALL INDIA 2013]

12. Recently you travelled from Bangalore city to Vasco in Vasco Express. To your dismay, you found that the coach was infested with cockroaches. Write a letter to the Editor, 'The Hindu' drawing the attention of the General Manager, Southern Railways, to the prevailing unhygienic conditions and asking for remedial action. You are Saroj/Saran, 5/31 Bangalore Cantt., Bangalore. **[ALL INDIA 2013]**

13. You are Prem/Parul of 16, TT Nagar, Bhopal. You would like to apply for the post of Marketing Manager in a reputed firm in Mumbai. Write a letter to the Public Relations Officer, Chantac Enterprises, Mumbai, applying for the job. Write the letter in 125 – 150 words giving your biodata.

[ALL INDIA 2014]

14. Recently you went to your native village to visit your grandparents. You saw that some of the children in the age group 5-14 (the age at which they should have been at school) remained at home, were working in the fields or simply loitering in the sheets. Write a letter in 120-150 words to the editor of a national daily analysing the problem and offering solutions to it. You are Navtej/Navita, M-114 Mount Kailash, Kanpur.

[DELHI 2015]

15. When cricket teams go abroad the members are allowed to take their wives, even friends along with them. Does this fact distract them or help them to focus on their game in a better way? If it is good, why don't we allow our athletes to enjoy the same privilege? Write a letter to editor of a national daily in 120-150 words giving your views on the issue. You are Navtej/Navita M-1 14 Mount Kailash, Kanpur.

[DELHI 2015]

16. You are Navtei / Navita, Secretary, Environment Club, Akash Public School, Agra. You, along with a group of students, went on a 3-day tour through Corbett National Park. You found how the tourists abuse the available facilities and thus endanger the environment. Write a letter in 120 - 150 words to the editor of a national daily highlighting the situation. Suggest ways through which the environment of the Park can be saved. [ALL INDIA 2015]

17. On Teacher's Day, you read in a newspaper that, privately owned and managed schools in small towns or even in the suburbs of metropolitan cities exploit their teachers by paying them just a fraction of their authorised salaries. This affects their performance in the classroom and thus the lives of their students. Write a letter in 120-150 words to the editor of a national daily raising your voice against such exploitation.

Suggest ways to solve this problem. You are Navtej/Navita,7l2 Taj Road, Agra.

[ALL INDIA 2015]

18. Yesterday you went to Sunrise Hospital, Market Road, New Delhi taking with you victim of a hit and run accident. There were chaotic conditions in the casualty department. The injured was attended to after a lot of precious time had been lost. Write a letter of complaint in 120-150 words to the Medical Superintendent. You are Karan/ Karuna, M-114, Mall. [DELHI 2016]

19. Lack of job opportunities in the rural areas is forcing people to migrate to cities. Every big city thus has a number, of slums in it. Life in these slums is miserable. Write a letter in 120-150 words to the editor of a national newspaper on how we can improve the living conditions in these slums. You are Karan/Karuna, M-114, Mall Road Delhi. [DELHI 2016]

20. Along with air and water pollution, our cities are also under an attack of noise pollution. Marriage processions, DJ's during wedding receptions, loud music from neighbourhood flats etc. are all source of noise which is not good for the old, the ailing and students. Write a letter in 120-150 words to the editor of a local newspaper describing the problem and making a request to the concerned authorities to solve it. You are Karan/Karuna, M 114, Mall Road, Delhi.

[ALL INDIA 2016]

21. In all big cities road rage, has become a serious problem. A minor scratch, a little push, or a small brushing past can lead to a scuffle sometimes resulting even in murder. Write a letter in 120-150 words to the Police Commissioner giving your views on the problem and its solutions. You are Karuna/Karan, M-L14, Mall Road, Delhi.

[ALL INDIA 2016]

22. In our society we do not give to our women the respect and status that they deserve. Women are stared at, stalked and even molested. We need to change the male mindset about women. Write a letter in 120-150 words to the editor of a national newspaper giving your views on the problem. You are Omar/Amna, A114 Mall Road, Delhi. 6

[DELHI 2017]

23. You want to spend a week-long holiday at Shimla in the month of October. You have decided to stay at Hotel Snow view. Write a letter in 120-150 words to the manager to book a room. Mention the dates, facilities in the room, food, sight-seeing facilities etc you will need. You are Amar/Amrita M114, Lake Road, Karnal.

[DELHI 2017]

24. Mountview Public School, Kalka is run by an NGO to give quality education to the children of the deprived sections of society. The Principal of the school feels that blackboards in the classrooms need to be replaced. She decides to ask the chairperson of the NGO named 'Education for All' for funds. Write her letter in 120 — 150 words. Her name is Shaweta Pandit.

[ALL INDIA 2017]

25. National Book Trust organised a week-long book fair at Anna Grounds, Chennai. You visited the fair and bought a few books. You were pleased with the arrangements, enthusiasm of the visitors and the fact that books have not yet lost their relevance in the world of the Internet. Write a letter in 120–150 words to the editor of a local newspaper to express your feelings. You are Lalit/Latha, 112, Mount Road, Chennai.

[ALL INDIA 2017]

26. You are Neeraj/Neeraja Shekhar, Principal, Vasant Public School, Pune. Your school has just started a music department. Write a letter to the Manager of Melody House, Pune, whole sale suppliers of musical instruments, placing an order for musical instruments for the school. Ask for a discount on the catalogue prices. (120-150 words)

[ALL INDIA 2018]

27. Bal Vidya Public School, Bhilai, urgently requires a post-graduate teacher to teach political science for which they have placed an advertisement in The Bhilai Express. You are Sanjay/Sanjana Sharma from 21, Vasant Marg, Bhilai. Draft a letter including a CV, applying for the advertised post. (120-150 words)

[ALL INDIA 2018]

28. You have realized the necessity of education and financial independence of women for their family, society and in turn for the nation. Write a letter to the Editor, The National Times' highlighting your ideas on the importance of education of women leading to a better status for them. You are Tarun/Taruna, B-7/9, Mall Road, Delhi. (100 - 125 words)

OR

You bought a refrigerator two months ago from Mohan Sales, Ashok Vihar, Bangalore. It has developed certain problems regarding its functioning. Cooling has stopped and it is making a lot of noise. Write a letter of complaint to the Manager asking him for immediate repair/ replacement of the same. You are Sachin/Shashi, 61 Pratap Enclave, Bangalore. (100 - 125 words)

[DELHI 2019]

29. You are Tapas / Tapasya of A-150, Mount Road, Chennai. You have seen an advertisement in the newspaper. 'The Chennai Times'for the post of Manager (Accounts) in Sundaram Westside, Chennai. Apply for the post with your complete biodata. (120-150 words)

OR

Write a letter to the Editor, 'The Indian times', Jaipur highlighting the need to tap the sports talent at a young age by sports teachers, coaches etc. so that it does not go unrecognized. Thus we shall have a large pool of young talented sports persons who can be groomed. You are poorva / Paras 78, Inderpuri, Jaipur. (120-150 words)

[DELHI 2020]

30. You are Chitra/Chetan Deshpande, residing at Akash Nagar, Agra. You come across the following classified advertisement in the newspaper. Write a letter, in about 120-150 words, applying for the position of a computer teacher at Sunrise Global School, Agra.

SITUATION VACANT

WANTED a qualified computer teacher for Sunrise Global School, Agra. Applicant must be post graduate in Computer Science with minimum 3 years of work experience. Mention additional skills and interests. Apply with full particulars within a week to the Principal, Sunrise Global School, Agra.

[DELHI Term II, 2022]

31. You have received an invitation to attend the prize giving ceremony for the Inter-School Science Exhibit Competition. Write a formal letter in 50 words to the Principal of Rose Public School, Simla informing him/her about your inability to attend the ceremony. You are Dr. Suri. Mention day, date, time and venue.

[DELHI 2023]

32. You are a resident of Pranihar Colony and a member of the Resident Welfare Association. During your morning walks, you have noticed that the parks are in a dismal condition. Due to the neglect, the parks are no longer safe for residents or children to play. Write a letter to the editor of your local newspaper in about 120-150 words, expressing your views on the situation and suggest ways of improving and maintaining the park. You are Satish/Sunaina, member RWA. Use the given cues along with your ideas to compose this letter.

Reason for Neglect	Efforts to be taken
Unpruned trees	Regular maintenance
No dustbins	Removal of broken benches
Stray dogs	Security tightened
Lack of security	Waste bins

OR

You are Prerna Seth, you saw the given advertisement in the newspaper and wish to apply for the position advertised.

Dimla Pvt. Ltd.

REQUIRED – an accountant with minimum 5 years' experience.
Job responsibilities – prepare salaries, account, record of income and expenditure.
Preferred skills & qualifications – B.Com., C.A. with knowledge of computers, especially Excel.
Send your bio-data within 10 days to Rajiv Arora, Personnel Manager, Dimla Pvt. Ltd., Nehru Enclave, Indore.
Write a letter to The Managing Director, Dimla Pvt. Ltd. along with your bio-data, expressing your interest in the situation vacant.

Write a letter to The Managing Director, Dimla Pvt. Ltd. along with your bio-data, expressing your interest in the situation vacant.

[DELHI 2023]

Solutions

1. 21, Civil Lines
    Bareily
    14th Feb, 2015
    The Dean
    D.P.I. School of Management
    Mumbai

    Sir,
    I am Ramola, a student of 3rd year of Graduation. I came across the advertisement for P.G. Diploma in HRM. I am wholeheartedly interested in

making my career at HRM and do this course. However, before moving ahead, I need some information and details about the course. First, what are the eligibility criteria for getting admission? Are candidates appearing for the final year graduation examination will be considered for the course? Is there any entrance test for the admission or the admission is on the marks basis? Please provide the fee structure. What is the mode of payment? Can it be paid by instalment?

Does school provide hostel facility? If yes, what are the charges? What are the prospects for placement? Is there any campus placement? Your on-time support will help me decide regarding admission to the esteemed institution.

Thanks

Yours faithfully

Ramola

2. 24, Hennus Road,
    Bangalore
    The Editor,
    Deccan Times
    Bangalore
    Sub.: About the Inadequate Parking Facility
    Sir,
    With due respect, I wish to say that I, Anoop own Ekta Music shop in the commercial street, M.G. Road. There are a good number of shops on both sides of the street which leads to a huge crowd gathering here for the shopping, on a daily basis. Most of the shopkeepers and customers come in their own vehicles. However, the parking facility is extremely inadequate. Vehicles are more than the alotted space. This causes great inconvenience to the people. Shopping in this area has become quite difficult as the passages get jammed by vehicles. An open field is lying vacant beside this area which can be used as a parking place. It can help reduce the problem of parking in the area. I would like to draw the attention of the concerned authorities to the problem and the solution suggested.

Thanks

Your's faithfully

Anoop

3. 15, Anand Colony
    Hyderabad
    4th April 2011
    The Principal
    Little Valley Senior Secondary School,
    Hyderabad
    Sub: Introduce of Vocational stream.
    Sir,

    I am, Rama, a member of the Parent-Teacher Association of the school. Through this letter, I wish to say that today the approach and the environment of education have changed immensely. Various job opportunities have been created, however they demand quite a different skill-sets. Traditional approaches of teaching and learning are not going to help in this regard. The need of the hour is that the conventional courses should be replaced with the vocational ones. Therefore, I would request you to consider subjects like computers, insurance etc. This could be put into a new stream as a vocational stream in the school. There are so many jobs in the area of computers, retails, marketing and insurance. These will help the students in preparing themselves for the job market.

    Thanks and Regards

    Rama

4. H.P. Engineering
    College, Tirupati
    14th April 2011
    The Manager
    Little Flower Company
    Hyderabad
    Sub.: Order for books
    Sir,

    Through this letter, I would like to place an order for four books on Management and Administration. As these books have been recently published by your company they aren't available in the market currently. Send forty-four copies of each book as soon as possible. Attach the bill with the books.

    An Account payee cheque has been attached with this letter so that you can immediately dispatch the books.

    Thanks

    Rohini

    Librarian

5. 27, W. E. A. Karol Bagh
    Delhi
    2nd March 2012
    The Librarian
    Brain Trust Library
    Karol Bagh, Delhi
    Subject: Application for discontinuation of Library membership.
    Sir,

    With due respect, I beg to state that I, Pritam, a member of your library with membership no. 5544, has been using the facility of the library since 2005 without any gap. I have deposited the membership fee for the year of 2012 which will be effective from 1st April 2012. However, I have shifted my residence from Karol Bagh to Faridabad due to transfer in the job.

    Now, I would be quite unable to use the library services in future. So, please cancel my library membership and return the membership fee of Rs. 5000/- (five thousand) as soon as possible. Hoping, you will do the needful at the earliest.

    Thanking you

    Yours Sincerely

    Pritam.

6. 13, W. E. A. Karol Bagh,
    New Delhi
    4th April 2012
    The Editor
    The Times of India
    B. S. Zafar Marg
    New Delhi
    Subject: Attention towards the cruelty against the stray dogs.
    Sir,

    I would like to use a column of your esteemed daily to draw your kind attention towards the cruelty against the stray dogs in our area by the people.

    Animals are man's best friends, but man is their worst enemy. For centuries, it has been a practice of man to be ruthless as he wants to only kill animals both for pleasure and to adorn himself.

But here, the story is different, the people of the area to rebuke these stray dogs, beat them badly with a stick. I have very strong feeling about the ill-treatment given to stray dogs at the hands of insensitive and apathetic people. It is not good for these stray dogs. Animals too have a right to live freely like humans. They also need our love, compassion, care and protection.

So, you are requested to consider the above-said subject and publish the same. So that the concerned authority may be made aware of such kind of cruelty against these stray dogs. These dogs should be protected from such callous people. Hoping a favourable consideration soon from your esteemed newspaper.

Thanking you,

Yours sincerely

Anu

7. 12, Kasturi Bai Street

Chennai-20

4th April 2012

Station Master

Anand

Subject: Complaint against the loss of my suitcase.

Sir,

With due respect, I beg to state that I was boarded in Navjiwan Express from Chennai. I was seated in compartment No. S-7, Birth No. 44 and seat No. 45. I had three suitcases. All of them were properly chained and locked. I travelled in the train whole night, the train was under the supervision of the compartment in charge. As the train approached at the Anand. I started to pick up my all luggage. But unfortunately, one of the suitcase was missing. The suitcase contained some clothes with cash and Jewellery of worth Rs. 50,000.

So, I request you to register my complaint to search my missing suitcase and take prompt action against the compartment in charge, and return the same at my address which is mentioned above.

Hoping for a favourable action to take place soon.

Thanking You,

Yours sincerely

Priya.

8. The Principal

ABC School

Delhi

4th April, 2012

Subject: Permission for Late Arrival of my son Akhil Arora.

Sir,

With due respect, I would like to inform you that my son Akhil Arora, Class XII-A has been selected by Delhi state to represent the state at the forth coming National Swimming Championship at Delhi in the first week of May.

The pre-competition of swimming coaching camp is being held from 14th April to 24th April 2012. This one month long camp will begin at 6.00 a.m. and continue till 9.00 a.m. and then again from 4 p.m. to 7 p.m. I do not want to neglect his studies altogether. But circumstances constrain him. Much though I want him to reach the school in time but I fear he may be late by two hours.

Keeping in view the circumstances detailed above, I request you to grant him permission to attend the school two hours late for a month. The grace shown by you will help him bring fame and reoute to the school and the family.

I hope you will grant my request.

Yours sincerely

(Vishal Arora)

9. 15, Udyog Vihar

Noida

4th April, 2013

The Editor

The Times of India

7, B.S. Zafar Marg

New Delhi

Subject: Rash driving by the DTC bus driver Noida to Delhi route.

Sir,

May I use a column of your esteemed daily to draw your kind attention towards the Rash driving by the DTC bus driver Noida to Delhi route.

Being a regular commuter of DTC bus route number 34 from Noida to Delhi for last five year, I have witnessed a lack of professionalism in DTC bus drivers on this route, especially in recent time. They never take care of the commuter's safety as they drive in zig-zag way. It is quite frequent now that we hear sad accidents taking place on this route.

Most of the driver's attitude is not good, they often use foul language, I guess some of them are illiterate and lack of proper training about professional etiquettes.

A new trend of rash driving and zig-zag driving is being observed among the drivers now a days. The department should provide a proper training, create awareness and also maintain the provision of punishment for the rash-drivers.

So, I request you to public the above said view points so that the top official of the Delhi Transport Corporation may get aware about this worsening situation. I am hoping a favourable consideration from you regarding this matter.

Thanks

Yours sincerely

Prakash

10. F-25, Shalimar Colony

New Delhi

4th April, 2013

The Editor

Time of India

Kasturba Gandhi, Marg

New Delhi

Sub: Driving without licence

Sir,

May I use a column of your esteemed daily to draw your kind attention towards the problem driving bikes by the school children without a valid licence. This is really a matter of concern. Many school going children drive around on bikes without a valid driving licence. They should understand that by doing this they are risking their lives and others too. They should understand that their lives are very valuable for their family and society. They are the future of the country. Parents should make their children understand that driving without proper licence is illegal and by doing this they are violating the law. Authorities should also come forward in this direction. They should launch an awareness campaign and make the children understand about the safety of lives. If this does not work, the children should be penalised with heavy fine as a deterrent.

Your's Sincerely

Amit

11. 20 Fort Road,

Mumbai,

14th April, 2013

Dear Raj Prakash,

I am well here and hope you must be doing well too. A lot of time has passed since I last wrote you a letter. This year, C.B.S.E. has introduced CCE examination system at secondary school examination in affiliated school of Mumbai. In which my school also falls. It is a foreign policy. The students of the school have lost the fear to fail in the examination.

Now a days they are not taking keen interest in their studies. The main reason behind this pattern is, the teachers are awarding good marks in Formatting Assessment. So, they need few marks to pass the examination in Summative Assessment.

Some students are unhappy, one of my junior is also among them. As he is a very laborious student, and had remained stood first from 6th standard. There is no fare system to award the marks.

I want to know your opinion about this system. Convey my regards to your mother and love to Ekta.

Thanking You

Yours sincerely

Narain

12. 5/31, Bangalore Cantt.

Bangalore

22nd March, 2014

The Editor

The Hindu

M. G. Road, Bangalore

Subject: Attention towards the unhygienic condition in VASCO Express.

Sir,

May I use a column of your esteemed daily to draw your, kind attention towards the unhygienic condition prevailing in Vasco Express which runs from Bangalore city to Vasco. In Vasco Express, the compartments of the train are not in proper hygienic condition. The cleaning department has not been working for last two years. There are regular complains that the coaches were infested with cockroaches. Being a regular commuter, I have also complained many times with other regular commuters to the General Manager of Southern Railway. They assured us that they would act but they did not do anything.

The passengers have been facing such kind of unhygienic problems and travelling in the train, as there is no alternate way to travel from Bangalore to Vasco.

So, you are requested to consider the above said matter and publish the same so that the top officials of the Southern Railway may get aware and commuters can get some relief.

I am hopeful of a favourable consideration soon.

Thanks

Yours sincerely

Saran

13. 16, TT Nagar

Bhopal

Dec. 20, 2014

Public Relations Officer

Chantac Enterprises

Mumbai

Subject: Job application for the position of Marketing Manager

Sir/Madam,

In reference to your advertisement in The Hindu dated Dec 18, 2014. I wish to apply for the position of Marketing Manager in your renowned organisation. I am a hard-working and an honest person who is passionate about marketing. I completed my MBA in 2012. Since then, I have been working with RP Communications as a manager. I am enclosing my bio-data and photocopies of certificates and testimonials for your reference. If selected, I assure you that I shall work with utmost devotion and sincerity to your full satisfaction.

Looking forward to hearing from you.

Yours truly

Parul

BIO-DATA

Name :	Parul
Father's Name :	Pappu
Address :	16, TT Nagar, Bhopal
Phone :	9134344444
Date of Birth :	27th September, 1989
Marital Status :	Unmarried
Educational Qualification :	MBA in Finance, Management School of Gurgaon, (98115) B.Com. in Accountancy, LU(90749)
Experience :	Manager at RP Communications (March, 2012 February, 2014)
Skills :	Excellent communication skills, ability to convince and influence people
Languages known :	English, Hindi and French
Reference :	Mr. D.N. Tripathi Chairman, KP

14. M-114, Mount Kailash Kanpur

3 March, 2015

The Editor,

The Times of India

Kanpur

Subject: Pathetic condition of children

Sir,

Through the columns of your reputed newspaper, I would seek to draw the attention of the government, NGOs and society at large towards the large population of children are not going to school. Children are the future of any country and a country that does not take care of this valuable resource suffers later. A successful nation is that which makes its youth strong enough to lift mighty responsibilities on their shoulders. Unfortunately, this is not the case in our country. Education, which is a necessity, is still a luxury here. Poor people hesitate to send their children to school. On a recent visit to a village, I couldn't help but notice the sheer number of children who should have been in the school, but were not. Children in the age group of 5-14 are supposed to go school to make a bright future. But in the villages, they are either seen loitering around or helping their parents in the fields, which is a very painful and depressing situation. It is high time that the government and NGOs take up the issue seriously and implement measures to solve it. Besides, literate villagers can also help by starting make shift schools to educate the children till reforms are made by the government.

Yours sincerely,

Navita

15. M-l 14, Mount Kailash

Kanpur

4 April, 2015

The Editor,

The Times of India

Kanpur

Subject: Difference in status of cricketers and other athletes

Sir,

Through the columns of your esteemed newspaper, I would like to express my views on the difference in the status of cricketers and athletes. Cricket is a very popular game in India and cricketers are idolised. The public as well as the officials are willing to give special privileges to them. The extent of their love is such that rules are easily bent for them. Cricketers are allowed to take their families with them when they go on tours, irrespective of the fact that this may distract them while playing. But when it comes to other games, Indian Government becomes rather stingy and the players do not get the same treatment. Why do we have two policies? I believe this is because cricket and cricketers are worshipped, while the other games and their players are ignored. Even the finances that are allotted to these games are either too less or are utilised by the officers themselves. The perspective of Indians needs a revolution and all the games need equal treatment, after all they all bring glory to the country. Government needs to implement measures to keep all the games at par.

Yours sincerely,

Navita

16. Akash Public School,

Agra.

4th April, 2015

The Editor,

The Hindu, New Delhi

Subject: The harmful effects of tourism on Corbett National Park

Sir,

With your kind consideration and this column of your reputed newspaper, I would like to draw the attention of the concerned authority to the widespread abuse of available facilities in the Corbett National Park by visitors and the consequential endangerment to the environment.

The visitors not only litter the place with non-biodegradable plastic packets and wrappers, but also, use woods from the forests for cooking purposes. Excessive trampling of the soil has been reported to have a harmful effect on the natural ecosystem. The tranquillity of the habitat, which is so crucial to the resident fauna, is habitually disturbed by tourists playing loud music in their safari jeeps and during their camps.

The Corbett National Park is the oldest in the country, established in 1936, to protect the endangered Bengal tiger. The public should be made aware of the fact that ecotourism should not be- facilitated at the cost of harming the environment. It is my request that this issue be immediately taken up by your esteemed publication to generate further awareness.

Yours sincerely,

Navtej

Secretary (Environment Club)

17. 712 Taj Road, Agra

2 March, 2015

The Editor,

The Hindu New Delhi

Subject: Exploitation of teachers in privately-owned suburban and small town schools

Sir,

It is quite a depressing state of affair that the teachers in most of the private schools in small towns and metropolitan suburbs are being exploited. Three years back on the occasion of Teacher's Day, this issue was brought to light in Prime minister's speech as well, bringing up that the appalling plight of teachers serving in such schools are paid a fraction of what their peers get in government schools.

This rampant malpractice certainly affects the performance of the teachers in the classroom, as most teachers take up other jobs to make ends meet and do not put in the requisite hours of teaching in the schools. The school trust pays these teachers much less than the amount they were promised, leading to frequent resignations and constant changes in the faculty. This has affected student's performances and led to an atmosphere of uncertainty in the schools, which is detrimental to the cause of education.

As a nation, which prides itself on revering its teachers, it must be noted that we cannot build a future for our students if we do not give due credit to our teachers. Therefore, I request your esteemed publication to take up this matter in order to investigate the issue further and mobilise the public towards calling for a complete overhaul in the education system of the country.

Thanking you,

Yours sincerely,

Navtej

18. M-114,

Mall Road, Delhi.

4th April, 2016

The Medical Superintendent

Sunrise Hospital

Delhi.

Sub: Chaotic conditions in the casualty department of Sunrise Hospital.

Sir/Madam,

Yesterday, I went to Sunrise Hospital, market Road, New Delhi taking a victim of a hit and run accident. I am very much shocked to see the chaotic conditions in the hospital's causality department. The injured person who was screaming was attended very leisurely resulting in loss of more blood. The patient got unconscious. This happened only because of not attending the patient in time. Hence, I request you to take-strict action against the hospital authorities. So, that, the situation won't get repeated.

Thanking you,

Karuna.

19. M-144

Mall Road, Delhi.

4th April, 2016

The Editor

The Hindustan Times, New Delhi

Sub: Miserable condition of people living in slums

Sir/Madam,

Through the esteemed column of your newspaper, I wish to draw the attention of the authorities to the people living in slums and their miserable conditions. Most of the slums in cities are cramped with the people migrated from rural part of the country. The very survival of these people has become very difficult with pathetic living conditions. This is mainly because of nit of education and hygiene. Their illegal occupancy has become a burden on resource. The, main reasons for their migration to cities from rural areas is lack of job opportunities and poverty. Government should discourage migration by creating opportunities in rural area. Even NGO's can adopt slums in order to make the life of these people better.

Thanking you,

Karuna.

20. M-114,

Mall Road

Delhi

4th April 2016

The Editor

Delhi Times, Delhi.

Sub: Problem of noise pollution

Sir,

On behalf of all the residents of my area, I would like to draw the kind attention of the concerned authorities towards the increasing noise pollution caused by marriage processions and DJ's. Our locality was one of the peaceful areas where there was no such problem till the last year. However, after the construction of a new convention centre, marriage processions are very common. Loud music keeps blaring up till night, which has disturbed the peace and tranquillity of the area.

I hope the concerned authorities will look into the matter and take apt steps in this direction to ease the situation.

Yours truly,

Karan.

21. M-114, Mall Road

Delhi

4th April, 2016

The Police Commissioner

Delhi.

Sub: Increase in crime on city roads.

Sir,

Through this letter I would seek your attention toward the road rages which sometimes even lead to murders. Day by day the numbers of vehicles are on upsurge the problems are also increasing innumerably. In such heavy traffic, it is so quite normal that the vehicles get minor scratches which results in fatal fights and even loss of a precious human life.

Its really hard to calm down such enraged people as they start scuffling with no time to even think. Even in a fit of anger, killing can't be justified. Before it becomes a normal part and parcel of our daily life in Delhi, one need to act. What I feel is sometimes it is because of poor traffic management and untrained drivers. I believe that we need to take certain measures to overcome this problem such as conducting traffic awareness week, appointing the traffic volunteers and also by effective traffic management etc.

I hope my views will be taken in good faith.

Thanking you.

Yours faithfully

Karan.

22. A 114 Mall Road

Delhi

June 16, 2018

The Editor

The Times of India

New Delhi

Subject: Safety of women

Sir,

Through the columns of your esteemed newspaper, I would like to draw the attention of all the well learned citizens of the nation towards the increasing incidents of eve-teasing in our Indian society. Whether it is a small girl or an aged lady or a college or office going woman, such incidents are creating a great sense of fear in the minds of all.

We do talk about women empowerment on a regular basis and ask everyone citizen of this nation to be a part of it. But, unfortunately, even after repetitive gender sensitization campaigns, the people are not learning. The woman is still considered the second gender in the society. We forget to realise that this second gender makes up the half of the population of the nation, and if they feel unsafe in the society, it would not take much time for the society to lose its existence.

India is now developing at a rapid pace and so should its society. The fight for women safety is not a fight of an individual or of a particular gender but is the fight of all the humans because if the society fails to serve half of its population, its end would not be too far.

Yours truly,

Amna

23. M114, Lake Road

Karnai

March 09, 2017

The Manager,

Hotel Snowview

Shimla

Subject: Rooms reservation request

Sir,

I am travelling to Shimla in the month of October with fifteen more people. I would like to book 5 rooms for the same. My itinerary details are as follows:

Arrival – October 12, 2017

Rooms required – 5 Double bedrooms including 2 suites

Departure: October 17, 2017

You are requested to confirm the reservations and let me know for further inquiries.

Yours truly

Amrita

24. The Principal

Mountview Public School

Kalka

13-05-18

The Chairperson

Education for All

Subject: Requesting Funds for blackboard replacement.

Sir,

I would like to thank you for providing the opportunities of a better study environment to our children from challenged background. Through this letter I would like to bring in your notice that the blackboards in our school have all worn out.

I feel all the blackboards should be replaced by white boards as they are chalk free and easy to maintain. Furthermore, I would also request you for a few projectors as they could also be used to make the learning more visual and application based.

I request you to release the funds as soon as possible. I am also attaching a quotation with the letter.

Thank You!

Yours

Shweta Pandit

25. 112, Mount Road

Chennai

13-05-18

The Editor

Delhi Times,

Subject: Books- Not yet, a Lost Cause

Sir

Through your globally recognized columns I would like to share an observation on Books in this internet clad era. Last week, National Book Trust organized a week-long book fair at Anna Grounds, Chennai.

The venue was divided into separate sections based upon the genre of the books. Each section had a separate theme. A few well-known writers also came upon to give guest talks and spoke about many behind the scene incidents. There were several activities organized in different theme sections.

The place was oozing with positive energy. I was overwhelmed to see so many people to turn up for the fair in this internet clad era. I was relieved to see that books are not yet, a lost cause.

Thank You!

Yours

Lalit/Latha

26. Vasant Public School

Pune

14th April 2018

The Sales Manager

Melody House

Pune

Sub : Order of musical instruments

Sir,

Our school has recently started its very own Music Department and henceforth we want to place an order for the bulk supply of musical instruments. As our relation with your store is about to start, we expect a handsome discount on the catalogue price. We are hopeful to get 18% special discount which is industry norm for the institutional buyers. Apart from that, cost involved in dispatch, fright and onsite installation should be borne by your store.

The list of instruments with their particulars and numbers is attached herewith.

1. Keyboards - 5 pieces

2. Drum sets - 3 set

3. Sitar - 1

4. Trampoline - 2 sets

5. Pianos - 2

6. Violins - 2

7. Flutes - 5

Please find enclosed cheque of Rs. 50000/- as advance, (which can be encashed once you agree to our terms). Rest will be paid after receiving the instruments. We will appreciate the delivery by 25th April 2018, as our new session starts on 26th of April 2018.

Yours faithfully

Neeraj

Principal

Vasant Public school

27. 21 Vasant Marg

Bhilai

4th April 2018

The Principal

Bal Vidya Public School, Bhilai

Subject: Application for The Post of a Post-Graduate Teacher

Dear Sir,

I have come across the advertisement in The Bhilai Express for the post of postgraduate teacher to teach political science. I would like to apply for the same. I feel that my experience and skills noticeably match the requirement. As asked, I have enclosed my resume with this letter.

Currently I am working as a political science teacher at St Jhon's High School since last 3 years. I have a Master's in political science and a B.Ed degree as well. I will bring with me the experience and the disciplined work culture that I have gained in last 3 years. In my current job, I am trusted with the responsibilities of class IX to XII. I remain open for feedback from my learners, mentors and peer teachers as it helps me grow better. I am sure that, given an opportunity, I can prove my efficiency in your school just as I have proved at my current work place.

I would be glad to have a demo session apart from the personal interview. Looking forward to a favourable consideration.

Sincerely,

Sanjana Sharma

Attachments: Resume and Work Experience Certificate

Resume

Full Name :	Sanjana Sharma
Father's Name :	Mr Mitesh Sharma
Date of Birth :	1 August 1984
Marital Status :	Unmarried
Educational Qualifications :	Post Graduation in Political Science & B.Ed
Experience :	3 years at St. Jhon's High School
Salary Expected :	90,000 per month
Languages Known :	English, Hindi and Marathi
Permanent Address :	21 Vasant Marg, Bhilai
Contact No. :	9744544544
E-mail ID :	sanjanasharma44@gmail.com

28. B-7/9

Mall Road

Delhi - 110001

2nd March 2019

The Editor

The National Times

147, Lajpat Nagar

Delhi 110006

Subject: Importance of education of women leading to a better status for them

Sir/Madam

Through the columns of your esteemed newspaper, I would like to express my views about the importance of education of women leading to a better status for them. In present times, it is important for the women to be educated, not only for the sake of gaining knowledge but also for providing them with a better stature and position in the society. Women today, are competent enough and are ready to work as equals.

For centuries, women were seen as mere caretakers thus education was not deemed important for them. This resulted in them being exposed and stuck in an abusive environment with no escape, as they were not independent. Their views were not taken into consideration and their voices were muted. Education acted as a revolutionary weapon and women had the means to get themselves heard. Women like Marie curie created a place for other women in science with her nobel prize in chemistry. Education provides a person with economic independence, respect, and power to bring a change in the society. When women started receiving education they contributed to the wokforce which was earlier operating at half the efficiency.

Educating women is just the first stepping stone towards their empowerment. Better status in the society means equal respect, income and standard of living. All of this has become of vital importance in a world like ours.

Thus, I hope my views find a place in your newspaper and make the people aware of the importance of education for liberating women so that they can stand as equals and conquer the world.

Thanking you

Yours Truly,

Taruna   [6]

OR

Sachin

61, Pratap Enclave, Bangalore - 560034

2 March 2019

The Manager

Mohan Sales, Ashok Vihar,

Bangalore - 560024

Subject : Complaint against a malfunctioning refrigerator

Sir

This is to bring to your notice that I had purchased a Samsung 255 litres double door refrigerator from your showroom via receipt number : SR4400 dated 6th November,2018. The appliance is still in the warranty period, therefore, I would like free servicing according to the terms and conditions of the agreement.

The refrigerator is not functioning properly : its cooling has stopped and it is making a lot of noise. The icemaker has stopped working, due to which food items, are getting spoiled.

This is the first time these problems have occurred. Kindly send a company authorised personnel to come and mend the refrigerator on a Saturday between 5:30 pm and 7:30 p. I await an earl and prompt action for you.

Yours sincerely

Sd/-

Sachin   [6]

29. 25, Mount Road

Chennai

Date- 5.01.2020

To,

The HR manager

Sundarama Website

112 Mint Road,

Chennai

Sub- Application for the post of Manager (Accounts)

Respected Sir,

In response to your advertisement in "The Chennai Times", dated January 2, 2020 for the post of Manager (Accounts), I wish to offer my candidature.

I'm interested in this post as I am working for the same position since two years and I am looking for a better opportunity.

I have done M.Com from the Chennai University. I possess good technical skills required for the position.

I'm attaching my resume for you review. I hope to hearing from you soon.

Thanking you

Sincerely,

Tapas/ Tapasaya   [6]

OR

78, Inderpuri

Jaipur

31st March, 2019.

The editor

The Indian Times

Jaipur

Sir ,

Sub : Need to tap the sports talent at a young age

Through the columns of your esteemed newspaper I would like to highlight the need for tap the sports talent at a young age by sports teachers.

Today is the age of globalisation and we see people making careers into various walks of life. Sports is one field that can offer a great career platform for those who possess the skill and talent for the same. Academics, no doubt are compulsory for one's life, but it does not mean that we ignore the talent that children possess in various other fields. Many students are dropping out from playing games and sports because they have lot of homework to do , besides in school all the teachers are forcing them to concentrate on academic than sports.

It is important that the sports teacher, coaches etc recognise the talent in a child and nurture it in such a way that one is able to live a fruitful life. Sports teach a lot to a person and most importantly the discipline that one develops during his/ her sports coaching remains with them on lifelong basis. Therefore it is important to encourage sports activities.

Hope you mention this article in your newspaper.

Yours faithfully,

Poorva/ Paras   [6]

30. Job Application

A-51, Akash Nagar

Agra

13th May, 20XX

The Principal

Sunrise Global School,

Agra

Subject: Application for the post of Computer Teacher

Sir,

This is in response to your advertisement in the Times of India dated 12 May 20XX, for the post of a Computer Teacher. I possess essential requisites for the aforementioned post and I wish to offer my candidature for the same.

I am a post graduate in Computer Science with an experience of 7 years, I am hardworking and honest person and have been fulfilling my duties with utmost sincerity. I assure you that I shall prove to be an asset to your school. I am also enclosing my resume for your perusal.

Thanking you

Yours sincerely,

Chitra Deshpande

Encl-Resume

RESUME

Name	: Chitra Deshpande
Mother's name	: Mrs. Sumegha Deshpande
Father's name	: Mr. Vimal Deshpande
Address	: A-51 Akash Nagar, Agra
Mobile Number	: 941XXXXXXX
E-mail Address	: chitra51@gmail.com
Age	: 30 years
Marital Status	: Married

Educational Qualifications :

Class	Board/ University	Percentage
X	CBSE	90%
XII	CBSE	82%
B.Sc.	Agra University	84%
M.Sc in Computer Science	DEI, Agra	79%

Additional Qualifications	: Well versed in C++, Java & Python; Well Equipped in Web Designing
Other fields of interest	: Reading & Travelling
Languages Known	: English, Hindi, Russian
Job Experience	: 5 years in Horizon Public School, Agra
References	: (a) Mr. Rakesh, Asst. Professor, IT Deptt., St. John's College, Agra
	(b) Mrs. Renuka, HOD, Computer Science, DEI, Agra

Chitra

(Signature)

[2 × 5 = 10]

31. ABC City

26 February, 2023

The Principal

Rose Public School

Shimla

Subject : Inability to attend Exhibit Competition

Sir,

Thank you for extending the invitation for the prize distribution of Inter-School Science Exhibition. I regret my inability to join you on 7th March, 2023 at your school auditorium at 2 p.m. because of some prior commitments.

I wish best of luck to the entire school team for the same.

Yours faithfully

Dr. Suri   [5]

32. Sunaina

Resident Welfare Association,

Pranihar Colony

XYZ City

26 February, 2023

The Editor

Dainik Bhaksar

XYZ City

Subject : Dismal condition of parks

Sir,

Through the column of your esteemed newspaper, I would like draw the attention of the municipal authorities of the city to the dismal condition of the parks of Pranihar colony.

As you are aware, Pranihar Colony is a residential area with a couple of parks that are used by the residents for walking, exercising as well as by children to cycle and play. These parks are a source of recreation for the residents of the colony.

However, because of neglect, the parks are now in a dismal condition. There are unpruned trees every-where giving the park a dilapidated look. Lack of dustbins has caused heaps of garbage in the park and this emanates foul smell and raises concern for hygiene. Moreover, the lack of security has made the park a home for stray dogs that often attack children who are afraid of going and playing in the park. It is therefore suggested that the parks be restored to a good condition by maintaining it on a regular basis, increasing the security, putting waste bins and also furnishing it with new benches and swings so that it becomes amicable for all the residents once again.

Looking forward to an early action by the concerned authorities.

Yours truly

Sunaina   [5]

OR

Examination Hall

26 February 2023

The Managing Director

Dimla Pvt. Ltd.

Nehru Enclave

Indore

Subject : Application for post of Accountant

Dear Sir,

In response to your advertisement published in ABC Newspaper, dated 23 February, 2023, I wish to be considered for the position.

I believe I have the educational qualifications and experience to carry out the mentioned responsibilities. I have attached my bio-data for your perusal.

I guarantee that if selected for the post, I would perform my duties with honesty and proficiency.

Thanking you

Yours faithfully

Prerna Seth

BIO-DATA

Name	: Prerna Seth
Father's Name	: Mr. Rajiv Seth
Date of Birth	: xx-xx-xxxx
Contact No.	: xxxxxxxxxx
Marital Status	: Unmarried
Educational Qualifications	: B.Com. PQR College C.A.
Work Experience	: 6 years as C.A. in a reputed at a chemical firm.
Skills	: Excellent communication skills, MS Excel, Tech-savvy

[5]

1. Article

Summary

Introduction:

An article is a written work which is published in electronic/printed form for spreading news and studying the results or academics. It is related to one subject, topic or theme.

Given are the points which should be kept in mind before writing an article:

(*i*) Arranging all the ideas in a sequence that come to mind after reading the topic.

(*ii*) Composition should be precise and clear. Every sentence should be linked to the previous one i.e. order should be systematic.

(*iii*) The article should be meaningful and should not exceed the word limit.

(*iv*) The opening sentence should be striking. Similarly the last sentence should be conclusive.

(*v*) The article should be well punctuated, simple with no grammatical error.

(*vi*) Descriptive or argumentative composition are usually formal. Sentences used should be complete. It is important to concentrate on the main points of the topic.

Format of an Article:

<table>
<tr><td>
Heading

-By ABC

....Introduction

....

....

....Content/Problem/Opinion

....

....

... .Solution/Conclusion

....

....
</td></tr>
</table>

PREVIOUS YEARS'
EXAMINATION QUESTIONS

1. Increase in the number of vehicles causes pollution and traffic jams. Write an article in 150-200 words for 'The New Indian Express', Delhi, highlighting the urgent need to solve these man-made problems, giving suitable suggestions. You are Madhav/ Madhuri.

[DELHI 2011]

2. In almost all big cities in the country there is a mushroom growth of slums where people are living in inhuman conditions. Write an article in 150-200 words about this problem suggesting steps to deal with it. You are Komal/Kartik.

[DELHI 2011]

3. The invention of mobile phone has brought about a revolution in the lives of the people in the country. If used properly it can be a blessing but if misused it can prove to be a curse. Write an article in 150-200 words on 'Mobile phone - a boon or bane'. You are Kartik/Krishna.

[ALL INDIA 2011]

4. With the rising number of people in almost all the big cities of the country, the rate of crime has also increased proportionately. The police need to be trained in new methodology of combating the crime besides changing its mindset. Write an article in 150 - 200 words on 'The role of police in maintaining law and order in the metropolitan cities'. You are Ravi / Ravina.

[ALL INDIA 2011]

5. Spurt of violence previously is known in Indian schools makes it incumbent on the educationists to introduce value education effectively in schools. Write an article in 150-200 words expressing your views on the need of value education. You are Anu/Arun.

[DELHI 2012]

6. Dance, as shown in some reality shows on TV, seems to be a mix of gymnastics and P.T. exercises. Actually, it is neither. India has a rich tradition of classical and folk dances. Write an article in 150-200 words on the need to have a reality show exclusively based on Indian classical dances. You are Anu/Arun.

[ALL INDIA 2012]

7. Write an article in 150-200 words for your school magazine on the topic, 'Obesity among School Children'. You are Mohini/Mohit.

[ALL INDIA 20 13]

8. You are Raman/Ruchika. Write an article in 150-200 words for your school magazine on the topic, 'Life without Modern Gadgets'.

[ALL INDIA 2013]

9. Your family has recently shifted from Kota in Rajasthan to Ernakulam in Kerala, where your house is situated in the midst of beautiful flowering plants and fruit-yielding trees. Every minute and every second, you are experiencing the joy of being in the lap of nature. Write an article in 50-200 words on the diversity of nature that you have experienced. You are Latha/Lalith of Class XII. [DELHI 2013]

10. Write an article in 150-200 words on the topic, 'Poverty is the cause of all evils, to be published in the Young World of 'The Hindu', Chennai.

[DELHI 2013]

11. Last week, as you were coming back from school you happened to see a huge plastic bag full of leftovers of food being flung into the middle of the road from a speeding car. You wondered how people can be so devoid of civic sense. Write an article in 125-150 words on why we lack civic sense and how civic sense can be inculcated in children at a very young age" You are Shiva/ Shamini. [ALL INDIA 2014]

12. You saw a stray dog beaten to death by a group of boys. Their act infuriated you and you scolded them for their cruel act. You decided to write an article on cruelty to animals. Write the article in 125-150 words. You are Nikhil/Naina.

[ALL INDIA 2014]

13. Education has always been a noble profession. Our ancestors received their learning at gurukuls and ashrams. Even in the near past pathshalas (schools) were associated with places of worship. Today, education is fast becoming commercialised. Parents have to shed out a lot of money on coaching classes, tuition fees etc. Write an article in 150-200 words on the State of Education, Today'. You are Karan / Karuna.

[ALL INDIA 2016]

14. According to 2011 census, literacy rate of hundred percent or around has been achieved by only a couple of states in India. Illiteracy, is found mostly among the old and the deprived sections of society. What can the youth do to spread literacy in society? Write an article in 150-200 words on 'Role of students in eradicating illiteracy.' you are Karuna/Karan.

[ALL INDIA 2016]

15. India is a land of diversity. One way in which it makes us feel proud of it is the number of festivals we enjoy. Write an article in 50-200 words on 'Festivals of India'. You are Karuna/ Karan.   [DELHI 2016]

16. Rising pollution, fast and completive lifestyle, lack of nutritious food etc. have caused health woes for a large section of our population. Providing health care used to be a charitable and ethical activity. Today it has become commercialized, a money spinning business. Write an article in 150-200 words on 'How to provide proper health care to the common man's. You are Karan /Karuna.   [DELHI 2016]

17. Our performance in Rio Olympics has told us that we do not pay enough attention to athletics and outdoor games. It is time we revised our attitude. Sports should be an important part of school's daily routine. Write an article in 150-200 words in 'Importance of Outdoor Games'. You are Sreeja/Thomas.   [DELHI 2017]

18. Every teenager has a dream to achieve something in life. What they are going to become tomorrow depends on what our youth dream today. Write an article in 150 – 200 words on 'What I want to be in life'. You are Simranjit/Smita.

[ALL INDIA 2017]

19. Recent floods in many metropolitan cities of the country during the monsoon season laid bare the hollowness of the claims of the civic authorities of their preparedness. The poor had to bear the brunt of the problem while no one was ever held accountable. Write an article in 150-200 words on the common man's woes during the monsoons and the need for accountability of the officials concerned. You are Sumit/Smita Verma.

[DELHI, ALL INDIA 2018]

20. Hard work and punctuality are essential for a happy and successful life. They help in meeting the desired targets of our life. You are Kavya/ Kanha. Write an article in 150–200 words highlighting the importance of hard work and punctuality in a student's life. [DELHI 2019]

21. The role of father is synonymous with strict discipline etc. but it is not completely true. The father fulfils his responsibilities affectionately for the family. Write an article in 150-200 words on the topic, 'Role of father in the family'. You are Dhruv / Deepa.   [DELHI 2020]

Directions (Q 22-28) : Answer any six of the seven questions given below with reference to the context.

Rashmi is President of her school Library Club. She decides to write an article on the need to develop the habit of reading as she strongly feels it is fading among the persent day students.

[DELHI Term I, 2022]

22. Select the option that lists an appropriate title for Rashmi's article.

(a) Develop reading habit to be successful

(b) Why is reading important

(c) Reading skill – A requisite to be a good communicator

(d) Reading is the best exercise for mind

23. Help Rashmi complete her ideas in the following sentence by choosing the right option.

Every book opens up new _______ of thoughts for the reader. Reading books is one of the _______ habits that helps one improve his or her focus.

(a) ideas, common

(b) dimensions, constructive

(c) doors, interesting

(d) views, best

24. What major reason can Rashmi state in her article for deteriorating reading habits among students?

(a) Academic pressure

(b) Sports

(c) Digital technology

(d) Friends

25. Select the option that lists suitable steps to be taken to improve reading habits among children.

i. Gift them books

ii. Take them on trips to a library

iii. Encourage them to read text books

iv. Create a reading space for children

v. Take children on field trips

(a) i, ii & iv

(b) i, iii & v

(c) ii, iii & iv

(d) i, iv & v

26. Select the option that best describes the importance of reading habit :

    (a) A book is a gift you can open again and again – Garrison Keillor

    (b) Reading is a conversation. All books talk, but a good book listens as well – Mark Haddon

    (c) The greatest gift is a passion for reading – Elizabeth Hardwick

    (d) Books are a uniquely portable magic – Stephen King

27. Read the following statements :

    (i) An article is a written piece of communication published for a large/targeted audience.

    (ii) An article is an interactive communication with a selected audience.

    (a) (i) is false and (ii) is true

    (b) (i) is true and (ii) is false

    (c) Both (i) and (ii) are true

    (d) Both (i) and (ii) are false

28. The title of an article must not be

    (a) clear and attractive

    (b) eye–catching

    (c) interesting

    (d) lengthy

29. You are Praveen/Prerna. Secretary, Eco-club of Bharati school, Lucknow. You write an article on the hazards of environment pollution for the school magazine. You may use the cues given below. (120-150 words)

> **Causes :** dumping of industrial waste in water bodies, improper disposal of e-waste and medical waste, indiscriminate construction work.
>
> **Solutions :** stricter laws / role of media in spreading awareness / initiative by N.G.O.

[DELHI 2023]

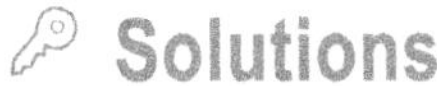 ## Solutions

1.   **Pollution and Traffic Jam**

(By- Madhav)

Science has been a great advantage to the human life. It has created wonders by inventing miraculous things. In the beginning of the civilisation the movement of man was very slow. But the invention of engine changed the life. Car, bus, trucks, two wheelers came and added movement to the life of the man. But the other side of the picture is no so attractive. Day by day the number of vehicles is increasing, and with this increase pollution and traffic jam are also increasing. Roads are become narrower. They are not fit for the rising number of vehicles. Jam roads have become regular sights. It takes an hour to cover one kilometre because of heavy jam. The number of increasing vehicles also causes pollution. Emission from traffic is causing a great danger to people and environment. Pollution is a source of many diseases. But no one is caring for this. Everyone wants to maintain status in society. One buys a vehicle and adds to pollution and traffic jam. There is urgent need to pay attention to these problems. Some strict laws should be made to regulate the traffic. Rule for issuing driving licence should be made strict. Some pollution free fuel should be made available or invented. Sharing of vehicle should be encouraged. It will reduce traffic jam as well as pollution.

2.   **Mushroom of slums and the inhumane life of people**

(By- Komal)

Big cities always attract people. People from small towns come to big cities to make future. But not everyone is born with golden spoon, in his mouth. In most of these people earning is very less. They are not able to make their both ends meet comfortably. They are not able to live at a proper place. This gives rise to slum. The Mushroom growth of slum have become a problem to the civic authority. These slums are very unhygienic. There is no proper house here, there is no electricity and water here. The condition of sanitation is very poor. People are living in inhuman condition which cannot be thought of. There is urgent need to pay attention to this problem. These slums should be made into regularised colony. Arrangement for proper sanitation should be made. People living in these areas are human beings. They also need care. They are poor but it does not mean that they should be overlooked by the authority. It is the result of improper development of the areas from where these people come. A little bit of development will discourage people to going to big cities. These ways can help in reducing slums.

3. **Mobile Phone-a boon or bane**

(By- Kartik)

Science has made the life of men very comfortable. Civilization started from scratch. But today men have everything for the comfort of life. Inventions of science are wonderful and useful. The invention of telephone is a such invention. Earlier phone started with base line. But today we have mobile phones. We can carry them wherever we go. It helps us in being touch with our family members and friends twenty-four hours. It is very useful when we are out of station. We can receive messages and calls anytime. We can inform the people at any point of emergency. Of course, it is a blessing if used properly. But there is other side of the coin. This picture is not very attractive. The blessing of mobile phone can be a curse if not properly used. If used unnecessarily it can be fatal. Radiation emitted by mobile phones can do damages to human life. It is a source of many diseases. It can create heart problem, leads towards impotency. So, we should use it sensibly so that we may take maximum advantage of this without any damage to our life.

4. **The role of police in maintaining law and order in the metropolitan cities**

(By- Ravina)

In big cities, maintaining law and order is not an easy task. People from small towns and villages keep coming to such big cities in search of jobs. No doubt, big cities offer a lot of opportunities to these people, but this influx of people creates problem also. The main problem is rising crime. Not everyone gets satisfactory job and these people indulge in crimes. In fact, the crime rises proportionately. Problem also lies in combating these crimes. The traditional way of dealing with crime is of no use. Now crimes are organised, so methodology should also be organised. Police needs to be trained, new methodology should be undertaken and mindset needs to be changed. Police plays an important role in maintaining law and order in metropolitan cities. But crimes can pose a serious, threat to these cities if not dealt with properly. So police must gear up itself with the changing circumstances otherwise the anti-social elements will have an upper hand.

5. **Value Based Education**

(By- Arun)

As is the saying, Value and Virtues are not hereditary they are learnt. The need is to inculcate the values in the young generation. As the tenets of tolerance, spiritualism, self-discipline and sympathy seemed to be swept by the tide of time.

In the materialistic pursuits, the essence of true life has eroded somewhere. But the big question is who should take the responsibility of inculcating the moral values in the young generation. A child roughly spends seven hours in school. It is the crucial time for the child, he/she can learn in the school sharing, team-spirit, kindness and companionship. Moreover, the subject moral science till middle section infuses the virtues in the child through stories, anecdotes and reactions to imaginary situations. In this direction, many schools in the wake of incidents like DPS Scandal etc. have taken steps to fill the moral vacuum among youngsters.

APS Secondary School is one such school which has implemented the value education in the school. The school conducts its assembly thrice a day based on value education. Skits story-telling, extempore unearths the hidden virtues in the children

Honesty, respect, sincerity and kindness among children is re-warded in the school assembly to boast others to follow the same path. Only the subject Moral Science or Literature do not aim at value education other subjects like Mathematics, Social-studies, Science etc. also aim at moral education.

As Gandhi rightly said that training of soul can be best given by a teacher. A teacher can influence the character of his student sitting forty miles away from him. In the school a teacher through words and actions can make the child learn the values at every stage. Moreover, celebration of days like grandparent's day, visits to old age homes etc. Hence, school plays a vital role in infusing virtues which cannot be ignored at any stage.

6. **Need of Reality shows that highlights the Indian traditional dance**

(By- Anu)

There are different viewpoints from people belonging to different walks of life and the impact of reality shows are paving its way today. The reality shows debate being held through the different medium has found more criticism against such crude shows on many national television channels. Nowadays, a popular show 'Dance India Dance' has become popular among the Indian viewers. But the dance shows in some reality shows on TV seem to be a mix of gymnastics and P. T. exercises. We are aware that India has a rich tradition of classical and folk dances. But these reality shows have forgotten the ethics of the traditions. While producers of the shows decided to provide better facilities to the participants and giving the medical aids to the general health problems. But, we should not have left the Indian culture. We need such kinds of new reality shows which should be based exclusively on Indian classical dances.

7. Obesity Among School Children

(By- Mohini)

Obesity among school children is attracting the attention of the Health Minister of India. The minister, of Health issued a rule to all school canteen all over the country that junk food should be banned to school children. All children go to school but they do not need much carbohydrate as they do not use that much energy to do work. What about the habit of eating pizza or noodles? French fries, burger and noodles are all carbohydrate and when taken in large quantity or more than what that person needs they will be converted into Fat and Stored in the body leading to obesity.

School children who are experiencing stress will like to eat more food that contain sugar and carbohydrate such as ice cream, chocolates, junk food and carbonated drinks. In short, excess of anything is bad.

Many South-East Asian nations including India are in a phase of an economic and nutrition transition. The nutrition transition is related with a change in dietary habits, declining physical activity and rising prevalence of obesity. Obesity in children and teenagers is gradually becoming a major public health problem in many developing countries including India.

There are quite a few studies stating prevalence of childhood and teenagers obesity and overweight from different parts of India (Maharashtra, Punjab, Delhi and South Indian states) that range from 3% to 29% and indicate that the prevalence is higher in urban than in rural areas.

8. Life Without Modern Gadgets

(By- Raman)

Technology has become a very important part our lives now a day. During the past few years, technology has evolved in many ways and is probably without a doubt better than ever before. People are always trying to find something new that will improve our lives dramatically. Some of the creations that have really changed our lives are the computer, telephone, mobile phone, tablet, internet, electronic mail and voice mail etc. Everything has a positive and a negative effect on our lives and so does technology. Technology may be very helpful but it can sometimes be very harmful.

In our modern society, people can't see themselves without computers and mobile phones. They used to be bulky, expensive and not very reliable machine but nowadays there are fast small and affordable and nearly every family has a computer. Now days, mostly everything is available on the internet. You can do shopping also over net. Electronic mails can be sent over a network and its much faster and takes up less time than to have to write a letter and then send. In case of emergency people can contact you even if you're not at home. In short, we have become slaves of modern gadgets.

9. Diversity of Nature

(By- Latha)

Nature is the part of the environment. It is divided into areas among the world. I was born in Kota which is in Rajasthan in the month of June. The temperature was about 48 degrees C. Everybody was worried about me. But I stayed there for about fourteen years and completed my secondary education from there. By chance, my father was transferred from Kota to Ernakulam that's why my whole family had to be shifted from there. In Ernakulam, I found the second heaven after the Kashmir. The atmosphere of here is very pleasant throughout the year. My house is situated near a garden. I am thankful to God who shifted me from scorching heat of Rajasthan. The flora and fauna is very different here. There are many flowering, medicinal and other sorts of plants.

We enjoy the sightseeing with my family every weekend. Greenery can be seen everywhere in Ernakulam. The weather condition is also suitable for the various types of harvesting. The ecosystem here is stable and the weather remains pleasant and conducive for the crops.

10. **Poverty is the cause of all social evils**

Poverty is the state of a life without having sufficient resources which are essential for survival. There are scores of people who are unable to meet the expense of the minimum necessities of life. Even getting a square meal for one time is tough for them. They can be easily seen engaged in trivial jobs to earn their food. They indeed have a miserable life which is worse than imagination in normal circumstances. Hunger and poverty are such compelling forces which make them shameless and they take on evil practice to battle with their circumstances. Undoubtedly, poverty leads to heinous crime like robbery thefts, murder, kidnapping and arson. Young boys selling tickets in black market or the kids who indulge in pick pocketing are the by-products of poverty. In the absence of proper amenities such as food, clothes and education, these children grow as antisocial elements of the society. Lack of good earning, they are bound to adopt ill-practices to earn their livelihood. They don't turn criminals as a choice but because of hunger and poverty. No wonders that most of the criminals are living in slums and poor colonies. It's poverty what makes them to accept in social evils and immoral practices. To eradicate social evils, one must lessen their sufferings and poverty.

11. **Lack of civic sense**

(By- Shiva)

Callousness and irresponsibility seem to be the order of the day. Modern society has given birth to indifferent individuals. People no longer think of the greater good of the society. They are driven by their selfish, individual needs. In India, people hardly follow traffic rules. They hardly, think twice before littering the streets. They have no respect for public property. Road rage and intolerance are rampant on the streets.

Inculcating a strong civic sense is the need of the hour. Parents must inculcate civic sense in

children at an early age. They must be taught the values of cleanliness, discipline, patience and tolerance. Parents must encourage their children to keep their surroundings clean. They must also learn to respect and abide by the rules at an early age. After all, children are the future of our country. Our country can progress only if we teach right values to our children.

12. **Cruelty to animals**

(By- Naina)

Treating animals with love and compassion is the moral duty of every individual. However, we often fail to fulfil this duty. Instances of animal cruelty are in abundance in our society. Poachers mercilessly kill animals for their skin, fur and teeth. This has led to the extinction of several species of animals which, in turn, has affected the ecological balance of our planet. Several companies use animals for testing medicines and cosmetics. Similarly, animals are often ill-treated and forced into performing circus tricks and other activities for our entertainment.

We must understand that co-existence and harmony between humans and animals are essential for our planet's survival. We must be more responsible and protective towards animals.

We must learn to love them. Steps should be taken by the government to ensure proper care, protection and shelter for the animals.

13. **The State of Education Today**

(By- Karan)

Education means the all-round development of man. It makes an individual responsible, sensitive and a decent human being. It has always been a noble procession. Our ancestors received their learning at gurukuls and ashrams. Even in the near past, schools were associated with places of worship. But today education is fast becoming commercialized. Modern education is merely academic and prepares students to acquire degrees or diplomas in general or specialized fields. There is no stress in the education to uplift the students morally, spiritually and physically. The students do not get even a chance to enjoy a game in the playground.

In these days education has turned into a successful business. As this is the age of cutthroat competition, everyone seems to be a rival here. Students are worried about their uncertain future. Parents want their children to become engineers or doctors. So, they send their children to coaching centres. These coaching centres spend a lot of money on advertisements and tempt their prospective customers. They guarantee sure success in the examinations. No doubt, their only aim is to mint money.

Coaching centres may be necessary for some students. But it kills drive, initiative and originality of brilliant students. Most of these coaching centres provide spoon-feeding for average students and they give stress on learning by heart.

14.   Role of students in eradicating illiteracy

(By- Karan)

In a developing country like India, about half of its population is illiterate. Although India produces the best doctors and engineers in the world, it remains In educationally back ward nation. Most of the people living in villages are illiterates. They can't read or write. Economic backwardness, ignorance as well as lack of opportunities have deprived them of literacy and knowledge. Education makes a man enlightened and perfect and helps him to prosper physically, economically and spiritually. illiteracy is a real handicap in the progress of a democratic society. Politicians and middlemen take advantage of these simple people by misguiding them with false promises. Illiteracy is the main cause of their exploitation. Students, the builders of the nation can play on effective role in removing the curse of literacy. They can organise classes in groups. Each one teaches one. By sparing an hour a day they can light the lamp of literacy in the lives of illiterates. Government should support the efforts of students as well as NGO'S who work for this cause. A continuous follow up is very neckwear to eradicate illiteracy till the roots.

15.   Festivals of India

(By- Karan)

India is the secular country having diverse, religions languages, customs and traditions. This is the reason why Indians celebrate many festivals throughout the year. Festival, celebration brings happiness and joy to all. This is the occasion which creates a gathering, where all the family members, relatives, friends can meet each another and share their happy moments. Festivals play an important role in our lives. As we are living in the materialistic world leading a mechanical life, all the time we are under stress. Festivals are those occasions which relieve us from stress and create a good mood in us. People belonging to different religions celebrate different festivals. The main religious festivals of Indians are Diwali, Holi, Ram Navami, Raksha Bandhan, Christmas etc.

In addition to the religious festivals, we celebrate the National festivals like Independence Day and Republic day, which are common to all the people living in India. Irrespective of religion, cast and creed, all Indians celebrate these festivals. These National festivals aim at promoting brotherhood. Thus, festivals are very important in one's life to know the traditional values and customs of a nation.

16.   How to provide proper health care
to the comman man

(By- Karuna)

'Health is wealth' Man living on this earth can enjoy his life only when his health is perfect. Only a healthy person runs, eats, works and sleeps properly. Of all the sectors in the world, health care occupies the first place. Basing on the importance of the sector it got commercialized. The private sector is the dominant health care provider in India. Private health care sector has over taken the Government sector. Most healthcare expenses are paid out of pocket by patients and their families which can be considered as health expenditure. Private medical sector remains the primary source of health care for 70% of households in urban areas and 63% of households in rural areas. This is because of large population. The other reason is all the govt., hospitals are overcrowded and they lack proper equipment and facilities. To provide proper health care to the common man, the government should increase the number of government hospitals, it should pass strict laws for private hospitals and in addition to these it should also create awareness on healthy lifestyles, nutritious food etc. in rural area. The government should also provide health care in schools. Only the dedicated implementation of necessary by the leaders of the nation can only bring a change.

17.   **Importance of Outdoor Games**

(By- Sreeja)

Games like cricket, hockey, tennis, football and badminton are outdoor games that are played in the open. They are games that involve physical activity and also a spirit of healthy competition. Outdoor games are important to relax ourselves and to charge our batteries, as the proverb goes 'All work and no play makes Jack a dull boy'.

In this age, where children are suffering from obesity, outdoor activities form an important part of their curriculum. Outdoor games also have long term benefits on health. They help the kids stay fit and healthy, and as they feel tired at the end of the day, they will sleep on time as well.

Outdoor games develop a competitive spirit and also boost up their confidence level and self-esteem. They learn to interact, and also to build strategies to win. In this tech savvy age, it is very important for the children to leave their televisions, laptops and videos games. They should go out and learn the importance of outdoor activities in their daily routine.

18.   **What I want to be in Life**

(By- Simranjit/Smita)

Every human being, since he was a child, has an ambition of something. Some people want to be a pilot, some to be a doctor or an engineer and the others want to be a teacher and the list continues. The goal of life should ideally defines ones' true self but, in today's world the case is totally opposite. One's ambition should be a combined mixture of the following four questions, 1- What a person loves to do? 2- What the person is good at? 3- What the world's needs are? and 4- What you can be paid for?. The combination of all of these four questions enables a person to lead a happy and fulfilling life. All the famous and successful people in the world have asked themselves based on the above four questions. The correct combination of each answer led them to this successful position. They are able to achieve so much just because they are happy doing that. Every young individual should think on all of the mentioned points. Believe me, you can achieve great heights.

19.   At least five people were killed as heavy monsoon rain deluged India's financial capital Mumbai, causing transport chaos and forcing schools and many offices to close on Wednesday. The coastal city of more than 20 million people is the latest to be hit by floods that have ravaged South Asia this monsoon season, affecting millions of people across India, Nepal and Bangladesh and killing over 1,200.Authorities in Mumbai said at least five people had died since the intense rainfall began on Tuesday, making roads impassable and briefly shutting the suburban rail network on which millions of commuters depend. India suffers frequent flooding during the June-September monsoon season, but international aid agencies say things are worse this year with thousands of villages cut off and people deprived of food and clean water for days. The sad thing is that our government is unprepared in spite of recurring floods every year. Who gets the blow? Not the rich, nor the politicians, but the poor people. Thousands of slum people have their lives devastated by floods every year. Those who were already the suffering and deprived classes suffer more deprivation. Think about poor aged people who are diseased. Think about pregnant women. Think about the children. Their world is totally decimated and the unscrupulous government hardly does anything to restore them. The government should take their responsibility seriously. There should be steps taken to deal with the floods way before the monsoon.

20.   **Hardwork and Punctuality : most desired virtues**

By Kavya

'Punctuality should not be limited to arriving at a place at the right time, it extends to taking actions at the right time'- this famous quote by author Kale Wood quintessentially sums up the importance of punctuality.

It is a student's responsibility to gain knowledge, learn new skills, and finally prove what he has learnt in the various assessments. Time is of utmost importance; assignments and projects to be submitted on time. Only, if the child is punctual in getting to school and attending his classes, will he learn all that the school curriculum has to offer. 'Time and tide wait for none'- be punctual and extract the maximum from each moment of your student life!

Punctuality and hardwork are two flipsides of a coin. Talent is natural aptitude for something, it could be a talent for singing or painting, etc.

But, talent is lost without hard work. We could have a skill, but its usefulness is proved only when it is utilised. To develop a natural skill further, a lot of hard work, persistence and punctuality is required. As human we are prone to procrastination, delaying things till the last moment arrives. Success comes to only those who are able to break this vicious behaviour cycle and become friends with hardwork and punctuality.

It has been statistically proven that many talented or gifted individuals fail to succeed because they don't have the drive to pursue and stay persistent towards their ambitions. In contrast to this many average yet hardworking and punctual individuals are able to achieve their goals. Hence, it is proved that hard work and punctuality are essential for a happy and successful life.   [10]

21. **ROLE OF FATHER IN THE FAMILY**

By: Dhruv/ Deepa

"Fathers provide not only support but also encouragement." Catherine Pulsifer

Talking about parenting, many attach immense importance to the role of a mother. But, what people usually forget is that the role played by a father in establishing a harmonious family is equally important. People tend to relate the persona of a father with a strict male whose job is to rule the family. This, however, is not always true.

A father, just like a mother also has a major role to play in the growth and development of a child. A father's role is to make sure that his children do not lack any of the necessities of life. A father has a profound influence on the social, emotional, and intellectual development of a child.

A father's participation in a son's life is crucial. This is because a father was once a young man and it is but obvious that he understands the needs or challenges that a male encounters. At times, children try to be a reflection of their father. Therefore it is important that a father conducts himself cautiously particularly when he is surrounded by his children.

In a nutshell, a father plays the role of a friend, philosopher and a guide to ensure that his family lives a life of contentment.   [10]

22. (b) This title will cover maximum facets of reading habit.   [1]

23. (b) New dimensions, constructive habits is most appropriate option   [1]

24. (c) Mobile phones, internet, computer are all examples of distractions/Digital technology
                                               [1]

25. (c) Gifting books and field trips not suitable options   [1]

26. (b) Reading has been composed to a conversation where both talking and listening are important.
                                               [1]

27. (b) An article is not interactive communication.
                                               [1]

28. (d) Title should be precise and crisp.   [1]

29. **Environmental Pollution- A Menace**

By: Prerna

Our environment is our mainstay and needs to be protected using every possible means. However, we as society are only causing this envir-onment to degrade. Environmental pollution is a rising menace and has become a major concern because the rate at which the environment is degrading, it would become impossible to sustain it for the future generations.

There are many causes of environmental pollution. One of the major causes is the dumping of industrial waste in the water bodies that results in the water as well as the air becoming contaminated. Another cause is the unchecked disposal of medical and e-waste which is not easily biodegradable. This waste only impacts the environment adversely, making it tough to sustain the environment.

The increasing construction work being carried out everywhere and the felling of trees for these activities are raising environment pollution levels to a very high level. Environment needs to be protected and every one must contribute to doing so. It is important to put into action strict laws and regulations to prevent the unchecked disposal of medical and industrial waste. People should be made aware of the adverse impacts of environment pollution via social media. NGOs and other government bodies should also put in efforts to minimise environmental pollution.   [5]

2. Debate

Summary

Debate is a formal discussion or an argument on a particular topic on which different people have different opinions.

Purpose: The main motive is to show the ability of presenting an argument.

Given are the points which should be kept in mind before starting a debate:

(*i*) Always begin the debate with "Honorable judges and my dear friends, day I am standing here to express my views for/against the motion "......."

(*ii*) The agreement or disagreement should be expressed clearly and forcefully.

(*iii*) Debate should always have logical reasoning to prove the points.

(*iv*) Relevant information should be used.

(*v*) Debate should be ended by writing 'thank you' at the extreme left end.

The expressions which can be used are given below:

(*a*) May I ask? Etc.

(*b*) Refer to your opponent's view

(*c*) In my opinion

(*d*) I'd like to argue

(*e*) Always stand for your view point either in favour or against.

Format of Debate/Speech:

> **Salutation:** Respected chairperson, honorable judges and all present here
>
> **Introduction:** Views for/against the topic
>
> **Body:** Views, facts, contradiction of opponent's arguments etc.
>
> **Conclusion:** Clarification stand mode

Some useful Tips:

- In a debate the content is presented differently than speech.

- In a speech the speaker's intention is to turn the audience to his/her own way of thinking on a particular topic.

- The tense used should be same throughout.

- Personal opinion should be given in a debate. Debate can be written in 1st person.

PREVIOUS YEARS' EXAMINATION QUESTIONS

1. The government has banned the use of animals in the laboratories for the purpose of dissection. Write a debate in 150 - 200 words either for or against this decision.　　[ALL INDIA 2015]

2. Some people feel that electronic media (TV news) will bring about the end of print media (newspapers). What are your views on the issue? Write a debate in 150 - 200 words either for or against this view.

   * use of visuals on TV

   * authentic and fast

   * not enough news for 24-hour telecast

   * may fabricate news

   * become repetitive and dull

   * even scandals become news

   * print media - time tested

   * analysed, verified news

   * editorial comments

   * cater to all interests　　[ALL INDIA 2015]

3. 'The policy of reservation of seats for admission to the professional courses is good for the deprived sections of society. Write a Debate in 150-200 words either for or against the motion.

   [DELHI 2016]

4. Brain drain is not a bane for a developing country like India'. Write a debate in 150-200 words either for or against the motion.

   [ALL INDIA 2016]

5. 'Private cars should be banned in the congested commercial areas of the cities.' Write a debate in 150-200 words either for or against the motion.

   [DELHI 2017]

6. "It is cruel to put stray dogs to sleep." Write a debate in 150 – 200 words either for or against the motion.　　[ALL INDIA 2017]

7. "Academic excellence is the only requirement for a successful career." Write a debate either for or against the motion. (120-150 words.)

   [DELHI, ALL INDIA 2018]

8. Write a debate in 150 - 200 words either for or against the motion: 'Capital Punishment should be abolished'. [DELHI 2019]

9. 'No detention policy for classes sixth to eighth is academically very unsound.' Write a debate in 150-200 words either for or against the motion. [DELHI 220]

Solutions

1. **Banning the use of Animals for Dtssection**

(Debate-for the motion)

Good morning everyone,

Today I am going express my views for the motion for banning the use of animals for dissection. No one is yet empowered to give life then why anyone should have the authority to take a precious life be it human or animal.

Many of us must be having pets at our home; don't you think that they emotionally react to joys and sorrows? Don't they make us laugh and cry? Then why to kill such creatures? Life is a gift of the almighty; no human should be allowed to take it away. With rapid changes or rather say the damage that the human race is inflicting on eco system has already put many species on the verge of extinction.

With the advancement of science and technology, it's possible to use simulators and AI to its best. By doing so, we would be easily able to impart the knowledge and understanding which one gains from dissecting animals.

I am a firm believer that using simulators would be better than killing an innocent creature that might have a family to live with, who has to bear unimaginable pain and suffering while being dissected. Ask these questions to your inner soul and let the entire system know, what is the answer that you got from your inner core.

Thank you all.

(Debate-against the motion)

Good morning everyone,

Today I am going express my views against the motion for banning the use of animals for dissection. Dissection of animals in the school laboratories provides a practical experience for the theoretical knowledge that students gain from books. They procure an opportunity to actually put their learning into practice. It should not be looked at as a wrongful practice because such an activity is meant to develop the student's knowledge of the elements and functions of the living being. The dissection of animals has a scientific purpose; it is a mode of hands-on education for students such that they learn outside of the pages of the textbook and actually look at what they are being taught. We should give more credit to the sensitivity and intelligence of our students so as not to believe that a dissection class will make them more prone to animal violence. Students should be taught the value of animal life by making them understand how an animal has the same kind of organs as human beings has that perform similar functions. The governing philosophy behind teaching students to dissect animals should be that life, whether human or animal, is the same; each living being is tied to each other by their inner similarity. Thus, a ban on dissection of animals in school laboratories would not be the best course of action in such a case. I hope my views on this topic were substantial enough to throw a light on this topic.

Thank You!

2. **(Debate-for the motion)**

Good morning everyone,

Today, I take the opportunity to express my argument in support of the topic 'Some people feel that electronic media (TV news) will bring about the end of print media (newspapers)'.

Ours is the era of speed and connectivity. Information is the propeller of our generation. One simply can't afford to lag behind in the race of cut throat competition. TV and mobiles along with hi-speed internet connectivity, enables us to get instant access to each and every information that we need in run time. Just for an example if there is an earthquake in any part of nation or sa world where our relatives and family members stay, won't be it ideal that we confirm there well being at that very time, or shall we wait for next morning to just even get to know that there was an earthquake.

The Government had recently announced such majors which has changed economical infrastructure in few hours, I wonder who will prefer to remain unaware in such an era. The 24x7 format of news is the truth of our time and the old and obsolete method late news is bound to go.

(Debate-against the motion)

Good morning everyone,

Today, I take the opportunity to express my argument against the topic 'Some people feel that electronic media (TV news) will bring about the end of print media (newspapers)'. TV news that strive towards authentic and fast reportage is always at the risk of fabricating its content to continue being in circulation. The governing principle for the 24-hours news format is that whether or not news constitutes the element of worthiness, it should be covered on the channel. If there is nothing worth reporting, then the content can be made sensational just to gain currency. It tends to become repetitive and dull. Scandals are allowed to become news and popularity becomes the main objective. The ambition of TV news to be the sole guardian of objective truth in the field of journalism can be considered to be a tall claim as more often than not it becomes a site for promotion of commercial products and sensational content in the garb of news. Print media is a time-tested medium of information dissemination, the time taken to publish engenders that the content of the report has been analysed and verified to offer a composite picture to the reader. Editorial commentary ensures an informed view on the issues at hand. Newspapers are not going to extinct any time soon; they are still a tried and time tested mode of receiving the world at our doorstep. Thus, electronic media can never overrule print media.

Thank you!

3.   *(Debate-for the motion)*

Good morning everyone,

Today, I take the opportunity to express my argument in support of the topic "reservation of seats for admission to the professional courses is good for the deprived sections of society". Those who have been deprived since ages and haven't got equal opportunities to compete for a better life must get opportunities to quality education at least. It's the education, which can empower them to uplift the society as a whole.

By giving reservation in quality professional education, which otherwise will be out of their reach due to its high cost, we can provide a level playing field to the deprived class. For holistic development of our nation we must provide opportunities to each section of our society to develop entrepreneurships.

Don't feed them for free, but educate them for sure. It will have its own cascade effects and the benefits will go deep down the socio-economical structure of our nation.

(Debate-for the motion)

Respected chairman, honourable members of the Jury and dear audience,

I stand before you to speak for the motion. The policy of reservation of seats for admission to the professional courses is good for the deprived sections of society. In the ancient India, the people in the society were divided into four sections based on their caste and creed. This inequality in society has created differences among people. The so called upper class people have started controlling the society and made the lower-class people their servants and untouchables which has created a long gap between these two sections of people in all aspects.

The deprived sections of society were not given equal opportunities. After Independence, the constitution has given importance to the deprived sections by introducing reservation for them. This is a boon to the weaker sections to excel themselves in all fields of knowledge. A country can only progress, if all sections of society contribute. It is a must in a developing country that the marginalized and weaker communities must raise to create equality among all. Getting a seat in a professional college is not easy. A sound financial stability is needed to join the coaching institutes and to get good books and material. The people belonging to the deprived sections lack this economical back up. So, they deserve reservation to get admitted into the professional courses.

Thank You.

4.   *(Debate-for the motion)*

I stand before you to speak in favour of the motion 'Brain drain it not a bane for a developing country like India'. Of course, its fundamental right of human race to vouch for the best available resources be it study or be it work. Undoubtedly India or such other developing nations are budding and are the future of world economy; however, this has happened because we have always been open to learn the best practices from the globe.

There are multiple reasons which make brain drain a natural phenomenon. In India, we also want reservation in education and job which leads to lack of genuine opportunities for many meritorious students. Also there is a serious lack of educational infrastructure and research facilities in India. Patriotism doesn't say you shouldn't thrive for your growth. Also, just sitting here our graduates are serving other countries in various BPOs. The world has turned into global village and it would be unwise to say that one shouldn't feel free to choose what and where he/she wants to work.

(Debate-against the motion)

Respected Chairperson, honourable members of the jury and dear audience,

I stand before you to speak against the motion 'Brain drain it not a bane for a developing country like India'. Having more and more money is the tendency inherent in every person in India. Most often, we rum to other countries for the sake of studies and earn money. In this regard I can firmly say that it is a wrong myth about which we are hankering after in vain. The developing India has become a hub for I.T industries. Cities like Hyderabad, Bangalore Chennai and Gurgaon are providing ample chances to the intelligent people with good salary packages in I.T industry. Even there is an enhancement and encouragement in the field of research.

Whenever the retrenchment starts in foreign countries, the Indians are at the forefront. They also treat us as second rate citizens. So, what a shame on our part to work on the soil of others.

I strongly feel that an Indian should not compromise his honour. Whatever position we may get in India, is always superiors to work in some alien country. Besides the surrounding and proximity to family gives one the feeling of at home and reduces the burden of being modern living.

5. Respected judges and teachers.

Today I stand before you to present my views for the motion on the topic given for debate. I believe that private cars should be banned in the congested commercial areas of the cities.

There is no end to the number of vehicles being driven around the city each day. Traffic jams have become a rather common problem and it has only increased in the last ten years. In my opinion, allowing private cars to congested commercial areas only adds to the problem. Long

traffic jams do not only mean consumption of extra fuel but it also means that more number of people would suffer from respiratory diseases due to pollution. If people take the public transport to work or hire a cab which runs on CNG and comes with an option of pooling, the problem of constantly rising pollution and heavy traffic jams can be reduced by many-folds.

The earth belongs to all of us and it is our duty to safeguard it and keep it clean for our future generations. Thus, the first step towards protecting our environment would be to stop abusing the available amount of petroleum and avoid creating pollution.

Thank you for listening to my views patiently.

6. Good Morning!

Today, I, Arjun Mittal, have got a golden opportunity to speak on the topic "It is cruel to put stray dogs to sleep".

Yes, it is cruel to put stray dogs to sleep. 'Euthanasia' is the commonly used term to describe the cruelty to put animals to sleep. It is a practice of putting an end to the life of an animal by giving him a poison or drug. Euthanasia should only be practiced if the dog is in excruciating pain and cannot be treated.

Humans have been domesticating dogs for many years. Dogs are known as man's best friend. They act as scavengers and thus maintain a balance in the ecosystem. They also protect human habitations from thieves and other threats. It is very important to take care of these human friendly species.

Humans should not consider stray dogs as a burden but as a part of their society. Thus, I will conclude by saying that Euthanasia should be stopped as every living being has an equal right to live.

7. Nowadays there is too much stress is put on academic qualifications. It has been projected as if this is the sole determiner of success in life. In our nation, for an example, jobs are secured by only those who accomplish well in their academic performance. No doubt, academic qualification is vital but it is not the lone factor to ensure success in life of an individual. Ability and the will power of person are also the crucial determiners of success. Skills can be characterized in many ways, for example, soft skills, language skills, and IT skills. There remains no guarantee that an individual with the most of top grades will

get hold of a job as many employers do employ workers based on their skills. There should be no ambiguity that academic qualification is solely based on one's performance in their respected schools, colleges or universities. Not everyone gets equal opportunities. For this reason, skills are far more significant in shaping a successful future. Furthermore, the determination and attitude of an individual is another deciding factor in one's life. As the famous quote goes, 'Where there's a will, there's a way ', there will be always opportunities for everyone to have successful life as long as they are willing to take on the challenge, no matter what their academic score is.

8. For the motion -

Goodmorning ladies and gentlemen! the motion tabled before the house today is 'indulgence of youth in the use of internet is a great bane for them' and I stand firmly against the motion. Today's youth has become addicted to playing computer games or chatting with their friends on social networking sites. Excessive indulgence of youth in the use of internet has made them a slave of the internet world. They have been affected negatively as they tend to experience only the 'virtual' and ignore the 'real' world. Their inter-personal relations suffer and they get distracted from work and study.

Cyberbullying and cybercrime have become real concerns today, especially when it comes to innocent youth. Indulgence of youth in the use of the internet is extremely dangerous because rumours can be spread and extreme religious sentiments can be hurt through internet, which in turn, can affect the mentality and perception of the future of our nation.

The Internet is used not only for beneficial purposes in all good sense, but it is also used by people with bad intentions to gather information available easily on various websites about the youth and use it for their personal benefit by blackmailing and threatening them. Thus, I would like to conclude that though the internet would be the best invention of the 20th century, it is more harmful than most other inventions done for liberating, educating and empowering the youth.   [10]

9. "The no-detention policy has created a wrong culture of promoting students irrespective of their academic performance. Owing to the policy, teachers, parents and students developed a laidback attitude towards academics, "said Vidyadhar Amrute, retired professor of Sathaye College, Vile Parle and member of the Mumbai geography teachers association.

The no-detention policy develops an ignorant and irresponsible attitude in a learner. Through this policy, a child does not pay heed to the fact that academics are an integral part of one's life. Moreover the learner in many cases have been observed loosing respect for their teachers as they are well aware of the fact that no matter what the teacher says, he/ she will be promoted to the next grade. This policy has brought down the learning abilities of the students and also questions the achievement of learning objectives that are designed while preparing a lesson plan.

Rekha Vijayakar, director, ADAPT-Able Disable All People Together, said, "Schools blindly promote academically weak children instead of holding remedial classes for them."   [10]

3. Speech

Summary

It is a formal address which is delivered to the audience.

Given are the points which should be kept in mind before writing a speech:

(*i*) Title should be given at the top.

(*ii*) Speech should begin with "Good morning to one and all present here, today I am here to express my views on the topic".................. .

(*iii*) The topic should be defined properly stating its causes, effects, the present situation and the solution.

PREVIOUS YEARS'
EXAMINATION QUESTIONS

1. Regular practice of yoga can help in maintaining good health and even in the prevention of so many ailments. Write a speech in 150-200 words to be delivered in the morning assembly on the usefulness of yoga. [DELHI 2012]

2. You are Raiendra Kumar, a social worker. You read an article in The Hindu on 'Health Care for Indian Workers'. Write a speech in 125-150 words on the importance of health care to be delivered at a public function to create awareness among the workers. [DELHI 2014]

3. Media has a strong hold on society. Write a speech in 125 -150 words on how media influences public opinion to be delivered in the school assembly. [DELHI 2014]

4. Mobile phone of today is no longer a mere means of communication. Music lovers are so glued to it that they don't pay attention even to the traffic while crossing the roads. This leads to accidents sometimes even fatal ones. Write a speech in 150-200 words to be delivered in the morning assembly advising the students to be careful in the use of this otherwise very useful gadget. Imagine of you are Principal of your school. [DELHI 2015]

5. Power shortage has become a norm even in the metropolitan cities. One way to face this situation is by preventing the wastage of power. Write a speech in 150-200 words on the importance of power in our daily life and how to save power at school and at home. Imagine that you are the Principal of your school. [DELHI 2015]

6. Write a speech in 150-200 words on 'Benefits of early rising' to be delivered by you in the morning assembly of your school. You are Karuna/Karan, Head Boy. [DELHI 2016]

7. Write a speech in 150-120 words on the topic, 'Discipline shapes the future of a student. It is to be delivered in the morning assembly. You are Karun/Karan. [ALL INDIA 2016]

8. Your PGT English Ms. Geetha is a short story writer also. 'Sky is not Far' is a collection of her latest short stories. This book has won a national award. Write a speech in 150-200 words you will deliver in her honour in the morning assembly. [DELHI 2017]

9. Holi is a festival of colours. It expresses pure and simple joy. Sometimes we start throwing coloured water and that too on strangers. As the Head boy / girl of your school write a speech in 150 – 200 words that you will deliver in the morning assembly of your school, describing why Holi is played and how it should be played. [ALL INDIA 2017]

10. You are Ali/Alia, Head girl/Head boy of your school. You are deeply disturbed by the rising cases of aggressive behaviour of students in your school. You decide to speak during the morning assembly about it. Write a speech on 'Indiscipline in Schools'. (150-200 words) [DELHI, ALL INDIA 2018]

11. Outdoor exercise or morning and evening walk during winter months has become difficult in the polluted atmosphere of the metropolitan cities. In such a situation indoor (team) games have become very important. Write a speech in 150 –200 words persuading your students to make more use of facilities for basketball, badminton etc. available in your school. You are Principal of your school. [DELHI 2019]

12. As per last census, the literacy rate in India was around 74%. In our day-to-day life, we find people who cannot even read or write. Looking at the gravity of the situation you decide to deliver a speech in your school morning assembly on the topic, "Each One, Teach One'. Write your speech in 150-200 words. You are Vinitha / Bejo. [DELHI 2020]

🔑 Solutions

1.   **Regular Practice of Yoga**

Respected Principal, teachers and friends,

Good morning to everybody, It's a great honour that I have been allowed to express my views in front of you all. Today I would like to discuss about the importance of Yoga in our daily life. Yoga is a conventional method of meditation developed by the sages and shadhus of ancient India. Yoga was practiced by them as an effective method of controlling their mental and physical activities. Yoga helps in development in the areas of physical, mental, social and spiritual health. A strong body carries a sound mind, and the mind remains clearly focused and stress remains under control. This helps us in maintaining our social eco system well. A healthy body allows you establish a direct connection with your inner soul. Be it children or victims of torture or another trauma, yoga benefits all.

2. Good Morning to all.

Recently, I read an article in The Hindu. I wonder why we hardly care for the health of other human beings, like the workers, around us and remain mute spectators to their misery. Often, the workers work in inhuman conditions, neglecting their health. The authorities must ensure clean and healthy working conditions for these people. It is the responsibility of the government to provide affordable healthcare services to these workers and their families. Indian workers should be taught the importance of cleanliness and hygiene. Many nongovernmental organisations can play a role in spreading awareness about health and hygiene. These workers play a major role in our life. We must understand and appreciate their contribution towards society. Access to basic health facilities is their right. Together, as responsible citizens, we should try to make their lives as healthy as ours.

Thank you!

3. Good morning to all.

Today, I stand here to voice my concerns on how media influences public opinion. Media is a powerful weapon in any democracy. It keeps people updated with the recent changes and development in the society and the world. It also helps them, understand these developments and build their opinion about the same. With the development of better methods of communication, the influence of media has increased. Consequently, its responsibility of delivering correct information has also increased. If people blindly believe in whatever either print or electronic media tells them, our democracy may suffer badly. As the media has the power to showcase both the facets of a piece of information, it should work towards helping

the common man to understand the pros and cons of any issue or event. Thus, one can clearly say that it is the responsibility of media and the media personnel to ensure that they direct their efforts towards building a constructive and balanced society and nation. Thank you

4. My dear students, a very good morning to one and all.

You might be thinking what I want to address today. I am here to discuss the obsession that has obsessed our current generation. On many occasions you might have seen people around you glued so much into their gadgets, especially mobile phones. Just last week, I read in a newspaper that a girl in Agra was hit by a car because she was too involved in her phone to notice a speeding car was heading toward her. Most of the time while crossing roads, children don't seem to notice the oncoming cars. With their earphones plugged in they don't seem to hear the blaring horns of the traffic. A lot of parents are seeing their youngsters dying even before they see the dawn of youth.. I would like to quote Albert Einstein, "I fear the day when technology surpasses human interaction, and we will have a generation of idiots." Children, you must know that you have a bright future and vibrant life ahead if you adhere to safety. Gadgets are for our convenience only; they should not lead us to death. Be safe and make your parents proud, not sorry.

Thank You!

5. My dear students, a very good morning to one and all!

The dwindling resources of today are giving all of us nightmares and the scariest one is loss of electricity. It won't be long before we are plunged into darkness and that too because of our own foolishness. Though electricity can be generated, it is not easy to do so and this fact needs to be recognised and realised at the earliest. We dread power failure but do nothing to save Power so that we may not face such a situation' It is high time we started saving power not only at school but at home too. Saving electricity will save fossil fuel too. We should switch off the lights and fans when not in use. We-all should make use of the daylight to do most of our chores and not forget to check the switches before we leave the room.

Remember, power needs to be saved and used efficiently for future use. Wasting power is going to leave us powerless in the future and I am pure no one would like that. So, children please heed my advice and save electricity. Set an example for others in doing so and lead the country to a brighter future.

Thank you!

6. Good Morning Principal, Teachers and my dear friends.

I take this opportunity to present my views on the topic 'Benefits of early rising.' In good older days people used to go early to bed and rise early from bed. This, habit is very energizing. It gives a positive start. The busy and hectic life of the present generation must inculcate this habit of early rising which relieves stress and tension. This early rising increases productivity and it helps in better time management. Even students can get many benefits out of early rising. Early morning is the best time to study as there won't be any disturbance. It is the ideal time to meditate and to do physical exercises which makes our body and mind fit and fine.

Thank You.

7. Respected teachers and dear friends

I am here to present my views on the topic, 'Discipline shapes the future of a student.' Discipline is a mean of keeping the things in. order. It inculcates in us a sense of duty and obedience. In the words of Swami Vivekananda:" Duty is obedience to the voice of conscience; discipline is necessary not only in schools and colleges but in all walks of life. Absence of discipline will lead to chaos and confusion in life."

Discipline is training, especially of the mind and character aimed at producing self-controlled obedience. It is absolutely essential to the growth and development of an individual and a healthy society. It is indispensable for one and all in every walk of life, it is highly necessary at home, at school, in the playground, in society, in army, in public life, in political party.

Discipline must be taught early in life. The home is the nursery, where we receive our first lesson of discipline, through obedience to parents and elders.

The value of discipline in the political, social and economic life of a country is no less important. Only a nation of disciplined people can rise to the occasion. An undisciplined nation invites its doom rudder or later. Hence, discipline is a precious treasure. Life without discipline is like a ship without a rudder and punishment.

8. I feel honoured and privileged to have been given the opportunity to stand before you all and say a few words of appreciation for our very own and beloved Ms. Geetha (PGT, English). What a person she is! She has not only inspired us to evolve as students and better human beings but has also, given us the courage to believe in our dreams and try to fulfil them.

On behalf of the students of our school, I am going to say something in the honour of the author of a national award winning book 'Sky Is Not Far'. The book is a collection of short stories penned by her. As the title itself suggests, the book is a set of stories which are not just tales but are an account of inspirational journeys, undertook by common people and achieving not so common goals in life.

Ms. Geetha, through her stories, not just the ones she has written in the book, but the ones she told us in class, has inspired each one of us and made us believe that sky is the limit and of course, 'it is not so far'. I am proud to say that I have been one of the students in her class, who has looked up to her and is a huge fan of her master pieces.

Thank you ma'am for mentoring us and making us believe that though life may not be a bed of roses, there is nothing which is impossible to achieve.

Thank You

9. Good Morning!

Today, I, Arjun have got a golden opportunity to speak on Holi. Holi is the festival of colours and victory of good on evil. Holi has roots very deep in our history. Let me start with a short story.

There was an evil king who used to worship his idol. His son used to worship the god. This made the king very angry. He tried to persuade him to worship his idol but failed every time. Finally the king asks his sister who could not be burnt to sit on the pyre with his son and so the sister did. But that day king's son was saved by the god himself. This depicts a win of good deeds over evil.

Now days the colours with which the people play Holi, are very dangerous chemicals. In a study it has been found the chemicals used in those colours are extremely dangerous to our skin and may even cause chronic diseases such as Cancer. So I would like to advise all of you to avoid using the hard colours and use herbal colours instead.

I would like to wish you all A Very Happy Holi!

Thank You!

10. Respected teachers and dear friends,

I Ali, being head boy of the school, would like to seek your attention toward increasing aggressiveness among students of our school. Our school has always been the talk of the town, mostly for good reasons. We have always felt pride while saying that we belong to this school. However, it is extremely unfortunate that nowadays, students of our school are being known for their aggressive behaviour. Be it in sports, competition or any other extracurricular activity, our students have shown some extremely disappointing traits of aggression.

Bullying, ragging are not something to be proud of. Unfortunately, these are rampant in our school. Our school has history of over a century. And it took almost same time to build its reputation, I humbly beg you all to not to decimate this hard earned respect and reputation of the institution. How we behave shows our upbringing and hence our behaviour represents our family values and I am sure no would like to bring bad repute to his/her family.

11. Good morning students and my dear teachers! As the Principal of this school, I would like to speak about the importance of indoor team games in this polluted atmosphere of the city. It is my duty to ensure that your health does not suffer due to the environment we are living in and the fatal combination of gases which we are inhaling these days . This advice will give you a better knowledge on how to live a healthy life in this metropolitan city.

It is said that outdoor exercise or a walk during morning or evening is good for your health but in winters , it has become more hazardous

than beneficial to play, exercise or walk in open areas. Thus, the need of the hour is that we start playing more of indoor (team) games and by indoor (team) games I don't mean games that require a computer screen.

During school hours, one must take advantage of the facilities provided here for playing basketball, badminton, tennis, squash, etc. as they will help you improve your health and and breathing by increasing stamina. The required gear and set-up for various indoor (team) games is available to you during sports period. Please make best use of this.   [10]

12. Good Morning Principal ma'am, teachers and my dear friends. Today I Vinitha/ Bejo of class XII C is here to share my thoughts on the topic "Each one teach one". "Each one teach one" is a famous historical proverb that originated in the United States during slavery when Africans were denied education, including learning to read. Many if not most enslaved people were kept in a state of ignorance about anything beyond their immediate circumstances which were under control of owners, the lawmakers and authorities. When an enslaved person learned or was taught to read, it became their duty to teach someone else, spawning the phrase "Each one teach one".

In India, also this campaign was launched to achieve the goal of 100 % literacy, especially among the adults. This campaign is still continuing in many backward areas. India is a fast developing country with the ambition of becoming a fully developed country as soon as possible. India is a densely populated country where a majority of people live in villages and education in villages is not given much importance. Already there are adults who are uneducated. Unless they are educated, the mission of achieving total literacy cannot be achieved. Thus adult education is very important.

These illiterate adults can contribute to the nation building by being literate in a far better manner. Open schools, skill development programmes, etc. are a few more initiatives taken by the Indian government to promote education.. We as citizens must contribute at our level in the literacy promotion programme.

[10]

4. Report

Summary

In a report the facts are presented in a systematic and well organized manner. It also deals with finding of an event that has already taken place somewhere in the past.

Given are the points which should be there in a report:

(*i*) The record of a sequence of events.

(*ii*) The interpretation of the importance of these records.

(*iii*) The result of the discussion or course of action should be discussed.

(*iv*) The conclusion should be mentioned appropriately along with the recommendations.

Format:

(*i*) Headline

(*ii*) Name of the report writer

(*iii*) Place and date of reporting

(*iv*) Opening paragraph

(*v*) Account of the event in detail

PREVIOUS YEARS'
EXAMINATION QUESTIONS

1. You are Cultural Secretary of PND Xavier School, Jamshedpur. Your school organised a debate on the topic, 'The impact of reality shows on the younger generation'. Write a report in 100-125 words to be published in 'The Times of India', Jamshedpur. **[DELHI 2011]**

2. A major bus mishap which left several people seriously injured took place at Nicholas Road, Nungambakkam, Chennai. Luckily no life was lost. Collect the infonnation from the eyewitnesses and send a report in 100-125 words to 'TheNungambakkam Times'. You are Vinod/Vinodhini, a reporter. **[DELHI 2011]**

3. You are Poorva/Partha, Cultural Secretary of your school, D.B. Senior Secondary School, Ambur. A week-long Music and Dance festival was organised by your school. Write a report in 100-125 words for your school magazine. Invent the details. **[ALL INDIA 2011]**

4. The Debating Society of your school has recently held a workshop on 'Continuous and Comprehensive Evaluation' (CCE) introduced for the students of Class X in all schools. The students discussed the assessment made by the school based on their participation in various activities and the system of grading. Write a report in 100-125 words for your school magazine. You are Parveen/Payal, Secretary of the Society. **[ALL INDIA 2011]**

5. Your school Commerce Association organised a seminar for class XII students of the schools of your zone on the topic, 'Rising prices create a crisis'. As Co-ordinator of the programme/ write a report in 100-125 words for your school magazine. You are Piyush/Priya of ABC School, Agra. **[DELHI 2012]**

6. A new indoor gymnasium has recently been constructed and inaugurate at APJ International School at Goa. As special correspondent of 'The Hindu' draft a report in 100-125 words on the gymnasium and the inauguration ceremony. **[DELHI 2012]**

7. Your school has recently arranged a musical night in the school auditorium. Write a report in 100-125 words on this programme, for your school magazine. You are Mahima/Mahesh, Cultural secretary of Vasant Vihar Public school, Itarsi. Invent the details. **[ALL INDIA 2012]**

8. You witnessed a fire accident in a slum area near your colony on Saturday night. You were very much disturbed at the pathetic sight. Write a report in 100- 125 words for your school magazine. You are Lakshmi/Lakshman, a student of P.D.K. International School, Madurai. **[ALL INDIA 2012]**

9. Your school, Sun Public School, Poona, celebrated 'Environment Day' on 5th November. Write a report on the Programme in 100-125 words for your school newsletter. You are Neeta/Naveen, Cultural Secretary of the school. Invent the necessary details. **[DELHI, ALL INDIA 2013]**

10. You are Deepak/Deepika, Secretary of Ahimsa Club, Parsva Public School, Delhi on 2nd October your school observed 'International Day for Peace and Non-violence', organizing various activities such as visit to Raj Ghats, Charkha spinning, lectures by eminent Gandhians etc. Write a report on the same in 100-125 words. **[DELHI, ALL INDIA 2013]**

11. Maxim Gorky School, Kodaikanal celebrated 'Nutrition Week' from 1st September to 7th September by arranging inter-school cookery contests, oratorical, painting and poster competitions, besides talks by eminent nutritionists and medical professionals. There was an overwhelming response from students and parents. Prepare a report in 100-125 words to be published in your school magazine. You are Arjun/Anita, School Pupil Leader.

[ALL INDIA 2013]

12. You are Roshan / Rohini, School Pupil Leader of Meerut Public School, Meerut. Your school joined a campaign organised by various agencies of your city to create awareness among people to conserve water. Write a report in 100-125 words highlighting the activities such as rain water harvesting etc.   [ALL INDIA 2013]

13. The Eco Club of your school launched a special cleanliness drive in the school and its neighbourhood. As Secretary of the club, write a report in 100-125 words giving details of the programme. You are Karan of A.M.M. High School, Hyderabad.   [DELHI 2013]

14. Incessant rain has caused irrecoverable damage in your area. As an active participant in the flood relief programme, write a report in 125-150 words on the different flood relief measures carried out. You are Krishan/Krishna

[DELHI 2014]

15. You have visited a book exhibition in your neighbourhood. Write a report in about 125-150 words on the exhibition. You are Rohan / Rohini.

[DELHI 2014]

16. You had attended a workshop on personality development for students. Many eminent personalities had been present. Write a report in 125-150 words on how the workshop proved to be beneficial. You are Rajesh/Rajshree.

[ALL INDIA 2014]

17. Last week the newly built auditorium of your school was inaugurated. As Deepak / Deepti Saha, the head boy/girl of the school, write a factual description of the auditorium in 125-150 words.   [ALL INDIA 2014]

18. MMD School, Nashik, recently organised a science symposium on the topic : 'Effect of pollution on quality of life'. You are Amit/Amita Raazdan, editor of the school magazine. Write a report on the event for your school magazine.

[DELHI, ALL INDIA 2018]

19. In your locality a blood donation camp was organized by an NGO – 'For Your Health'. Many people visited the camp and donated blood. Write a report in 150 – 200 words for a local newspaper covering the arrangements, doctors' team, refreshment served etc.   [DELHI 2019]

20. A programme on 'Swachh Bharat Mission' was organized in your school on Mahatma Gandhi's birthday. Posters were prepared and pasted in the colony near your school. A procession was taken out. School premises and its surroundings were cleaned by the students. Public was advised to make the mission successful. Write a report on the programme in 150-200 words. You are Srinivasan / Latha.   [DELHI 2020]

21. You are Sunil/Megha, School Leader of Sudheer Public School, Chennai. On the completion of 25 years of meritorious service to the cause of education, your school celebrated its Silver Jubilee with great pomp and show. The celebrations lasted three days and in the true tradition of the school, each day was devoted to a noble cause of service. Special attention was paid to Children with special needs, Old Age Homes and Orphanages. Students shared experiences of voluntary service and the Theatre Club put up short skits highlighting social concerns. Write a report in 120-150 words about the event to be published in your school magazine.

[DELHI Term II, 2022]

22. Write a Report for the school magazine on a one day inter-school cricket match held in Suraj Public School, Chalapuram, Calicut. You may use the inputs given below.

> Day, date, time, venue, scores of each team, outstanding individual scores, prizes and awards. You are Sujatha/Anil – Students reporter. (120-150 words)

[DELHI 2023]

✐ Solutions

1.   The impact of reality shows
on the younger generation

(Report by- Sumit)

On April 4th, a debate was organised on the topic of "The impact of reality shows on the younger generation" at 10 A.M in the school auditorium. Students of about fifteen schools had participated in the debate. They expressed their views in favour of or against the topic.

The District Magistrate of our district presided over the debate. The panel of judges declared the outstanding participants. Students from St. Jhon's Senior Secondary secured all the top three slots of the competition .Prizes and certificates were given away by the chief guest. He delivered a short but impressive speech by saying that there are positive-and negative aspects of everything.

2.   **Bus Mishap**

(Report for The Nungambakkam Times)

(By- Vinodhini)

Today morning a major bus mishap took place at Nicholas Road, at Nungambakkam. Many people got seriously injured in the accident. As per eye witnesses accident took place at around 7 a.m. At that time traffic was heavy. Everyone was in a hurry. All of sudden a bus came at a high speed and collided with the divider. It broke the divider and went to the wrong side. On the wrong side, it hit a shop and collided with many standing vehicles. Of course there was hue and cry everywhere.

Several injuries were reported. The police was immediately informed by the public. Ambulances reached, and the injured were carried to the nearby hospitals. People said that the driver was drunk and lost control of the vehicle. He also had fatal injuries. However, there was something good as no life was lost in this accident.

3.   **Music and Dance Festival**

(Report by- Poorva)

A week-long Music and Dance festival was organised by our school, D.B. Senior Secondary School, Ambur on March 19 to mark the annual cultural week of the school. Students from several other schools also actively participated in various events. The venue for the week-long functions was primarily the school campus. An eye-catchy pandal was constructed for the festival. Theme based lighting and sound arrangement were among key attractions. Audience were present to the capacity of most of the Pandals. Music and dances of various genres were performed. Kathak, Bharatanatyam, Odissi and Disco were prominent in the dance section,. Students of Mt, Carmel girl's school performed Kathak well. Entire audience was mesmerised with the performance. Western classical enthralled the audience to the core.

A musical play presented by Gargi school gave the finishing touch to the festival. No doubt, the same was chosen for the best performance of the festival.

Many celebrities graced the occasion and cheered the students. With the concluding speech of the principal, the festival came to its end.

4.   **Workshop on CCE and Grading System**

(Report by- Poorva)

On June 20, our school organised a workshop on continuous and comprehensive evaluation. It was held by the debating society of the school. The students discussed the assessment based on their participation in various activities. Many students appreciated the move. They said that study is a continuous process. It takes one complete year to finish one academic year. So, evaluation of the students should be continuous. Multiple choice questions will encourage the students to study the books regularly. Formative activities give students opportunity to participate in various activities like, debate, discussion. It was a good workshop which helped a lot in understanding the continuous and comprehensive evaluation.

5.   **Rising Prices Creates a Crisis**

(By- Piyush)

Today, the Commerce Association of ABC School, Agra organised a seminar on "Rising prices create a crisis". The current era has become a difficult one for the common person who finds it increasingly impossible to meet his daily needs. A price rise in essential commodities tends to have its cascade effects. Price of commodities e.g. LPG, pulses, vegetables, fruits etc. are sky-rocketing and meeting end needs has become a distance dream. The drastic changes in economic policies lead to hike in prices of commodities. The increase in the price of petrol and diesel affect the entire economic structure of the nation. With liberalisation and globalisation, there has been in increased entry of multinational and other corporate giants into -our country. The government should ensure that the rich do not enjoy these services at the cost of the poor. To ensure equity, higher taxes should be levied on these companies and subsidies should be given to indigenously produced options.

This will ensure a bare minimum level of quality of life for the population of lower socio-economic status. The government should also seriously boost the marketing and sales of its own agriculture produces. This will ensure a favourable environment for domestic agriculture growth. Policy decision makers should keep the poor person in mind at all times.

6. The APJ International School at Goa, constructed the indoor Gymnasium for the school students and staff. The school organised the opening ceremony, the chief minister of Goa, inaugurated the indoor gymnasium of the school. The school principal welcome the chief guest with-garland. A short speech was delivered on the history of gymnasium. The first indoor gymnasium in Germany was probably the one built in Hesse in 1852 by Adolph Spies, an enthusiast for boys and girls gymnastic in school.

Today, a gymnasium is common in virtually all American Colleges and around the world. So, it is very important for the overall development of the children. The chief guest also stressed on the education of gymnastic. He also praised the Principal for devotion and initiation of gymnastic education in the school. Principal Mr Mitesh Kumar gave the vote of thanks at the end of the celebration.

7. Musical Night

(By- Mahima,

Cultural Secretary)

Our school arranged a musical night in the Vasant Vihar Public School, Itarsi at school auditorium on the eve of foundation Day. Eminent citizens and Parents of the students were invited. The broad casting Minister of the state was the chief guest and the popular music composer A. R. Rehman was the guest of honour. The Programme was started at 6 p.m. The programme was initiated with the tune of Patriotic song. The students presented a variety of entertainment programmes. The gathering liked the folk songs of different states in their local costumes. Folksongs/gazals and geets were highly applauded. A play depicting the problem of educated unemployed was also presented. It was a realistic play. The parents and students were highly motivated. At the end, the principal gave the thanks note and the musical night came to an end successfully.

8. Slum area Destroyed in Massive Fire

(By- Lakshmi, P. D. K.

International School, Madurai)

On Saturday night, the colony slum near my colony was gutted in a fire due to short circuit. Most of the people in the area have got serious burn injuries. At least ten people have died, about 150 have been admitted in various hospitals. About 500 people have been left rendered homeless in this tragic incident. The area has become unhygienic. To help these unfortunate victims of fire, the CSR club of our school has given them money, clothes, food and other material so that they may carry on their lives without feeling depressed. Free medical service has been provided to the wounded. A group of volunteers have been posted to look after those admitted in the hospitals. Other voluntary organizations have also come forward to help the victims. The situation in the area is very miserable. The government should take care of this issue on war footing.

9. Environment Day

(By- Neeta)

Our school celebrated 'environment Day' with great zeal in the school campus and its nearby areas from 3rd April to 8th April, 2013. The aim was to sensitize the students and the neighbourhood people to preserve and conserve the environment. The entire week saw frenzied activities and the school campus wore a green look.

The plantation drive was inaugurated by the chairman of the school, Dr. K.H. Jain marked the beginning of the event. 'Each one-plant one-adopt one' was the motto infused among the children. On the second day, DDE, District East, Mr. K.M. Sinha along with education officer Mrs V. L. Vinayak planted the saplings in the school ground. They appreciated the school's endeavours-to make the future of our nation, environment conscious and nature lovers.

Afterwards, the Eco-club in charge along with house coordinators planted the saplings. The praefectorial team took pledge to tend the saplings. It was followed by a rally of the students and teachers with placards accompanied by slogan shouting were a sort of wake-up call. The 'Nukkad-Nataks based on cleanliness, plea to stop the usage of-polythene bags and replacing it with eco-friendly products stirred the people's conscience. On the concluding day, inter-house debates and declamation contests were organised. To disseminate the message among the tiny-tots, the drawing and fancy-dress competitions were held. The colourful attire of children as trees, flowers, mountains presented lively environment. The small gestures of the future citizens aimed at turning the green movement to mass movement.

10. International Day for Peace & Non-Violence

(By- Deepika, Secretary,

Ahimsa Club)

Yesterday on 2nd October, Our school Ahimsa Club organised the 'International Day for Peace and Nonviolence' in school premises from 10 a.m. to 12 p.m. The function was started at 10 a.m., the education minister of Delhi was the Chief Guest. Our school principal welcomed him with garland. Speeches on the life of Gandhi were delivered by some students. Many positive aspects were also reflected in the speech. A stage play was played on the life of Gandhi. How he helped the people in Champaran was also discussed. Some eminent Gandhians were also present on the occasion. They all highlighted over the non-violence and peace. They also advised the students to resolves the matter with peace. A team of students was sent to Rajghat to observe the situation and various activities. They provided the information to our principal over the phone. The popular song was also sung by the student to remember the Gandhi. At the end of the function, the Chief Guest distributed the Prize for the best performance. The principal gave the thanks note to the students and all invitees.

11. Nutrition Week

(By- Arjun,

School Pupil Leader)

Our School health club organised and celebrated the Nutrition week from 1st September to 7th September, as usual, every year. This year some special attraction was the arranging inter-school cookery contests, oratorical, Painting and Poster Competitions. Besides these activities, some eminent nutritionists and medical professionals from AIIMS talked about the importance of Nutritious food. There was an overwhelming response from students and parents. The weekend programme was a grand success. At the end of the weekend, the prizes, certificates were distributed among the students by the Health Minister of Kodaikanal.

12. Conserve Water

(By- Rohini, Pupil Leader,

Meerut Public School)

Last week, our school participated in a campaign organised by various civic agencies of the Meerut to spread awareness among the public at large to conserve water. Water is essential for every human being. As we all are aware that water level is depleting day by day. So, these agencies forced the people to utilize the PWD water supply only for drinking. For bathing and washing advised them to use boring water. Besides that, they also highlighted the activities such as rainwater harvesting etc. The commissioner of MC of Meerut appreciated the campaign and gave the certificate to some students and agencies to encourage such kind of activities in future also.

13. Special Cleanliness Drive Programme

(By- Karan, Secretary, Eco club)

The Eco club of J.D.V.M. High School launched a special cleanliness drive in the school and its neighbourhood from Dec 1 to Dec 15. Almost all the students from junior to the senior sections participated in this drive with immense enthusiasm and fervour. During this span, they were told the significance of cleanliness with the help of street plays and skits. Moreover, they were given the task to keep their surroundings clean, which included their school building, house, the streets, roads, parks etc. Several competitions on cleanliness were conducted by all the four houses. Most interestingly, students along with their teachers went out and swept the neighbouring streets encouraging others to participate too. They sprayed mosquito killing sprays in the drains to avoid procreation of mosquitoes. It was indeed, an impressive effort taken by them to create awareness about this serious issue.

14. Flood Relief Programme

(By- Krishna)

The incessant rain in the past few days has caused major damage in our area. Most of the low-lying areas have been flooded, causing irrecoverable damage to the properties. A flood relief programme was organised on 4th April to aid the victims of the flood-affected areas. Everyone came forward to make generous contributions. The donations made were in the form of money, clothes, food and other basic requirements. We distributed the donations to the victims. The Chief Minister too announced a definite amount of relief for the victims. The volunteers also helped us in moving the victims to the relief camps, set up on the outskirts of the city. We are expecting more donations from the people of the city over the next few days.

15.   Book Exhibition

                                    (By- Rohan)

The Residents Welfare Association of Nehru Nagar organised the Fifth Book Exhibition in the community centre of the locality. The two-day long exhibition started on February 25 and attracted over five thousand book lovers from all over Delhi. Renowned publishing houses participated in the fair. Books written by well-known writers were on display. The book stalls were systematically divided. The exhibition also offered heavy discounts on some children's books. People were excited to get access to some of the rare books that were on display. The event was graced by the presence of the renowned writer and novelist Chetan Bhagat.

16.   Workshop on Personality Development

                                    (By- Rajshree)

Last week, a weeklong workshop on personality development was organised by our school. The students of class IX, X, XI and XII actively participated in the workshop. The aim of the workshop was to prepare the students for their future and to equip them for the bigger challenges in life. The workshop proved to be a great success. The students were addressed on various topics like self-analysis, body language and etiquette. Several activities and group discussions were conducted to help the students with their communication and public speaking skills. The workshop was also graced by the presence of eminent personalities like Javed Akhter and Amir Khan. They interacted with the students and spoke to them about the importance of interpersonal skills. The students left the workshop beaming with confidence and optimism.

17.   New Auditorium

                (Report by- Deepak Saha, Head boy)

Last week, Mr . Ramesh Bidhuri, the MP of South Delhi inaugurated the newly built auditorium of our school. The auditorium boasts of all modern amenities. It has several gates so as to avoid any chaos while entering or exiting the auditorium. The seating space has been designed to accommodate about 5000 students.

The seats are comfortable and placed on slopes for a better visibility of the performances on the stage. Special care has been taken to build the stage of the auditorium. The lighting system, which includes dramatic lights, spot lights, etc., and the digital sound system have been installed by a leading brand. The highly equipped auditorium became an instant hit with the students and was even highly appreciated by honourable guest.

18.   Science Symposium at MMD School

                                    (By- Amit)

The two days Regional Level CBSE Science Symposium with the theme "Effect of Pollution on the Quality of Life" was hosted by MMD School, Nashik on 14-15th April. The event witnessed young fervent participants from various part country putting up 44 exhibits displaying how environmental pollution is affecting our life.

Science and technology minister of union government inaugurated the symposium. He was quite amazed by the presentations and thanked the participants. The exhibits by the different schools showed the thorough research and preparation done by their pupils.

Meaningful seminars, debate sessions and group discussions were highlights of different sessions. The best thing was that the students not only highlighted the challenges about the environmental pollution but also suggested various practical solutions which could be effective in adding the life of the earth.

Each of the participants was facilitated with certificates and mementos. Portraying rich cultural heritage of the state host pupil enacted a Nukkad Natak on environmental pollution. Visiting dignitaries applauded the students for their novel ideas and enthusiasm which would help the world to become a much better place to live in.

19.   Blood Donation Camp in ABC Colony

                            -By the correspondent

Thursday, 28 March 2019, New Delhi- A blood donation camp was organized in the community hall of ABC Colony by the NGO - 'For Your Health' on 25th February 2019 between 10:00 am and 2:00 pm. The camp was a great success as people from all age groups above 18 came forward and participated in the camp. Even the members of the residential committee showed their support by donating blood.

Various street performances and melodious songs were performed by the NGO volunteers to attract the attention of the residents towards the camp. An efficient team of doctors and nurses gave knowledge on various aspects related to blood which are not commonly known by people apart from it being a vital fluid in the human body. A healthy human being can donate blood once in eight weeks. Many lives can be saved through voluntary donation of blood in the blood donation camp. The blood collected in such camps is of utmost importance during natural calamities and medical emergencies. The arrangements were well taken care of. Each donor was supplied with milk and glucose biscuits to regain strength.

Accidents and mishaps happen regularly, blood shortage is a common occurrence in hospitals. if citizens take required initiative by donating blood in such camps many lives can be saved. The camp was closed by a short speech by the President of the residential area. All the people, agreed that such camps should be organised regularly.   [10]

20. Programme on Swachh Bharat Mission

By: Srinivasan/ Latha

Our school organized a programme on Swachh Bharat Swasth Bharat Mission on the 150th birth anniversary of Mahatma Gandhi. The programme aimed at creating an awareness among the students and general public regarding Cleanliness and its benefits. Under this programme, all the students from 9th to 12th participated. As a part of this Cleanliness Drive, we had to clean the whole school.

Students were divided into different groups to clean several areas of the school. Students also prepared posters that were pasted in the nearby locality. In order to make the general public aware about the importance of cleanliness, a procession was taken out.

The programme concluded with words of appreciation by the school Principal and a pledge ceremony for keeping our surroundings clean. The teachers and people of the nearby locality appreciated the efforts of the students   [10]

21. Silver Jubilee Celebration

- by Sunil, School Leader

On the completion of 25 years of meritorious service to the cause of education, Sudheer Public School, Chennai, celebrated its Silver Jubilee with great pomp and show. The celebrations lasted three days and in the true tradition of the school, each day was devoted to some noble cause of service. Special attention was paid to Children with Special Needs, Old Age Homes and Orphanages. On the first day, the Theatre Club put up short skits highlighting social concerns. On the second day, a grand fete was organised. The students arranged some fast-food stalls and also some interesting games. A total amount of Rs. 25,000 was collected through this fete. The entire amount was contributed to the Old Age Homes and Orphanages. On the third day, the students shared their experiences of voluntary services. These activities of the school were highly acclaimed by one and all. The programme ended on a cheerful note and was a huge success.   [5]

22. Inter-School Cricket Match

By: Sujatha

Suraj Public School, Chalapuram

Calicut

26 February, 2023:

Last Monday, an inter-school cricket match was organised by our school and played in our school grounds. It was a very thrilling match with the best players of both school teams putting the best show possible. Our school won the toss and chose to bowl. The batsmen batted brilliantly and put up a score of 145 runs in twenty overs. The opposite team then came in to bat and the match was decided on the last bowl when the opposite team needed 3 runs and hit the bowler for a four to win the match. The star batsman ABC of our school scored a brilliant 34 runs of just 12 balls and was given a prize for the same. The winning team lifted the trophy and also the opportunity to host the best match. It was a great nail-biting match and the spectators thoroughly enjoyed it.   [5]

Literature Textbooks and Long Reading Text

PROSE

1. The Last Lesson

Summary

Introduction:

Franz, who is one of the two key characters of the story, didn't want to go to school fearing that Mr. Hamel, his French teacher would ask questions regarding Participles and he was certainly not prepared for it. Mr. Hamel's ruler and scolding had an impression on Franz. Though Franz was more inclined to spend a day out of school, however, he landed into the school. On his way to school, he saw a huge gathering at the Town Hall's notice board but he chose to ignore it as he was of opinion that this board always served bad news related to war. In fact when a blacksmith told him there was no need of going to school. Franz took it as if he was making fun of him. Once he reached the school he noticed a change in the school atmosphere. The absence of noise and chants of lessons by the learner made him suspicious. The day resembled to be a Sunday for the school. Students had already taken their seats in the classroom. Franz saw Mr. Hamel walking with the ruler under his arm and naturally got scared of it. But to his surprise, Mr. Hamel was polite and courteous in welcoming him. As Franz took his seat, he noticed that Mr Hamel was wearing his green coat and the silk cap which he usually wore on functions only. He remained puzzled until Mr Hamel read the notice which came from Berlin and stated that French wouldn't be taught any further in the schools of Alsace and Lorraine. This made Franz realise how he had missed the opportunities to learn and he was apologetic on wasting time and not to learn French. Franz hardly knew to read and write French. Franz now realised that why there was so much crowd on the notice board of Town Hall. The books which seemed like a burden to him earlier looked like old friends now. His feeling for Mr Hamel also changed; he didn't have any bitter memory of the cruel ruler and his cranky nature. Franz was also able to understand why his teacher had put on his best cloth. He could easily relate the presence of elderly people in the classroom as they were there to show respect to M Hamel, as he had served them for forty years. When Franz turn came to recite the lesson, he spoke a few words only and that too with mistakes, however, Mr. Hamel didn't scold him. In fact, on the contrary, he urged him to not to take opportunities for granted as if there is plenty of time to do things. He pointedly connected it with national pride by asking how they would feel when they would be mocked for being Frenchmen but unable to even read or write French. However, Mr Hamel didn't put the entire onus on him only but he also highlighted the reluctance of parents to encourage their children to go to school and instead taking them to farms and mills. Mr Hamel was honest in accepting that even he himself used to ask learners to water his plants rather than asking them to study. He also confessed that whenever he had to go fishing he used to declare a holiday for the learners. Then he highlighted the importance of the French language. He described it as the most beautiful language with the clearest and the most logical structure in the world. He linked language with national pride and said that when you are enslaved you need to keep your language and culture alive. Their language was the key to their freedom from slavery.

Though this was his last class in the school, he taught grammar and writing. Franz felt that the teacher taught his best that day as if he wanted to give all that he knew. As the church clock struck twelve, it was time to close the school. Due to his emotional state, Mr Hamel couldn't say the last words however he wrote "Vive La France"

PREVIOUS YEARS'
EXAMINATION QUESTIONS

▶ **Short Answer Type Question**

[1 Mark]

1. "I had counted on the commotion to get to my desk without being seen." In the light of Franz's statement select the option that rightly brings out his intention.

   (a) He tried to avoid his friends

   (b) He tried to cheat his teacher M. Hamel

   (c) He did not want to face the villagers in the class

   (d) He wanted to escape M. Hamel's scolding.

   [DELHI TERM I, 2022]

▷ **Short Answer Type Questions**

[2 & 3 Marks]

2. Why were some elderly persons occupying the back benches that day? [ALL INDIA 2017, 2014]

3. Why did Franz not want to go to school that day? [DELHI 2017]

4. Who occupied the back benches in the classroom on the day of the last lesson? Why? [DELHI 2015]

5. What tempted Franz to stay away from school? [DELHI 2014]

6. How did Franz react to the declaration that it was their last French lesson? [DELHI 2013]

7. What changes did the order from Berlin cause in the school? [DELHI 2012]

8. How did M. Hamel say farewell to his students and the people of the town? [ALL INDIA 2012]

9. What was Franz expected to be prepared with for the school that day? [DELHI 2011]

10. Franz thinks, "Will they make them sing in German, even the pigeons? What does this tell us about the attitude of the Frenchmen? [All INDIA 2011]

11. How did M. Hamel make his last lesson a special one ? What did he emphasize in it? [DELHI 2019]

▷ **Long Answers Type Questions**

[6 Marks]

12. Our native language is part of our culture and we are proud of it. How does the presence of village elders in the classroom and M. Hamel's last lesson show their love for French? [ALL INDIA 2016]

13. Our language is part of our culture and we are proud of it. Describe how regretful M. Hamel and the village elders are for having neglected their native language, French. [DELHI 2016]

14. Everybody during the last lesson is filled with regret. Comment. [ALL INDIA 2015]

15. Educating children is the responsibility of society. Justify the statement in view of "The Last Lesson". [DELHI 2019]

16. When do the residents of Alsace realise how precious their language is to them? [DELHI 2023]

🔑 **Solutions** ______________________________

1. (d) Under normal conditions, M. Hamel wouldn't allow any late comers in the class. [1]

2. To pay respect to the language teacher M Hamel. He was leaving the school after serving for forty years. [3]

3. Franz was expected to be prepared with the rules of participles which he hadn't prepared and hence he was scared to go to school that day. [3]

4. Villagers occupied back benches in the classroom as they all wanted to pay respect to M. Hamel for his dutiful services to the school children for last forty years. [3]

5. As Franz was late that day he feared of being scolded by the school teacher. This unwillingness was further strengthened by the warm weather and chirping of birds as well. [2]

6. Franz was full of regrets when he came to know that his teacher M. Hamel was leaving after serving the school for forty years. He wished he could have timely learnt his French lessons and he wanted to apologize. [2]

7. The order from Berlin brought the school to almost standstill; the regular hustle-bustle was no more there. The teacher became more caring for the learners. Learner and elderly villagers were apologetic for not paying much attention to learn French when it was easily accessible. [2]

8. He tried his best to arouse the patriotic feelings among the students and the elderly of the village who were present by linking the French language with national pride. He urged them to safeguard the language and tried to impart all his knowledge to the present audience. He made a hand gesture to declare the end of the class after writing ' Vive La France' (Long live France). [2]

9. He was supposed to be prepared with a speech on participles which he hadn't prepared. [2]

10. Franz thinks, "Will they make them sing in German, even the pigeons?" This denotes the fear among the Frenchmen that the invaders

would try to force German on them using unnatural practices but to him French was as natural to native people as cooing was to the pigeons. [2]

11. On the day of the last lesson the village elders had occupied the backbenches in the classroom. They regretted not coming to attend school when they had the chance to. Their language and identity was being taken away from them. They were Frenchmen who wouldn't know how to speak French. As M. Hamel said Alsace had a habit of putting things to last. They had come to pay respect to M. Hamel's forty years of dedicated service [3]

12. In the story, 'The Last Lesson' when the French districts of Alsace and Lorraine had passed into Prussian hands and they received an order from Berlin, that only German was to be taught in the schools of Alsace and Lorraine, then they started realising how precious their language was to them. They also learnt how important is the language and culture of one's own country. The incident actually arouse the feeling of patriotism among the mass. [2]

13. Native language helps a person to express his/her feelings, emotions and thoughts in the most lucid and friendly manner. All feels proud of their language. As M. Hamel declared that henceforth only German would be taught in the schools of Alsace and Lorraine, he praised French as the most beautiful, the clearest and most logical language in the world. He arouses the feeling of patriotism by writing 'Vive LA France' on the board. Presence of elderly to pay tributes to the French teacher shows that they all were having the same feeling of missed opportunity to learn the language when it was easily accessible. By arousing patriotism, M. Hamel and by being present in class the elderly of the village, all of them showed their love for the native land and language. [6]

14. We respect our cultures; hence we respect our language and we are proud of it. M.Hamel blamed himself and natives for neglecting their native language French. Many times he had given a holiday when he wanted to go fishing and he even asked the students to water his flowers. Hamel also found fault with the parents who had sent their children to work instead of

making them attend school. On the last day of the French lesson, all the village elders attended the class and they showed regret for neglecting their native language. All of them sat quietly on the back benches of the classroom. They come with their primers and they tried to listen and understand whatever Hamel taught. Hamel appealed that they hold fast to their language, a key to their freedom. [6]

15. As per the order from Berlin, only German was to be taught in the schools of Alsace and Lorraine. Mr. Hamel, the village people and his students were regretful. The villagers were apologetic about not learning the French lessons when they were easily available. Most of them were engaged in their profession to earn a living, as a result, they ignored their French lessons. Everyone present in the classroom had always thought that they had enough time to learn the language. But in the last French lesson, everybody was apologetic of their mistakes.

Now they had the realization of how little they knew their native language. Everyone attended the last lesson to express their respect for their native language, the dutiful teacher and their beloved country, none of which was theirs now. [6]

16. The story "The last lesson" is narrated by a French boy, Franz who dislikes studying French and hates his teacher M. Hamel. On reaching his class, he is surprised to see that the elders of the village who have come to the classroom to attend the last lesson of French as Berlin ordered that French language would no longer be taught in schools in the French districts of Alsace and Lorraine. Franz at this time starts feeling guilty that he did not pay attention to his own language.

M. Hamel confesses his guilt about not being able to create the love for native language among his students. The chapter throws light on the role that the society needs to play particularly in educating the children. One's personality is mostly the product of the type of society that one is born and brought up. Therefore, it is imperative that the society attaches due importance to education as it is education only that will prepare a child to be self reliant and contribute to the nation and world at large. [6]

2. Lost Spring

Summary

Introduction:

The first part talks about the writer's impressions about the life of the unfortunate rag pickers. She meets Saheb, a rag picker, every morning. Saheb along with his family migrated from Bangladesh as their farms and homes have been swept away by a flood caused by a storm. After observing that he always keeps searching for something in the heaps of garbage the author asked him, why he did it? To which his reply was " I have nothing else to do". When advised by the author to go to school, he told that there is no school in the nearby area. Though she never intended to open any school, she told Saheb that she was going to open a school, which made him happy.

In sharp contrast to his name Saheb-e-Alam, he used to wander barefooted on road in the company of his poor friends. The author came to know that they all desired to have footwear, however, they did not have any proper ones.

Some people argue that it's due to tradition that they walk barefoot, however, the author doesn't agree to it. For her, it was more about poverty. The Rag pickers reside in Seemapuri. The author visited that place. Seemapuri, located on the outer Delhi, however, looks a different world altogether.

It's a colony where tens of thousands of rag pickers reside. Their houses are temporarily made of mud and plastic. Though they are enlisted voters, civic amenities are far from their reach. Wherever they find a livelihood, they put their tents there. Garbage is the main source of survival for them. The same garbage was termed as wrapped in wonders, as they occasionally 10 rupees note or sometimes a coin or so.

The author then outlines the dreams of Saheb. Standing in front of a tennis court, he aspires to play tennis a day in his life. One of the rich people had given him his discarded shoes as well. Even though the shoe had a hole in it, still it was in sharp contrast to his faded clothes. Saheb wasn't bothered about the hole, as for him wearing that shoes itself was like a dream come true.

One fine morning, the author met Saheb at a milk booth to find that neither he had his carefree look nor the happiness that was usually visible on his face. He was carrying a steel canister which looked far heavier or him than the plastic bag he used to carry. On enquiry, the author came to know that he had joined a tea stall and now he would earn 800 rupees and he would also be getting all his meals. However, all this hadn't charmed Saheb as he had lost his freedom and he was no more his own master.

The second part of the chapter is a story of Mukesh, a child labourer in a bangle-making glass factory in Firozabad. Mukesh wants to be a mechanic as he aspires to be his own master.

Firozabad is a famous city for manufacturing bangle; every second house is involved in bangle making. Several generations have passed doing the same work i.e. making bangles for women. Working around furnaces, welding glass is the most integral part of their life cycle. There is a lack of awareness with regard to rules prohibiting child labour. Often they even lose their eyesight. The author feels that if the laws were enforced appropriately then more than twenty thousands of childhood could be saved.

They live in a miserable state as the lanes leading to their homes are stinky and choked with garbage. Animals and humans co-existed in such areas.

The family has several health issues. Women were frail. Father was a tailor at first then worked as a bangle maker. He wasn't able to make the house completely or to send his children to school. As generations, he also passed the skill of bangle making to his children.

From the words of Mukesh's grandmother, one can easily feel that they have accepted their poor condition as their destiny. They accept it as their destiny as they are born in bangle maker caste. The author sees another girl Savita, making mechanical moves of arms as if she is just a machine. Her mother has not had even a full meal in her whole life.

Poverty, unfulfilled wishes, apathy and injustice are all that they feel. They have a fear of doing anything else as the entire administration will not allow them to do anything new.

The author sense some hope when she sees a dream of becoming a motor mechanic in Mukesh's eyes.

PREVIOUS YEARS'
EXAMINATION QUESTIONS

▶ Short Answer Type Questions   [1 Mark]

(Q. 1 to 5) : Read the extract given below to attempt the questions that follow :

Mukesh insists on being his own master. "I will be a motor mechanic", he announces.

'Do you know anything about cars?' I ask.

"I will learn to drive a car," he answers, looking straight into my eyes. His dream looms like a mirage amidst the dust of streets that fill his town Firozabad, famous for its bangles. Every other family in Firozabad is engaged in making bangles. It is the centre of India's glass blowing industry where families have spent generations working around furnaces, welding glass, making bangles for all the women in the land it seems. Mukesh's family is among them. None of them know that it is illegal for children like him to work in the glass furnaces with high temperatures, ...

[DELHI TERM I, 2022]

1. What does the author try to convey by the expression 'being his own master'?

    (a) Mukesh is disobedient to the elders

    (b) Mukesh is adamant in his behavior

    (c) Mukesh takes his own decisions

    (d) Mukesh does not listen to others

2. Through the expression "..... looking straight into my eyes" the narrator is trying to convey

    (a) Mukesh displayed no fear in his eyes

    (b) Mukesh was not feeling shy while speaking to the narrator

    (c) Mukesh was conversing in a very friendly manner with the narrator

    (d) Mukesh displayed his courage and determination in expressing his opinion

3. 'His dream looms like a mirage', This indicates

    (a) Mukesh has no clear vision of his dream

    (b) His dream is distorted and misleading

    (c) His dream is illusive and elusive

    (d) Mukesh's dream is different from others

4. "None of them know that it is illegal for children to work in glass furnaces". Select the inference in reference to the above statement.

    (a) The children are innocent and do not realise the hardships of life

    (b) Their illiteracy and ignorance are exploited by the unsurpulous businessmen

    (c) They have no one to support them legally to get out of the situation

    (d) The children are ready to work in glass furnaces due to their poverty

5. Select the option that lists the facts about Firozabad.

    i. Almost all the families are engaged in bangle making.

    ii. The children work as motor – mechanics.

    iii. The children work in a hazardous situation.

    iv. Firozabad is the centre for car making.

    (a) i & ii

    (b) ii & iii

    (c) i & iii

    (d) iii & iv

6. 'The young men echo the lament of their elders.' Select the option which indicates Anees Jung's view on young men.   [DELHI TERM I, 2022]

    (a) They don't take any initiative

    (b) They are as poor as their elders

    (c) They are as helpless as their elders

    (d) They don't support their elders

▶ Short Answer Type Questions
[2 & 3 Marks]

7. What does the reference to the chappals in 'Lost Spring' tell us about the economic condition of the rag pickers?   [ALL INDIA 2016]

8. Describe the irony in Saheb's name.
[DELHI 2016]

9. What did garbage mean to the children of Seemapuri and to their parents?
[ALL INDIA 2015]

10. What job did Saheb take up? Was he happy?
[DELHI 2014]

11. What explanation did the children offer the writer for not wearing footwear ? Did she agree to it ? (Lost Spring) [DELHI 2020]

▶ Long Answer Type Question

[5 Marks]

12. 'Last Spring' and 'Indigo' bring out how the common man is a victim of exploitation. Explain. [DELHI 2023]

▶ Long Answer Type Questions

[6 Marks]

Answer the following questions in 120-150 words :

13. "For the children it is wrapped in wonder, for the elders it is a means of survival." What kind of life do the rag-pickers of Seemapuri lead? [ALL INDIA 2017]

OR

Garbage to them is gold. How do ragpickers of Seemapuri survive? [DELHI 2017]

14. **Give a brief account of the life and activities of the people like Saheb-e-Alam settled in Seemapuri.** [DELHI 2011]

15. What kind of life did children living in Seemapuri lead ? [DELHI 2020]

16. And in dark hutments, next to lines of flames of flickering oil lamps, sit boys end girls with their fathers and mothers, welding pieces of coloured glass into circles of bengles. Their eyes are more adjusted to the dark than to the light outside. That is why they often end up losing their eyesight before they become adults. [DELHI 2023]

(i) Complete the sentence with reference to the extract :

Their eyes are more adjusted to the dark than to the light outside because _____

(ii) Which of the following would NOT be true ?

(a) The hutments were shining and inviting.

(b) The children's lives were as bleak as their surrounding.

(c) There were no electricity connections.

(d) The boys and girls had got used to the dark.

(iii) The bangle workers lose their eyesight before they became adults because

(a) they already have poor eyesight.

(b) they work in dim light.

(c) they are married in childhood.

(d) they are malnourished.

(iv) Which of the following most nearly means 'adjusted' in the context of the extract?

(a) conditioned

(b) favoured

(c) accepted

(d) reconciled

(v) 'Flickering oil lamps' suggests _______.

(vi) What is the antonym from the extract of the word 'rarely' ?

🔑 Solutions

1. (c) Mukesh is his own master and has a brain of his own to take his own decisions. [1]

2. (d) Mukesh wasn't scared of anyone and was determined to do something in his life. [1]

3. (c) Elusive- indefinable and abstract; illusive-imaginary and unreal [1]

4. (b) Corrupt businessmen are exploiting the illiterate and ignorant poor people. [1]

5. (c) ii & iv are absolutely false. [1]

6. (c) The young people also are in a sorry state, equally ignorant of their rights due to poverty and Illiteracy. [1]

7. The narrator, Andes Jung asks Saheb why he doesn't wear 'Chappals'. He simply answers that this mother didn't buy them. There is a tradition to stay barefoot in villages and slums. It seems merely lame excuse to explain away a perpetual state of poverty. The economic condition of these rag pickers is not so well. [3]

8. The full name of Saheb is Saheb-e-Allam which means "Lord of the Universe". He doesn't know the meaning of his name. The irony here is this Saheb is a ragpicker and a refugee from Bangladesh. He is not the Lord of the Universal all. [3]

9. Garbage was a means of survival to the people of Seemapuri. However, it held a different meaning for the children, for whom it was a mysterious package that held unknown valuables.   [3]

10. Saheb took up a job at a tea-stall. He was not happy because working for a master meant sacrificing his freedom and his 'carefree look'. Even though he earned 800 rupees and all his meals, he was less contented than before.   [2]

11. It is not lack of money but a tradition to stay barefoot, is one explanation offered by the children. The author did not agree to it as she felt that it was only an excuse to explain away a permanent state of poverty.   [2]

12. The proses 'Lost Spring' and 'Indigo' reflect the exploitation of the poor by the powerful. Lost Spring talks about a poor rag picker of Delhi, a bangle maker of Ferozabad. Similarly, the prose Indigo talks about the poor and emaciated peasants and their worst living conditions. Both the texts show how a common man becomes a victim of hunger and helplessness. For Saheb, the garbage is like gold to him. He and hundreds of thousands of other children like him lead a pathetic life living in mud structures with roofs of tin and tarpaulin, with no running water and no drainage. Similarly, In Indigo Rajkumar Shukla is a sharecropper who grows crops on other's land with a meagre share. But in the end both the stories reflect a ray of hope when Mukesh thinks differently and starts dreaming. Likewise, Rajkumar Shukla with his never ending hope convinces Gandhiji to fight for their rights to get their share of happiness and contentment. Thus, both the stories on one hand portrays the victimisation of the poor, but on the other hand it conveys the readers a ray of hope.   [5]

13. Seemapuri is a place in the suburbs of New Delhi. Mostly the refugees, who came from Bangladesh in 1971 live here. It is a hub of almost 10,000 rag pickers. They don't have citizenship and hence no basic amenities, still, they are happy. They manage to secure food which is more important than citizenship. Basically, it's a slum where rag picking is their only way of survival as they don't have any other means of income. As per the author, it is their "daily bread, a roof over their heads, even if it is a leaking roof" which is equivalent to gold for them. Apart from this, for the kids it is "wrapped in wonder" as they, occasionally find "a rupee, even a ten-rupee note".   [6]

14. The story, "Lost Spring" written by Anus Jury revolves around the pitiable condition of poor children who have been forced to live in slums and work in very dirty conditions. The first part of the story tells the writer's impressions about the life of poor ragpickers who have migrated from Bangladesh but are now settled in the Seemapuri area of Delhi. The writer watches a boy named Saheb every morning in his neighbourhood. The boy looks for some coins and other things in the garbage heaps. Rag picking for them means survival, garbage to them means gold. It is a thing wrapped in wonder. When they find a silver coin in a heap of garbage, they feel happy. They have always hoped to find more.   [5]

15. The glass bangle industry was nothing more than a death trap. Thousands of men, women and children work in dingy cells with no light and air, rising temperatures and hot glass furnaces. They slowly lose their eyesight and immunity. Even after all of this most families like that of Mukesh's are not able to manage two square meals a day and a roof over their heads. Like Mukesh's grandmother most of them are fatalists accepting this to be a god given lineage. They are burdened by the stigma of caste and poverty. They don't have any leaders who can start cooperatives. They are unaware about the labour laws that prohibit such living conditions.   [6]

16. (i) They regularly work in flickering dim lights, in dark hutments so they are more adjusted to the dark.   [1]

   (ii) The correct option is (a) i.e. the hutments were shining and inviting.   [1]

   (iii) The correct option is (b) i.e. they work in dim light   [1]

   (iv) The correct option is (a) i.e. conditioned   [1]

   (v) The dim lights.   [1]

   (vi) 'often'   [1]

3. Deep Water

Summary

Introduction:

The story, "Deep Waters" reveals to us how the author conquered his dread of water and mastered swimming with the inner will and self-determination. He had built up a fear of water since his early years. At the age of three or four years, the author had gone to California with his dad. On a particular day, the waves thumped him down and he was almost drowned. The author was extremely frightened yet his dad who knew there was no damage. This left a permanent impression on the author's mind regarding the dread of water.

Afterwards another episode, more frightening, amplified his fear, while he was attempting to get over his fear of swimming in the Y.M.C.A. swimming pool in Yakima. On that day while he was sitting tight, a major kid all of a sudden played an unsafe trick and pushed him into the water. The author was unpleasantly unnerved. He went down nine feet into the water. His lungs were brimming with the unreleased air. When he reached the base, he hopped upward energetically. He came up yet gradually. He attempted to seize something like a rope, however, got a handle on just at the water.

He endeavoured to yell but to no use. He went down once more. His lungs hurt, head throbbed and he became bleary-eyed. He felt incapacitated with fear. All his organs were incapacitated. Just his heart revealed to him that he was alive. Again he endeavoured to hop up. Be that as it may, this time his appendages would not move by any means. He searched for ropes, steps and water wings however all was futile. At that point, he went down once more, the third time. This time all endeavours and dread stopped. He was moving towards serene passing. The author was in peace. When he came to awareness, he was lying near the pool with young men close-by. The fear that he had encountered in the pool never left him. It frequented him for quite a long time and years to come. It spoilt many of his campaigns for kayaking, swimming and angling. It spoilt his delights in Maine Lakes, New Hampshire, Deschutes, Columbia and Bumping Lake and so on.

In any case, the author was resolved to vanquish his dread. He took the assistance of a swimming trainer to get the hang of swimming. The trainer showed him different activities fundamental in swimming step by step. He put his face submerged and breathed out and breathed in raising it above water. He rehearsed it for a little while. He needed to kick with his legs for half a month in the pool. Finally, he joined every one of these activities and influenced himself to swim. He got the hang of swimming yet the dread continued. So profound goes our youth encounters! So frightful is the dread of dread! At whatever point he was in the water the dread returned. Henceforward the writer endeavoured to threaten dread itself. He attempted to confront the new test. At the point when dread came, he went up against it by asking it mockingly with respect to what it can truly do to him? He dove into the water as though to oppose the dread. When he embraced fearlessness the dread was vanquished. He confronted the test intentionally in different spots like the Warm Lake. He vanquished it finally.

The encounters of the writer project some critical light on specific parts of life. Encounters of agony or delight in adolescence stay in the sub-cognizant personality and impact our emotions later as well. The dread of water followed up on the author in that way. Indeed, even subsequent to being a specialist in swimming, the writer felt dread though there was no reason for it. When he embraced bravery, the dread vanished. That shows a large portion of our feelings of dread is vincible. Dread makes perils where there is none. The writer's encounters additionally affirm the notorious truth, "Where there is a will, there is a way."

PREVIOUS YEARS' EXAMINATION QUESTIONS

▶ **Short Answer Type Questions: [1 Mark]**

(Q. 1 to 5) : Read the extract given below and answer the questions that follow : [DELHI TERM I, 2022]

I went to the pool when no one else was there. The place was quiet. The water was still, and the tiled bottom was as white and clean as a bathtub.

I was timid about going in alone, so I sat on the side of the pool to wait for others.

I had not been there long when in came a big bruiser of a boy, probably eighteen years old. He had thick hair on his chest. He was a beautiful physical specimen, with legs and arms that showed rippling muscles. He yelled.

"Hi Skinny! 'How'd you like to be ducked?

1. What impression do you form about the narrator?

    (a) He is a beginner in swimming lessons.

    (b) He has made friend during his swimming lessons

    (c) The big boy was well build and handsome.

    (d) The narrator lacks courage and confidence to enter the pool alone

2. The description of the big boy by the narrator is one of

    (a) Complaint

    (b) Admiration

    (c) Criticism

    (d) Poise

3. Select the option that lists the probable reason for the big boy's behaviour towards the narrator.

    (a) his intention to frighten the narrator

    (b) his desire to give him a surprise

    (c) The place was quiet and odd

    (d) The narrator was skinny and alone

4. The figure of speech in the expression 'as white and clean as a bath tub' is ________.

    (a) Metaphor

    (b) Alliteration

    (c) Simile

    (d) Irony

5. The writing style of the narrator indicates that the passage can be classified under a/an ______.

    (a) Interview

    (b) Autobiography

    (c) Fiction

    (d) Short story

6. "And then sheer, stark terror seized me".

    [DELHI TERM I, 2022]

    Which of the following options has used the same figure of speech as in the underlined phrase above?

    (a) See <u>waves roared frighteningly</u> on a stormy night.

    (b) Fear <u>is a poison</u>

    (c) He roared <u>like a lion</u> in anger

    (d) I am <u>frightfully sorry</u> for my mistakes

7. 'But the jump made no difference'. Select the option that reflects the tone of Douglas.

    [DELHI TERM I, 2022]

    (a) fear

    (b) regret

    (c) anger

    (d) grief

▶ **Short Answer Type Questions:**

[2 & 3 Marks]

8. Why did Douglas' mother recommend that he should learn swimming at the YMCA swimming pool? [DELHI 2015]

9. How did the instructor turn Douglas into a swimmer? [All INDIA 2013]

10. Why did the Douglas go to Lake Wentworth in New Hampshire? How did he make his terror flee? [All INDIA 2012]

11. Why was Douglas determined to get over his fear of water? [DELHI 2011]

12. Which factor led Douglas to decide in favour of Y.M.C.A pool? [All INDIA 2011]

13. Which two incidents in the life of William Douglas before he was ten years old created an aversion in his mind to water? [DELHI 2019]

14. How did Douglas' experience at the beach in California affect him ? (Deep Water) [DELHI 2020]

▶ **Long Answers Type Questions:**

[6 Marks]

15. Fear is something that we must learn to overcome if we want to succeed in life. How did Douglas get over his fear of water?

    [DELHI 2018]

16. The story "Deep Water" has made you realize that with determination and perseverance one can accomplish the impossible. Write a paragraph in about 100 words on how a positive attitude and courage will aid you to achieve success in life. [DELHI 2014]

17. How did Douglas develop an aversion to water?

    [DELHI 2012]

🔑 Solutions

1. (d) "I was timid about going in alone, so I sat on the side of the pool to wait for others." [1]

2. (b) "He was a beautiful physical specimen." This shows his admiration. [1]

3. (d) The way that boy addressed the narrator showed that he wanted to take advantage of his skinny frame and loneliness. [1]

4. (c) Simile is the figure of speech in the mentioned expression. [1]

5. (b) First person narration. [1]

6. (a) Terror is personified and so are the waves. [1]

7. (b) The jump was ineffective as the water was still around him and there was no sign of hope of survival. [1]

8. The overpowering force of the waves at the California beach stired aversion for water in Douglas. His mother warned him against swimming into the deep water of the treacherous Yakima River. So, she recommended that he should learn swimming at the YMCA Swimming Pool. [3]

9. The instructor started training Douglas with great caution. He tied a belt around him with a rope attached to the belt which went through a pulley that ran on an overhead cable. Douglas was made to swim in water for hours and hours. To exhale underwater was taught. He also taught him how to inhale by coming out of the water. [2]

10. Douglas was not certain whether all the fears had been conquered or not, even after the training of six months and practicing. As a result of this doubt, he went to Lake Wentworth and swan two miles. He felt the fear only once when he was in the mid of the lake. He had put his face under and saw never-ending water. Though the fear returned, however, in a smaller intensity. He laughed out and dismissed terror. [2]

11. Douglas was determined to get over his fear of water because it had ruined his fishing trips. He could not enjoy water sports like canoeing, boating or swimming. [2]

12. The Y.M.C.A. Pool was an ideal place for Douglas to learn swimming. It was safe and it was only two or three feet deep at the shallow end. Since it was nine feet deep at the other end, the drop was gradual. [2]

13. The poet's mother had told him that the Yakima river is treacherous and kept fresh in his mind the details of each drowning. Therefore, the poet chose the YMCA swimming pool which was two to three feet deep in the shallow end and nine feet on the deeper end with the drop being gradual. [3]

14. Douglas developed an distaste to water in his early childhood. This was because when he was three or four years old, his father took him to a beach in California. The waves knocked him down and swept over him. This made him fearful and fear of water got entrenched in his heart and mind permanently. [2]

15. Initially, Douglas tried to conquer his fear of water on his own, however, as this didn't fructify, he got a trainer for him who worked in a systematic way. Under his guidance, Douglas learnt to remain at ease in water. After that, he exhaled and inhaled water and was less afraid of putting his head under water. Step by step, he gradually mastered all the skills to have a complete experience of swimming. Within a span of six months he had conquered his fear of water.

Douglas journey highlights the importance of overcoming fear in order to be successful in one's life. [6]

16. In the story "Deep Waters" we see Douglas overcoming his childhood fear of water through determination, perseverance and hard work. Thus, this story shows that with a positive attitude and strength of will, we can accomplish almost anything. All of us may fear something or the other. But, when we conquer the fear through courage, we become victorious. And a victory, emerging from the bitterness of failures- and hardship of enduring them for a long period of time, has its own meaning and charm. It might seem to be a long and gruelling journey, however, it will definitely conclude in success. [5]

17. It was in his early age of three or four years when Douglas developed an aversion to water. It followed the incident when he went surfing with his father. He was holding his father tight still the powerful waves knocked him down. He was almost choked, drowned and swept away. Though his father was there, however, the fear of water struck deep into his heart. This fear had done a long-lasting damage on Douglas' mind. [5]

4. The Rattrap

Summary

Introduction:

A rattrap peddler used to sell small rattraps. His clothes were all torn. He looked like a starved man with hollow cheeks. He used to make wiretraps. Sometimes to survive he used to steal and beg. The world was cruel to him. He was homeless as well.

He was given to meditation and led a very lonely life. As he was thinking about his rattraps, he discovered a new theory. The world itself seemed to be a rattrap to him. The world offers land, clothes, joys and riches to trap people. As soon as anyone touched them the trap closes on them. He found it so funny to think of people who were already trapped and who were on their way to reach the bait.

One cold evening in the month of December he saw a cottage. He knocked at the door to get shelter for that night. A lonely old crofter was the owner of the cottage. The crofter was so kind to him that he welcomed him and served him hot porridge to eat and tobacco to smoke. The peddler came to know from the crofter that he had a cow and that he sold her milk and cream. He also told the peddler that he received thirty kroner as payment in the previous month. After showing the money to him he hung the pouch of money on a nail in the window frame. The next morning the peddler left the cottage and the crofter locked his cottage and went out.

The peddler was tempted to steal the money and he came back to the cottage, smashed the window and stole the money. As he did not find it safe to walk along the public highway he went into the woods. He kept on walking and moved in circles but could not find the way. He was tired and the forest seemed to be a rattrap in which he was caught. He laid down on the ground to die as he thought that his end was near now.

After some time he heard thumping of a hammer's strokes. He was aware that the sound was coming from some iron mill. He stood up and started walking towards the sound. He went into the forge after opening the gates. It was Ramsjo Ironworks.

The blacksmith did not notice him. The owner of the work was on his visit and he came to the forge. It was he who after a careful observation at the peddler's face felt certain that the peddler was Captain von Stahle, one of his old regimental comrades, who had fallen on evil days. He invited the peddler to his home with him for the Christmas. But the peddler was afraid so he denied and the Ironmaster went home. The ironmaster's daughter Edla was sent by him to invite the peddler to come home. She came in a carriage with a large fur coat. She spoke very softly to him and convinced him to go along with her for the Christmas Eve. On the way, he was repentant for stealing the crofter's money. This act of stealing had put him in a trap.

As he sees the old regimental comrade in his home, the ironmaster was extremely happy. He was treated well, fed well and also provided him with respectful work. The servant was asked to cut the peddler's hair and arrange a bath for him. The peddler wore the ironmaster's fine suits. As soon as the ironmaster saw him in daylight he felt that he had made a mistake. The peddler wasn't certainly Captain von Stahle. The ironmaster thought that the man had cheated him and he thought of handing him over to the sheriff.

According to the peddler, he did not show what he was not. He was not quite keen to visit the home of the Ironmaster. Even at that point in time, he was willing to wear his worn-out clothes and leave. He also told the ironmaster that the world was a rattrap and he too might be tempted by the big bait and caught in the trap. He was asked to leave his house by the Ironmaster.

Edla obviously didn't like her father's stance and thought that it was not right to turn away the man whom they had invited for the Christmas. As a result, she stopped the peddler and her father had to give in. Edla served food to the peddler. During the Christmas party in the evening, he was also given some Christmas presents and he received them thankfully. The peddler came to know from Edla that the coat was also a Christmas present. Edla not only showed her kind gestures but also assured the peddler that he would be welcomed again if he wished to spend another Christmas Eve with them.

Next morning when the Ironmaster and his daughter went to the church there they came to know that the peddler was a thief who had robbed the crofter. The ironmaster was certain that their silver was taken by the peddler. Edla was sad about it. But as they reached home they came to know that the peddler had left their house. However, nothing was taken from there. In fact, to the contrary of expectations, a Christmas present for Edla was left by him. As soon as Edla opened the present she found a rattrap in which he had left the crofter's money behind. This made Edla happy. There was a letter as well, which was addressed to Edla. In the letter, the peddler had thanked Edla for her kindness. He had also requested to return the money to the crofter. He stated his upbringing was like a captain and that is what enabled him to come out of the rattrap in which he was trapped. The letter was signed as Captain von Stahle.

PREVIOUS YEARS'
EXAMINATION QUESTIONS

▶ Short Answer Type Questions

[2 & 3 Marks]

1. What do we learn about the crofter's nature from the story, 'The Rattrap'?

[ALL INDIA 2016]

2. Why did the peddler derive pleasure from his idea of the world as a rat trap?

[DELHI 2014]

3. Why did the peddler decline the invitation of the ironmaster? [DELHI 2012]

4. Why was the crofter so talkative and friendly with the peddler? [DELHI 2011]

5. Why was the peddler surprised when he knocked on the door of the Cottage?

[ALL INDIA 2011]

6. The iron master accuses the peddler of not being quite honest. What does the peddler say to justify the situation?

[DELHI TERM II, 2022]

7. Explain the metaphor of the rattrap.

[DELHI 2023]

▶ Long Answer Type Question

[4 Marks]

8. In Edla's dealing with the peddler, she was compassionate and generous. Discuss with reference to the story 'The Rattrap'.

[DELHI TERM II, 2022]

▶ Long Answer Type Questions

[6 Marks]

9. The peddler believed that the whole world is a rat trap. How did he himself get caught in the same? [ALL INDIA 2017]

10. The peddler thinks that the whole world is a rattrap. This view of life is true only of himself and of no one else in the story. Comment.

[DELHI 2017]

11. How did the peddler feel after robbing the crofter? What course did he adopt and how did he react to the new situation? What does his reaction reveal? [All INDIA 2013]

12. How did the crofter tempt the peddler to steal his money ? How did it change the peddler's life? [DELHI 2019]

13. Why did the Crofter repose confidence in the peddler ? How did the peddler feel after betraying the crofter ? [DELHI 2020]

14. "I am thinking of this stranger here," said Edla "He walks and walks the whole year long, and there is probably not a single place in the whole country where he is welcome and can feel at home. Wherever he turns he is chased away. Always he is afraid of being arrested and cross-examined. I should like to have him enjoy a day of peace with us here-just one in the whole year."

(i) Complete the following sentence with the most appropriate option :

Edla wished the Pedlar to have a peaceful day because __________

(a) the Pedlar had worked for Edla.

(b) the Pedlar had not been released from jail.

(c) the Pedlar had been staying at the forge.

(d) the Pedlar had always been looked with suspicion.

(ii) Select the suitable word from the extract to complete analogy.

single : multiple :: abroad : ___________

(iii) In the above extract, Edla comes across as

(a) conscientious

(b) pretentions

(c) compassionate

(d) selfless

(iv) Based on the above extract, choose the statement which is true.

(a) relationships are rattraps.

(b) money is important in the world.

(c) criminal is not born but made

(d) christmas is a time of charity

(v) In the context of the given extract, which day is referred to in the expression 'just one in the whole year'?

(vi) What does the expression 'he is cross examined' suggest?   [DELHI 2023]

🔑 Solutions ___________

1. The Crofter was a generous host and a good companion. He was an old man without wife or child. He was a lonely man always in search of a good company He was happy to get someone to talk to his loneliness. So, he served the peddler food and pipe. He made every effort to make his guests comfortable.   [3]

2. The peddler derived happiness from the idea of the world being a giant rat trap as he was never treated in a kind manner by the world. And for this reason, he had hard feelings for the world and felt pleasure by thinking ill of it, by comparing it to a giant rat trap.   [2]

3. Being aware of the fact that the Ironmaster had mistaken him as his old comrade, the invitation from the ironmaster did not please the peddler. As the stolen money was with him, he was scared and frightened as well.   [2]

4. The crofter was friendly with the peddler because he lived alone without a wife, child or companion. He suffered from loneliness.   [2]

5. The peddler did not expect to receive the kind of hospitality he received from the crofter. He usually used to meet sour faces and was turned away without even a word of kindness.   [2]

6. When the ironmaster accused the peddler of not being quite honest, he spoke in his defence and explained that he had never tried to pretend as ironmaster's acquaintance. So he was not at fault. All along he had upheld that he was a poor trader and had pleaded to be allowed to stay in the forge. However, no harm had been done by his stay. Hence he was willing to put on his rags again and go away.   [2]

7. The metaphor is the poetic device which shows comparison of two different things with similar characteristics. Similarly in the prose, The Rattrap, the author signifies that the whole world exists only to trap the people by setting baits in the form temptations which lead to be caught in a vicious trap. The author cites the example of baits like luxuries which lure a human and make him commit crime leading to get punished. All the good things are cheese rinds offered to a rat (human) to make him get trapped. In this way no one can come out of the trap.   [2]

8. Answer ANY TWO of the following

In Edla's dealing with the peddler, she was compassionate and generous, This act of kindness by Edla towards the peddler altered his outlook towards the world. Edla had understood in the very first meeting that her father was muddling up with someone's identity to be his acquaintance. She understood this since she had observed the peddler very keenly. She knew he was either a thief or a deceitful character; however, she persuaded him to accompany her to her house to spend the Christmas Eve with them.   [4]

Earlier the peddler used to think that the entire world is a big rattrap and that everything in life is a big bait. But Edla made him realize that she could see the real human being behind the swindling rattrap seller by bringing him to their house and asking him to be a part of their family at least for a single day. She also supported him when his identity was revealed. All this made the peddler see a very new side of the world. She wanted the peddler to enjoy Christmas Eve and be at ease. She even invited him to be their guest on the next Christmas. He began to realize that there are good people in the world too and that he must henceforth change his way of looking at the world.   [4]

9. The life of the peddler is of loneliness. This thought of being absolutely alone made the peddler a cynic. After the theft of money, he tried to flee through the forest but soon got lost. He remembered his own thoughts and comprehended that he had trapped himself in the rat trap. He was tempted by the bait, the thirty kronor bills. The ironmaster and especially his daughter's kindness failed to make the peddler positive about the world. The rat trap seller articulated himself strongly realising that the worldly bait had, once more, tempted and trapped him. Unlike the other characters in the story, peddler is the only one who gave up to the loneliness and as there was an absence of the emotional bonds, the human relationship of love and empathy, it made him the skeptic and made him believe the world was a rat trap. [6]

10. The peddler had a lonely life. By being completely alone, he became a cynic. When he ran to the forest to escape after stealing money, he got lost. In such conditions of despair, he reflected on the world as a giant rat trap. A sense of realisation came to him that he was caught in the rat trap as he allowed himself to be tempted by the bait, the thirty kronor bills. The kindness of the ironmaster and especially his daughter failed to make any difference in the peddler's world. And, this made him a cynic who considers the world as a rat trap. [6]

11. After robbing his host crofter, the peddler was amused with his act. He did not have any harsh feelings that he had broken the trust reposed in him by the crofter. He thought only of his own safety. As he realised the danger of being caught by the police along with the thirty kronors, he decided to leave the road, and run into the woods. In the initial few hours, the woods didn't cause any difficulty. Gradually, it became hard as the forest was big and confusing. The trails were twisted back and forth. Though he was walking he did not find any end of the wood. He realised that none of his efforts to get out of the forest was fructifying. The forest seemed like a prison from where he could never escape. This reaction of the peddler shows the quandary of human nature. Temptations often lead to evil. And the fruits of evil seem amusing initially, however, they deny a man of his kindness and push him into the rat trap. [6]

12. The peddler had always been a victim to the apparent atrocities of this cruel world, he liked to think ill of it and its citizens. He thought the world was a rattrap and everyone was attracted to the lands, riches, joys it had to offer. But the kindness of Edla completely changed him. Initially he had been given shelter under the belief that he was an old friend of the owner of the ramsjo ironworks. However when the next day his identity was discovered the owner suggested giving him away to the police, it was only because of Edla that her father agreed to host him for Christmas. For the first time the tramp slept peacefully and had a hearty meal. The young girl didn't care about his identity and served him with pleasure. She, gave him new clothes and offered him to come back next year. In the end, the peddler completely changed and returned the money he had stolen. [6]

13. The Crofter reposed confidence in the Peddler because he was lonely, living alone and earning a living with his cow. He wanted someone with whom he could share his feelings, even trusting him to the "extent of showing the Peddler where he had kept his money. The Peddler betrayed this trust by robbing the money and eloping. However, when the Peddler went through the forest instead to avoid detection, he got lost and returned to the same place again and again. Ultimately the Peddler realized that he was like a rat caught in a rattrap and that the whole world was like that. The bait he had fallen for was the Crofter's money and he could not escape with it. [6]

14. (i) (d) the Peddlar had always been looked with suspicion [1]

 (ii) home [1]

 (iii) The correct option is (c) i.e. compassionate [1]

 (iv) The correct option is (c) i.e. criminal is not born but made [1]

 (v) Christmas eve [1]

 (vi) The expression 'he is cross examined' suggests that Peddlar and his identity have always been questioned because of suspicion. [1]

5. Indigo

Summary

Introduction:

In December 1916 there was the annual convention of the Indian National Congress. A poor illiterate peasant came there and he complained about the injustice suffered by the peasants in Champaran. He met Gandhiji there and told him about the problems. As Gandhiji had many engagements so he did not give any assurance to Mr. Shukla. But the peasant was determined and he followed Gandhiji wherever he went. Gandhiji was so impressed that he fixed a date.

Both of them went to Patna by train to meet a lawyer Rajendra Prasad. The lawyer was out of town. But the servants already knew Shukla as he had been there several times. The servants made both of them stay on the ground as they mistook Gandhiji for another peasant and untouchable. They did not allow them to draw water from the well.

Gandhiji decided to break his journey to camp at Muzaffarpur as he wanted to get more information about Champaran sharecroppers. At Muzaffarpur, Gandhiji stayed in the house of a government teacher, Mr. Malkani. In those days Indians were afraid to show sympathy to the supporters of the home rule. As the news of Gandhiji's arrival in Muzaffarpur spread the sharecroppers started coming to Muzaffarpur to see him. They briefed him about their problems. Gandhiji chided the lawyers for taking high fees from poor peasants. Gandhiji thought that the most important thing was to free the peasants from the fear of British landlords. Champaran district was divided into estates of which the English people were the owners and the Indians worked as sharecroppers on their land. The sharecroppers were compelled to plant 15% of their land with indigo and the entire harvest was surrendered to the landlords as rent.

In the meantime, landlords heard that Germany had developed synthetic indigo. So they offered to release the sharecroppers from the obligation to harvest indigo but asked them to pay the compensation. Some peasants agreed and some resisted. As the peasants learnt about the synthetic indigo so those who paid the compensation asked for their money back. The dispute between the landlords and sharecroppers arose. The landlords hired thugs and the sharecroppers engaged lawyers.

Gandhiji wanted to know the exact situation so he visited the secretary of the British landlords association. But he was refused the information as he was an outsider.

Gandhiji called on the commissioner of Trihut division. He was rude to him and asked Gandhiji to leave Trihut immediately. Gandhiji made Motihari his headquarter. He started his investigations. A peasant who was maltreated in a nearby village so Gandhiji decided to go there to know the fact but was stopped by the police. He was served a notice to leave Champaran but Gandhiji denied. Gandhiji was summoned to appear in the court. Gandhiji sent the report to the Viceroy.

The peasants got to know that Gandhiji was in trouble so they gathered around the court building. This baffled the British authorities. They felt powerless. In the court, Gandhiji pleaded guilty. He read out a statement and asked for a penalty. The judge let Gandhiji go free as the delivery of judgement would take several days.

Gandhiji's lawyer friends told him they would follow him to jail if he went to jail. Gandhiji was pleased. He declared that the battle of Champaran was won.

The Lieutenant Governor of the province decided to drop the case against Gandhiji. This was the victory of Civil disobedience. Gandhiji and lawyers proceeded to conduct an enquiry and recorded the statements of thousands of peasants. After long interviews, the Lt. Governor constituted an official commission of enquiry through the indigo peasants' complaints. The commission comprised officials, landlords and Gandhiji as the sole representative of the sharecroppers.

There was serious evidence against the British landlords which were collected by the commission and that made the landlords very nervous as a result they agreed to refund the peasants' money that they extorted illegally.

The landlords offered 25% of it to which Gandhiji agreed. It was a moral victory. The landlords abandoned their estates which went back to the peasants. This was the end of indigo sharecropping in Champaran.

Gandhiji also decided to remove the social and cultural backwardness in Champaran. During his seven months stay in Champaran, Gandhiji kept a distant watch on the Ashram.

Charles Freer Andrew who was a devoted follower of Gandhiji came to Champaran. Gandhiji's lawyer friends wanted Charles to stay on to help them but Gandhiji refused the idea as he did not want to take help from an Englishman in their fight. Gandhiji taught a lesson of self-reliance.

PREVIOUS YEARS'
EXAMINATION QUESTIONS

▷ **Short Answer Type Questions**

[2 & 3 Marks]

1. Though the sharecroppers of Champaran received only one-fourth of the compensation, how can the Champaran struggle still be termed a huge success and victory?   [DELHI 2018]

2. Why was Gandhiji opposed to C.F. Andrews helping him in Champaran?   [DELHI 2016]

3. Why did Gandhiji feel that taking the Champaran case to the court was useless?   [DELHI 2014]

4. Why did Gandhiji not accept C.F. Andrews' help during the Champaran movement?
     [DELHI 2019]

5. Why has Raj Kumar Shukla been described as being resolute ? (Indigo)   [DELHI 2020]

6. Gandhi effectively managed to redress the problems of the indigo sharecroppers with the Lieutenant Governor. What did he achieve?
     [DELHI TERM II, 2022]

7. Describe the role of Raj Kumar Shukla in Indigo.   [DELHI 2023]

▷ **Long Answers Type Question**

[4 Marks]

8. Gandhi not only alleviated the economic conditions of the Champaran people but also their social and cultural background. Justify?
     [DELHI TERM II, 2022]

▷ **Long Answer Type Questions**

[6 Marks]

9. Why is the Champaran episode considered to be the beginning of the Indian struggle for Independence?   [ALL INDIA 2014]

10. Exploitation is a universal phenomenon. Poor indigo farmers were exploited by the British landlords to which Gandhiji objected. Even after our independence we find exploitation of unorganized labour. What values do we learn from Gandhiji's campaign to counter the present day problems of exploitation?   [DELHI 2013]

11. Give an account of Gandhiji's effort to secure justice for the poor Indigo sharecroppers of Champaran.   [All INDIA 2012]

12. Why do you think Gandhiji considered the Champaran episode to be the turning point in his life?   [All INDIA 2011]

🔑 Solutions

1. Even though the sharecroppers of Champaran got only one-fourth of the compensation, yet it seemed like a huge victory because it made the farmers fearless. So far, they had never even dreamt of resisting the Britishers, but now they were on the street in countless numbers. Of course, this was a declaration of the end of terror. As it liberated the peasants from slavery and fear, there remains no ambiguity regarding its success.   [3]

2. Gandhi was opposed to C.F Andrews helping him in Champaran because the support of Englishmen would show the weakness of heart of Indians. Gandhi wanted Indians to rely on themselves and to be self-reliant.   [3]

3. Gandhiji believed that the peasants were crushed and fear-stricken. He felt that taking the Champaran case to the court was useless as the actual relief for the peasants would come when they become free from fear.   [3]

4. Primary schools were opened in six villages of champaran and an appeal was made for teachers. Gandhi's pupils, along with their wives and teachers from distant parts of the country, volunteered to work. His son Devdas and wife Kasturba also taught rules on personal cleanliness, hygiene and community sanitation. His wife also taught girls how to wear clean clothes.   [3]

5. Rajkumar Shukla is described as being 'resolute' because he wanted Gandhiji to accompany him to his district named Champaran. Gandhiji was busy at that time and had several engagements. But Rajkumar Shukla never left Gandhiji's side. He followed him whenever he went. [2]

6. Gandhi effectively managed to redress the problems of the indigo sharecroppers with the Lieutenant Governor. As a result the landlords withdrew their claims over their estates and reverted back to the farmers. The farmers learnt courage and realised that they too, had defenders. The landlords obliged to surrender part of their money and prestige. Thus, Gandhi broke the deadlock between the farmers and the landlords. [2]

7. Rajkumar Shukla was the farmer who was the guiding light of the Champaran Kisan Movement. He is the one who is the epitome and symbolization of the Indian Freedom struggle and the role of Gandhiji. He was a sharecropper who was though illiterate but resolute. His efforts made Gandhiji to reach to Champaran which resulted in the first successful civil disobedience movement, which became one of the major landmarks in the history of India's freedom struggle. [2]

8. Answer ANY TWO of the following

There is no denying the fact that Gandhi's loyalty was not to abstractions. It was a loyalty to living human beings. The Champaran episode turned out to be an episode of moral victory. Gandhi agreed to take 25% as a refund which the landlords offered as he explained that money was not important. The refund by the British stated that they were agreeing to what the Indians said. They were no longer dreaded by the Pasants. [4]

Gandhi didn't leave Champaran after this victory. During his stay there, he had realised that the people of Champaran were culturally and socially backward, so he decided to work on this front. He decided to open primary schools so he appealed for teachers. A couple of his disciples volunteered themselves as teachers. Gandhi also took help of a doctor. Some basic ailments of the villagers were treated. Not only this, Gandhi's wife Kasturba also joined him in this movement and also taught the rules of personal cleanliness and community sanitation to the women. He

kept a distant watch on his ashram also from this place and called for regular financial accounts, He even wrote to them that it was time to fill in the old latrine trenches and dig the new ones. Thus, with his firm determination and persistent efforts, Gandhi was able to bring changes in the ordinary man's life. [4]

9. The Champaran episode is considered to be the beginning of the Indian struggle for independence because, for the first time, farmers and peasants rose against the Britishers. The peasants had always been oppressed by their British landlords, but they lacked the courage to revolt. Now under the leadership of Gandhiji, they became aware of their rights. A small farmer, Rajkumar Shukla, who hailed from a small district, Champaran, helped bring about a very major change. Likewise, many other peasants from the villages fought audaciously and contributed in their own way to the movement. Their cumulative effort eventually resulted in their winning the battle of Champaran and to finally free themselves of the sharecropping arrangement. This success also proved, for the first time, the effectiveness of Gandhi's method of non-violence and noncooperation. [6]

10. Exploitation continues in un-organized sectors such as farm workers, construction site labourers, housemaids or helpers at 'dhabas' paid too little for the quantum of work done in unhygienic surroundings. Gandhiji has shown us the way to counter the present day problems of exploitation. He helped the Champaran sharecroppers by infusing courage and freedom from fear. He taught them to be confident which in turn enhanced their self-esteem. In a violence-ridden world, he taught the sharecroppers to move towards their goal in a peaceful and tolerant manner. They become independent and self-reliant. These values helped them improve their quality of life and can bring relief to present-day problems of exploitation. [6]

11. On receiving reports of exploitation of the poor sharecropper peasants at the hands of British planters, Gandhiji went to Champaran. Initially, he tried to get the facts. As expected, the British landlords, along with the commissioner of Tirhut, didn't -co-operate. Gandhiji got a briefing about the court cases of these peasants.

Along with the lawyers, Gandhiji collected a deposition by about ten thousand peasants. Other pieces of evidence were also taken into account. The entire area pulsated with the activities of the investigators and forceful protests of landlords. As a result, Gandhiji was summoned by the lieutenant governor. Consequently, an official commission of inquiry was appointed to mull over the indigo sharecroppers' situation. Gandhiji solely represented the peasants. The official inquiry commission gathered a huge quantity of evidence against the big planters, As a result, they had to agree, in principle, to make refunds to the peasants. This was a moral victory of the peasants which gave them a sense of empowerment.

They acknowledged their rights and garnered courage. In the following years, the British planters gave up their estates which then went back to the peasants. The peasants were then masters of their land. **[6]**

12. **The British planters wanted some excuse for prolonging the dispute with the peasants. However, Gandhiji proved too wise for them. The deadlock was ended by accepting what the planters wanted. Even so, the British had to compromise with their pride. The peasants now had courage. They believed that they had rights which they could defend. Gradually, the British planters left their estates. These estates now came back to the peasants. After this episode, Gandhiji told the British that they had no authority to order him in his own country. He was ordered to leave Champaran but Gandhiji refused. So, the government had to relent.** **[6]**

6. Poets and Pancakes

Summary

Introduction:

Poets and Pancakes is an excerpt from *My Years With Boss*, authored by Asokamitran. Asokamitran worked in The Gemini Studios. His duty was to cut out and preserve newspaper clipping on a wide variety of subjects in files.

Set up in 1940, Gemini Studios was located in Madras (Chennai). Film making was its infancy in India. Asokamitran's writing style is both rambling and humorous. He shares his experiences of themake-up department of the studios. It was located at the upstairs of a building, which earlier had been Lord Clive's stables. There were quite a few buildings known to be Clive's residences, although Asokamitran did not believe it to be true because Clive's stay in India was very short. Since he lived in Madras for still shorter time, he couldn't have lived in all these houses.

'Pancakes' was a brand name attributed to a make-up material, which was extensively used in truckloads by the make-up department at the Gemini Studios. Although it was used in bulk, it made decent looking boys and girls ugly.

Talking about the make-up department, he talks of his office boy, who was, in fact, a grouwn-up man of forty. He aspired to become a top star or a director but remained an office boy. He put the blame of his failed aspirations on Subbu who was regarded as No. 2 in The Gemini Studios.

Kothamangalam Subbu was a man of talent having various occupations. He was a talented person. He was a poet, novelist, actor and a film maker. He was loyal to his boss and had no aspirations of making it big.

Then he tells us of the legal advisor who was a member of the story department and ruined the careers of various actors unwittingly. He wore western clothes and looked odd among khadi-clad writers and poets, who were averse to communism.

Throwing light on the concept of communism, the author speaks of the arrival of Moral Re-armament Army at the studios. It was a sort of counter-communism movement. It presented plays in the studios. Although their plays influenced Tamil dramas, their anti-communism failed to have any effect. Later, when an an English poet visited the Gemini Studios, nobody could comprehend what the poet said or what the purpose of his visit was.

The poet, which the author discovered, was the editor of the periodical, *The Encounter*. He visited the Studio in regards to the essay he wrote on the disillusion with communism.

'Pancakes' was the brand name of a make-up material, which was used by the Gemini Studios in abundance. Many well-known dresses must have used that material. It was used by make-up artists for transforming decent looking men and women into hideous monsters. In fact, it was used because most of the film-shooting was done on the sets, and the studios and lights required every single pore of the faces of the actors and actresses closed. A strict hierarchy was maintained in the make-up department to make the player look ugly. The chief make-up man made the hero and heroine ugly. His senior assistant made the second hero and heroine ugly and so forth. It was the office boy's job to make the crowd players ugly.

The make-up department had an office boy, although he was a forty year-old man. He had joined the studios years ago. He believed that he had a great talent and hoped to become a star actor, director, screen writer or lyrics writer. Gaining no success, he became frustrated and blamed his disgrace on Gemini Studios. The make-up department, located at the was at the upstairs of a building, was known to be one of Robert Clive's stables. The make-up room looked like a hair-cutting salon because of its ambience, comprising of large mirrors and lights, which gave out intense heat. The person who underwent make-up had a miserable experience of being scorched like that in hell.

Long before AIT began broadcasting programmes on national integration, the make-up department presented a picture of the same subject. In the beginning, the department was headed by a Bengali and was later succeeded by a Maharashtrian who was assisted by people from different parts of India.

Due to its nature, the author's job seemed insignificant to many at the Gemini Studios. He was usually seen tearing newspapers. Everybody walked into his cubicle to give him some or the other work to do. Sometimes, the office boy would recite his poems to him, to impress the author through his talent, which was being wasted because of Subbu.

Due to Subbu's stature, the office boy was frustrated and jealous. It was Subbu who presented various practical ideas to the boss whenever any difficulty arose in presenting a scene.

Subbu was a good poet and a novelist, too. He could write poems of high order. But he deliberately suppressed his talent to write for the masses. He had written a novel in which he recreated the mood and manner of *Devadasis* of early 20th century. He had created life-like characters too.

Subbu was also an excellent actor but never aspired to get the leading roles. Whatever minor roles he played, he acted better than the leading-role actors.

Subbu was a large hearted and a loving man. Several friends and relatives stayed with him for long periods, and he always served them well and also lent money to support them. But the office boy despised him, perhaps he appeared to be a sycophant.

Although Subbu was always seen with the Boss, he was a member of the story department. Besides writers and poets in the story department, there was a lawyer too. Officially, he was known as legal adviser. But people called him by an opposite name. Once the legal adviser unwittingly, ruined the career of a talented actress.

It happened when one day the actress, who was not seasoned in worldly wisdom, lost her temper on the sets. She spoke angrily against the producer and the legal adviser switched on the recorder. When she paused, he played back the record. . The actress was shocked to to hear her own voice. Although she had not said anything offensive, she never appeared on the stage again.

The legal adviser was always dressed in formals. At times, he wore a coat too. He appeared odd among khadi clad poets and writers. The poets and writers worshipped Gandhi, although they had no direct affiliation to him or his ideas. They were averse to the concept of communism an had a notion that a communist does not love anybody and was an anarchist.

Anti-communist feelings were widespread in South India. Moral Rearmament Army was a sort of anti-communism movement. It visited Gemini Studios in 1952. They were about 200 people belonging to at least 20 nationalities. They presented two plays 'Jotham Valley' and 'The Forgotten Factor' in the most profession almanner. The play impressed the Gemini family of 600 and the citizens of Madras.

Their message was simple but the sets and costumes were excellent. Its influence stayed for many years. The Tamil drama imitated the sunrise and sunset scenes presented by MRA. The scenes were presented on a bare stage with white background and a tune played on the flute. But the MRA did not influence the outlook of the Gemini bosses and the enterprises continued without any change. The staff had enjoyed hosting the MRA.

After a few months, another guest arrived at the Gemini Studios. He was an Englishman and nobody knew who he was. Some said he was a poet, a poet of whomthey had not heard. Some believed that he was an editor because the top men of *The Hindu* were taking the initiative.

But he was not the editor of any of the newspapers which the staff of Gemini Studios had heard of.

The boss, Mr. Vasan, warmly welcomed the English-man. Mr. Vasan read a long speech of democracy and freedom. Then the Englishman spoke. His accent made it impossible for the people to understand him. They also failed to understand the purpose of the Englishman's visit and it remained a mystery. . Tamil films were made for simple people who could not be expected to have any interest in English poetry.

The author saw a notice in *The Hindu*. *The Encounter*, a British periodical, was organizing a short story contest. The author had never heard of the periodical but wanted to send an entry. Inorder to gather some information regarding the same, he visited the British Council Library. At the Library, he found copies of *The Encounter* and learned that its editor was Stephen Spender, who had visited the Gemini Studios. After a few years, the author had retired. One day, he saw a pile of low-priced paperback edition of *The God that Failed* and bought a copy, which contained six different essays of six different writers. They described writers' journeys to communism and their disillusioned return. One of the writers was Stephen Spender. The whole mystery of Spender's visit was then cleared. Mr. Vasan was not interested in his poetry but was interested on his views on communism.

PREVIOUS YEARS'
EXAMINATION QUESTIONS
▶ Short Answer Type Questions
[2 Marks]

(Answer the following questions in about 30-40 words each)

1. What does the writer mean by 'the fiery misery' of those subjected to make-up?

2. What is the example of national integration that the author refers to?

3. What work did the office boy do in the Gemini Studios? Why did he join the Studios? Why was he disappointed?

4. Why did the author appear to be doing nothing at the Studios?

5. Why was the office boy frustrated? What did he show his anger on?

6. Who was Subbu's principal?

7. Subbu is described as a many-sided genius. List four of his special abilities.

8. Why was the legal adviser referred to as the opposite by the others?

9. What made the lawyer stand out from others at Gemini Studios?

10. Did the people at Gemini Studios have any particular political affiliations?

11. Why was the Moral Rearmament Army welcomed at the Studios?

12. Name one example to show that Gemini Studios was influenced by the plays staged by MRA.

13. Who was the Boss of the Gemini Studios?

14. What caused the lack of communication between the Englishman and the people at Gemini Studios?

15. Why is the Englishman's visit referred to as unexplained mystery?

16. Who was the English visitor to the Studios?

17. How did the author discover, who the English visitor to the Studios was?

18. What does The God That failed referred to?

19. Why was Kothamangalam Subbu considered No. 2 in Gemini Studios?

20. How does the author describe the incongruity of an English poet addressing the audience at Gemini Studios?

▶ Long Answer Type Question

[4 Marks]

21. **Read the extracts given below and answer the question that follow each of them.**

    He could'nt have addressed a more dazed and silent audience – no one knew what he was talking about and his accent defeated any attempt to understand what he was saying.

    (i)   Identify the chapter. Who is 'he'?

    (ii) What was 'he' in real iife ?

    (iii) How did the audience react to his speech?

    (iv) Why was his speech not a success?

▶ Long Answer Type Questions

[6 Marks]

(Answer the following questions in about **125-150** words each)

22. What do you understand about the author's literary inclinations from the account?

23. The author has used gentle humour to point out human foibles. Pick out instances of these to show how this serves to make the piece interesting.

🔑 Solutions

1. The people who were subjected to make-up had to face intense heat which was a result of the various incandescent lights. The author refers to the intense and scorching heat as 'the fiery misery'. [2]

2. The example of national integration that the author refers to is the make-up department which had a diverse environment. People from various parts of India worked there together. [2]

3. Whenever there was a crowd shooting in the Gemini Studios, the office boy mixed paint and slapped it on the crowd players. He had joined the Studio years ago with the hope of making it big in the film industry as a writer, director or lyrics writer. He was disappointed because his talent was being wasted away as he had failed to gain much success. [2]

4. The duty of the author at the Studio was to cut-out and preserve relevant newspaper clippings on a wide variety of subjects. Doing such a meager job, he appeared to be doing nothing except tearing newspapers. [2]

5. The office boy felt that he had a great talent which was being wasted away as he was made to rot in a department that was fit only for barbers and perverts. Failing to making it big in the film industry led to frustration. He blamed Kothamangalam Subbu, who was No. 2 in the Studios, for his neglect and disgrace. [2]

6. The Boss, Mr. Vasan, was Subbu's principal. [2]

7. Subbu is showcased by the author as a man of many talents. Some of his specialties included always being ready with a solution to every problem. Subu was a poet and a novelist capable of writing complex form of poetry and prose. One of the best things about Subu was his helpful and cheerful nature, even in the face of failure. [2]

8. The legal adviser never helped anybody to solve a legal problem. Moreover, he created legal problems for others. For example, he ruined the career of a talented actress through his action. When she heard her recorded voice, she felt she had committed a crime. He was also opposite to others in terms of his dressing sense. All the poets and writers wore khadi clothers. He, on the opther hand, wore formals. [2]

9. The lawyer was a member of story department. All members wore khadi dhoti and long khadi shirt. But the lawyer wore trousers, shirt and tie. Sometimes, he wore a coat too. It was this formal attire that made him stand out from other people of Gemini family.

10. No, the people at Gemini Studios had no particular political affiliations. Although they wore khadi and worshipped Gandhiji, but they did not have affiliations to a particular political thought. [2]

11. The Moral Rearmament Army were welcomed at the studios because they presented two plays in a very professional manner. The set and their costumes were appreciated and imitated for years at the Studios. [2]

12. The Studios, in their play Jotham Valley, were particularly influenced by the sunset and sunrise scenes presented by MRA. The scenes were presented on a bare stage with a white background and a tune played on the flute. These scenes were imitated at the Studios. [2]

13. Mr. Vasan was the boss of the Gemini Studios. [2]

14. People at the Studios were unable to comprehend what the Englishman was talking about. Moreover, his English accent made it impossible for people to understand him. This led to a lack of communication between the people and the Englishman. [2]

15. Nobody was able to understand the purpose of the English poet's visit to the Studio. Tamil films were made for very simple people who were not expected to develop a taste for English poetry. Thus, the visit remained an unexplained mystery. [2]

16. The English visitor of the Studios was Stephen Spender. He was an English poet and an editor of *The Encounter*. [2]

17. There was a contest organized by **The Encounter** to which the author wanted to send an entry. In order to get an idea about the periodical, he visited the British Council Library. Therein, he found copies of *The Encounter* and saw the name of the editor of an article. He recalled it as the Englishman who had visited the Gemini Studios. [2]

18. The God That Failed is a collection of six essays by six different writers. They all describe their journeys into communism and their disillusioned return. [2]

19. Kothamangalam Subbu was a man of many talents. The Boss always sought his opinion in tough situations. Subbu was considered No. 2 in the Gemini Studios because he was always seen with the Boss and was very close to him. [2]

20. The Studios made Tamil films for simple people who had no interest in English poetry and it was not expected that the Englishman's visit and speech could cultivate an interest in it. So, the author could not see any logic in Englishman's addressing the audience at Gemini Studios. [2]

21. (i) The name of the chapter is 'Poets and Pancakes'. He refers to an English poet. [1]

(ii) Stephen Spender [1]

(iii) Everyone was left bewildered. [1]

(iv) The people at Gemini studios found it difficult to understand the poet's accent. His visit remained an unexplained mystery. [1]

22. The author's job at Gemini Studios was to cut out and preserve newspaper clippings on a wide variety of subjects. Naturally, his work honed his literary taste. Given the nature of his work, he must have had a good knowledge of English literature. He has also named quite a few English poets in this account. He must have been sending his prose pieces to different papers and periodicals. He surely sent his entry to a short story contest organised by *The Encounter*. Even after his retirement, he was still very much inclined towards literature, which is evident from the incident where he aw a pile of low-priced edition of 'The God That failed' and bought a copy. All these incidents throw light on his inclination and interest in literature. [6]

23. There are a number of instances of gentle humour in this piece. Especially the description of the make-up department that consumed truckloads of pancakes (they did not eat them, of course) is very interesting. The make-up room with mirrors and lights looked like a hair cutting salon. The make-up department was a symbol of national integration because there was a gang of people from different parts of India. This gang of nationally integrated make-up men could turn any decent looking person into a hideous crimson hued monster. There was a strict hierarchy in the make-up department in the task of making actors ugly. There was an office boy (though he was not a boy but a grown up man of forty). He had joined the Studios years ago in the hope of becoming a star actor, or a top screen writer, director or lyrics writer. He came to the author to enlighten him how great literary talent was being wasted. But the author prayed for crowd, shooting all the time to get rid of a genius of a bore. [6]

7. The Interview

Summary

Introduction

In our times, 'The Interview has always held a special significance. An interview is a journalistic practice and we rely on it to gather information about our contemporaries. Essential as it may be, celebrities and recognized people despide being interviewed. For them, it is an invasion of their privacy. They feel it diminishes them in some way. Some of the well-known writers even refused to be interviewed.

In spite of not being found of it, celebrities have been interviewed. Some of them were interviewed repeatedly.

This is an excerpt of an interview with Umberto Eco. The interviewer is Mukund Padmanabhan of

The Hindu.

Part-1: Christopher Silvester

The invention of interview took place more than 130 years ago. Since then, many celebrities have been interviewed. Some of them were interviewed repeatedly.

Some people praise the practice. Others, especially the celebrities, despise its functions and methods. As per the people who praise the process of interview believe it to be a source of truth. Its practice is an art. In our times, we get all the information about our contemporaries through the interview.

Celebrities believe that interviews invade their private lives and, in a way, diminishes them. The celebrated writer of *Alice in Wonderland*, Lewis Carroll, condemned the interview and never consented to be interviewed. Similarly, Rudyard Kipling considered the interview as an assault. Even H. G. Wells referred to it as an ordeal and Saul Bellow described it as thumbprints on his windpipe.

It is ironic that although some celebrities despised the interview, they themselves interviewed other celebrities. H. G. Wells interviewed Joseph Stalin and Rudyard Kipling interviewed Mark Twain.

Despite having advantages and disadvantages of the interview, its practice has become commonplace in journalism. The interviewer holds a very powerful and influential position.

Part-2: Umberto Eco

Umberto Eco's interview by Mukund Padmanabhan

Umberto Eco is a university professor. He has authored five novels and has published over 40 academic works. His novel 'The Name of the Rose' got huge success. Mukund Padmanabhan of *The Hindu* interviewed Eco.

Padmanabhan began the interview by reminding Eco what David Lodge once said about him. He had remarked, 'I can't understand how Eco can do all the things he does'. He wanted to know how he (Eco) could do so many things at a time. In response to this Eco said that although he seemed to be doing several things, he was always doing the same thing. He explained that he had some philosophical interests which he pursued through his academic works and novels.

Then Eco revealed his secret. He said that there are a lot of empty spaces in everybody's life, which he referred to as interstices. Suppose a visitor was coming to him. Before the visitor reached from the elevator to his room, Eco would have written an article, which amazed Padmanabhan.

Padmanabhan said that Eco's writing style was distinctively different from the regular academic style which was impersonalized, dry and boring. Umberto Eco told him that when he had presented his first doctoral dissertation, he told the story of his research, including his trials and errors. One of the professors highly praised it. Eco learnt, at the age of 22, how scholarly books should be written. They should have a narrative style, which was the case in Eo's essays. To satisy his taste for narration, he started writing novels at the age of 50, which was a continuation of his narrative style. Mukund told him that his novel "The Name of the Rose' made him from an academician to a famous novelist. Though he had written only five novels against 40 scholarly works, people knew him only as a novelist. Mukund wanted to know if it hurt him.

Eco replied that it hurt him because he always considered himself an academician, and always identified himself with the community of academics. He participated in academic conferences but never went to the writers' meetings. But most people had read his novels. He had reached a far larger audience through novel than his works on semiotics. But he could not expect a million people to read scholarly works on the concept of semiotics. a scholarly work as semiotics.

Mukund said that The Name of the Rose is a serious novel. Although it was a detective story, it had elements of metaphysics, theology and medieval history. The novel became widely successful. Mukund wanted to know if he was puzzled by its popularity.

Eco replied that publishers and journalists were puzzled because, according to their belief, people only liked trash. But some people like difficult reading experience too. There are six billion people in this world and The Name of the Rose-sold only 10 to 15 million copies, which was a very small number of readers.

Then Mukund put him the final question. He wanted to know if the novel had huge success because it dealt with period of medieval history. Eco replied it could have been one of the reasons. Many books had been written about the medieval history before this novel. His publisher felt that it would not sell more than 3000 copies because in their country nobody had seen a cathedral or studied Latin but around three million copies were sold in the US.

Eco felt nobody could predict the success of a novel. Had he written the novel ten years earlier, or ten years later, things might have been different. It was the time of the writing which was favourable to its popularity.

PREVIOUS YEARS' EXAMINATION QUESTIONS

▶ Short Answer Type Questions [2 Marks]

(Answer the following questions in about 30-40 words each)

1. What are some of the positive views on interviews?

2. Why do most celebrity writers despise being interviewed?

3. What is the belief in some primitive cultures about being photographed?

4. What do you understand by the expression "thumbprints on his windpipe"?

5. Who, in today's world, is our chief source of information about personalities?

6. Do you think Umberto Eco likes being interviewed? Give reasons for your opinion.

7. How does Eco find the time to write so much?

8. What was distinctive about Eco's academic working style?

9. Did Umberto Eco considered himself a novelist first or an academic scholar?

10. What is the reason for the huge success of the novel, *The Name of the Rose*?

11. Interviews are necessary. Justify the statement.

12. Do you think Eco's non-fictional writing style is a departure from regular style? Give reasons.

13. What did Eco learn at the age of 22 that he pursued in his novels?

14. What makes 'The Name of the Rose' a serious novel?

15. What does Eco think of the readers of his novel 'The Name of the Rose'?

▶ Long Answer Type Question [6 Marks]

(Answer the following questions in about 125-150 words each)

16. Every famous person has a right to his or her privacy. Interviewers sometimes embarrass celebrities with very personal questions.

🔑 Solutions

1. Interviews are a source of truth. These days, it is a tool through which we get a vivid impression of our contemporaries. It is regarded as supremely serviceable mode of communication. [2]

2. Most celebrity writers despide being interviewed because they see it as an unwarranted intrusion into their private lives. Celebrities believe that it somehow diminishes them. [2]

3. Some primitive cultures believe that if you are photographed, your soul is stolen. [2]

4. The phrase was used by Saul Bellow amd it means that it was as if he was being strangled while being interviewed. [2]

5. In today's world, the chief source of information about personalities of different people is interview, the interview, one man asking questions of another. [2]

6. Yes, Umberto Eco does enjoy being interviewed. According to the text, it seems as if he is at ease with the interviewee. He patiently tries to answer each question in full without harshness. [2]

7. Eco manages his time very well, he does not waste a second of his time. He tries to fill his empty time with productive work. Even while he is waiting for someone, he would write something before his visitor reaches him. [2]

8. Eco's style of academic writing is interesting, narrative and personalized. His work stands apart from the regular academic style of writing, which is depersonalized, dull and boring. [2]

9. Umberto Eco considered himself an academic scholar first and then a novelist. He identified himself with the academic community and actively participated in academic conferences, but did not attend writers' meetings. In his own words, he was a university professor who wrote novels on Sundays. [2]

10. *The Name of the Rose* is a very serious novel. At one level, it is a detective story. At the other level, it also delves deep into mythology and metaphysics. It is set in a period of medieval history. Of course, there are people who like serious reading material, yet the novel's huge popularity remains a mystery. Umberto feels that perhaps the time of its publication was favourable. [2]

11. Despite the drawbacks of interviews, they are considered a supremely serviceable medium of communication. Being an art, it is a source of truth. It is through these interviews that we get to understand our contemporary celebrities and others. [2]

12. Eco's non-fictional writing is not depersonalized and boring like his scholarly works. He adds a a playful and personal touch in it, which is a departure from his regular style and makes him stand apart from other authors.[2]

13. At the age of 22, Eco learnt that scholarly books should be written in narrative style: by telling the story of research. He learnt that there should be a narrative technique employed in scholarly writing. He later employed this technique when he wrote novels at the age of 50. [2]

14. Despite being a detective story, 'The Name of the Rose' is a serious novel as it delves in to metaphysics, theology and medieval history. . [2]

15. According to Eco, there are readers who don't like 'trash' and like to have difficult reading experiences, which is contrary to the beliefs of journalists and publishers. The novel sold more than 15 million copies and is regarded as a serious work, where the readers like the reading experience which is not easy. [2]

16. Interviewers want to present exclusive and intimate details about the famous person they are interviewing. Some interviewers focus on the achievements and the public life of the individual. They try to be objective in their approach as well as assessment. However, there are others who cross the line and invade private lives in order to make their interviews spicier. In their zeal to present a good copy, they embarrass the famous person with personal questions. At times, this leads to aversion as well as irritation of the interviewee at the silliness of the person. If they shout, they are accused of being rude and proud, and if they keep mum they are labelled as arrogant. It is always essential to respect the privacy of an individual. [6]

8. Going Places

Summary

Introduction:

Sophie and Jansie are classmates and friends. Sophie is filled with fantasies and desires. She is a daydreamer who dreams of owning a boutique after school or hopes to be a fashion designer or an actress too. Jansie who believes that they come from a poor financial background becomes sad as she knows that they have no other option but to work in a biscuit factory. Jansie who is more realistic tries to pull Sophie to the reality that she needs a lot of money to have a boutique. But Sophie is not discouraged.

Sophie declares at her home that when she would have earned some money she will have a boutique. Her father retorted that he will thank her if she could buy a decent house for the family. Sophie has a younger brother Derek who also scoffs at her impractical idea. He says that she thinks money grows on trees. Her mother who is bent over the sink could only sigh. Sophie has an elder brother Geoff with whom she shares all her secrets comfortably.

Danny Casey, an Irish young football player who plays for United is her hero. She thinks about him all the time. She tells her brother Geoff that she had a chance meeting with Danny Casey in the arcade. Geoff tells their father about their meeting. Her father calls them as her wild stories but Sophie asserts that it is true. Her father tells that she would be in trouble if she talked like that. According to her father, Danny is a promising player but is too young.

Geoff is an apprentice mechanic who travels to work every day. According to Sophie, it is a fascinating world which her brother visits.

Sophie shares with her brother Geoff that Danny has asked her to meet again in the next week. But Geoff did not believe her as Sophie was too young and Danny must be having a lot of girlfriends. Sophie makes Geoff promise that he would not tell their father about the date.

Geoff told Jansie's brother about Sophie's and Danny's meeting. So one day when Sophie came across Jansie, Jansie was curious to know all about that. After a few talks, Sophie discovers that Jansie knew nothing about their date. Then Sophie tells Jansie about her meeting with Danny Casey. She tells Jansie to keep it a secret as she did not want her neighbours to talk about all this. Sophie was very afraid of her father and she tells Jansie that if her father came to know about it, he will murder her. Sophie along with her father and brother went to watch the United. Danny scored the second goal there which made Sophie proud of her hero and her father was also very happy and they all three went to the pub to celebrate.

Sophie decides to meet Danny. After dark, she goes to the decided place. There was a wooden bench under a tree. She sits and waits for Danny there. She imagines him coming out of the shadows. As Geoff had doubted that Danny would come at all so she thinks she would tell Geoff that he was wrong. She is excited but he does not come. Slowly and disheartened she walks to the arcade. There she imagines him once again and asks him for the autograph and like the last time this time as well she discovers that they don't have a pen and paper. Then Danny disappears.

PREVIOUS YEARS'
EXAMINATION QUESTIONS

▶ **Short Answer Type Questions**

[3 Marks]

1. Why did Jansie discourage Sophie from having dreams? [ALL INDIA 2017]

2. What was Sophie's ambition in life? How did she hope to achieve that? [DELHI 2017]

3. Why did Sophie long for her brother's affection? [ALL INDIA 2014]

4. Why did Sophie like her brother, Geoff more than any other person? [ALL INDIA 2013]

5. Why did Sophie not want Jansie to know anything about her meeting with Danny Casey? [ALL INDIA 2012]

6. Why didn't Sophie want Jansie to know about her story with Danny? [DELHI 2011]

7. What thoughts came up to Sophie's mind as she sat by the Canal? [ALL INDIA 2011]

▶ **Long Answer Type Questions**

[6 Marks]

8. In one's approach to life one should be practical and not live in a world of dreams. How is Jansie's attitude different from that of Sophie? [DELHI 2018]

9. Every teenager has a hero/heroine to admire. So many times they become role models for them. What is wrong if Sophie fantasies about Danny Casey and is ambitious in life? [ALL INDIA 2016]

10. Teachers always advise their students to dream big. Yet, the same teachers in your classrooms find fault with Sophie when she dreams. What is wrong with Sophie's dreams? [DELHI 2016]

11. Sophie lives in a world full of dreams which she does not know she cannot realize. Comment. [ALL INDIA 2015]

12. Has Sophie met Danny Casey? What details of her meeting with Danny Casey did she narrate to her brother? [DELHI 2014]

13. Attempt a character sketch of Sophie as a women who lives in her dreams. [DELHI 2012]

14. What did Sophie tell her father and her brother about her 'meeting(s)' with Danny Casey? How did each of them react?　　[DELHI 2019]

🔑 Solutions

1. As they belonged to lower middle-class, Jansie wanted to bring Sophie to the ground. Jansie thought that being rational would help Sophie realize her dreams.　　[3]

2. Sophie wished to rise above her middle-class status and to obtain sophistication. She aspired to open a boutique or become an actress or fashion designer. Though she belonged to a middle-class society, she never missed in taking a plunge because she was not one who accepts regrets in life. The dreams sometimes proved unachievable to Sophie but she took the refuge of dreams to fulfil her desires. She gracefully maintained the balance between reality and dreams, and in this way, lived her unachievable dreams.　　[3]

3. Geoff was an introvert and did not speak much. Sophie envied her brother's silence as she thought that he had access to a world that she had never got a chance to visit. She craved to be a part of her brother's world. Hence, she longed for his affection.　　[3]

4. Sophie was extremely fond of her brother Geoff. while Dad and Derek represented the squalor of their present existence, Geoff was the only person who offered a ray of hope in her life. He symbolized freedom as he visited places she had never been, to Sophie hoped that he would introduce her to his exotic and promising world for which she believed she was made.　　[3]

5. Jansie was inquisitive. She had an interest in knowing every detail about others. Also, she feared that Jansie would spread the news everywhere. As a result, Sophie simply didn't wish Jansie to know about her story with Danny. This might be due to mutual jealousy and one-up man ship on her part. Sophie was apprehensive to learn that Geoff had told her story with Danny to Jansie.　　[3]

6. Sophie knew that Jansie wouldn't believe her so easily and she wouldn't keep it a secret.　　[3]

7. Sophie was interested in a boutique. For this, she needed money. So, she thought that she should become an actress as there was real money in that. Then she could have a boutique also.　　[3]

8. Jansie and Sophie are just opposite in characters and have an overall different way of living life. On one hand Jansie is more pragmatic and down to earth person, on the other hand, Sophie lives in a fantasy world and can be best termed as a daydreamer. Jansie understands the fact that an ordinary person like her can only work in a biscuit factory. To its contrast, Sophie denies the truth and has goals of becoming a manager, an actress or a fashion designer.

Sophie is a daydreamer and her world is imaginary. There is nothing wrong in dreaming big but one has to work equally hard as well.

To make her dream come true, Sophie needs to work hard rather than of dreaming of a bright and successful life. Accepting the reality, that she is a middle-class person is going to help her. Undoubtedly, she would have hard times due to her poor financial condition, but with sincere devotion and resolution, she could certainly attain a level from where she would actually have the company of successful people like Danny Casey.　　[6]

9. Sophie is a school going girl. She lives in a dreamy world which has a distant relation with the harsh realities of her life. Her dreams are beyond her reach or her means. She thinks of having a boutique. Then she entertains the idea of being an actress. She even wants to become fashion designer. Here, she is very different from her classmate and friend Jansie. Jansie is realistic and practical. She knows that both of them have been earmarked for the biscuit factory.

Sophie's romantic dreamy nature leads her to hero-worship. The hero of her dreams is the Young, Irish footballer Danny Casey. She has developed a romantic fascination for him. Geoff cautions her that Casey is a celebrity. Many girls like her run after Danny. But she is an incurable dreamer. She thinks of him all the time. She sits for hours imagining Danny Casey coming to her. She knows that he will never come. She becomes sad but helpless. This is the point where she went wrong. She might have moved forward towards her destination by doing hard work.　　[6]

10. Sophie was a middle-class girl who aspired to be big. She wished to own a boutique after finishing her school. This would help her to achieve a glamorous and stylish lifestyle. She thought money could be saved by working as a manager,

or by becoming an actress because there is huge money in it. She was romantic in nature, who was far from reality. Saddy, Sophie did not even have a good house for her. Her father worked hard to meet the needs of the family. Her mother was also a hardworking housewife. However, Sophie aspired to doing something beyond all this and wished to have the costliest shop and a royal life. She also wishes to explore the places she had never seen. These places allured her towards them as they were far and unknown. Her dreams were certainly unrealistic.

[6]

11. At the very beginning of the chapter Going Places, Sophie tells Jansie that she aspires one day she would own a boutique or be an actress. If ever she becomes an actress, she would still run the boutique as actresses normally need not work full time. It's obvious that Sophie loves to live in her dream world. One can think that these dreams were still achievable, however, her desire about Danny-Casey highlights that she is completely lost in her fantasy world. She is a firm believer that she has met Danny Casey despite no one taking her words seriously. She has no doubt about her capability of achieving her dreams.

[6]

12. No, Sophie has not met-Danny Casey in reality. One day, in an attempt to gain Geoff's attention, Sophie narrates a cooked-up story about accidentally meeting Danny Casey at the Royce's. Geoff, however, refuses to believe her. So, she describes Danny Casey's physical appearance to make her brother believe her story. She tells Geoff that she was also willing to get an. autograph for little Derek, but she did not have a pen or a paper for the same. Then, Sophie claims, that the two of them talked about the clothes at Royce's. She ends her story by saying that Danny has promised to meet her again.

[6]

13. Sophie is a school going girl. She lives in a dreamy world which has a distant relation with the harsh realities of life. Her dreams are big and beyond her reach or her means. She thinks of having a boutique. Then she entertains the idea of being an actress. She wants to even become and fashion designer. Here, she is very different from her classmate and friend Jansie. Jansie is realistic and practical. She knows that both of them have been earmarked for the biscuit factory.

Sophie's romantic dreamy nature leads her to hero worship. The hero of her dreams is the Young, Irish footballer Danny Casey She has developed a romantic fascination for him. Geoff cautions her that Casey is a celebrity. Many girls like her must run after Danny. But she is an incurable dreamer. She thinks of him all the time. She sits for hours imagining Danny Casey coming to her. She knows that he will never come. She becomes sad but helpless. This is the point where she went wrong. She might have moved forward towards her destination by doing hard work.

[6]

14. Sophie was a dreamer and unrealistic. She dreamed of becoming an actress like Mary Quant or opening a boutique. She hero worshipped Danny Casey and made stories of meeting him. Jnsie on the other hand was a practical girl, she was aware of her economic conditions and knew that she and Sophie have been earmarked for the biscuit factory. Hearing about Sophie's unrealistic expectations made her sad. Sophie felt that the world was waiting for her arrival, she was living in her own illusion.

[6]

1. My Mother at Sixty Six

Summary

Introduction:

Right at the outset of the poem with the usage of words like "parent's home", the underlying tone of nostalgia is inculcated into this poem. The overarching idea of mortality also finds its first prologue in the poem. The poetess Kamala Das realises while accompanying her mother on an emotional roller-coaster drive that she is at the ripe age of sixty-six.

The poetess then paints a gloomy but realistic image of ageing, by portraying her mother as a dozing ageing lady whose mouth is open in a carefree sleep and a face turned pale in course of the passing of time.

1. Driving from...
....
....
....................................though away.

It was previous Friday when the poetess' mother accompanied her on her way back to Cochin to board a flight. Her mother was sitting beside her. As her mother went into deep sleep, her mouth opened and the colour of her face seemed pale and the colour of ash, as if of a dead body. This triggered panic in the poetess. She was in an unparalleled pain realizing that her mother won't survive for long.

2. .... and
....
....
..............................Smile............

In order to overcome her fear, she looked out of the window. The young green trees, the cheerful children seemed to be in sharp contrast to her ageing mother.

After reaching the airport and getting cleared from the formal security check, the poetess again looked at her mother who appeared weak and resembled the moon of a late winter night. This revived her childhood fear of permanent separation from her mother. However, the poetess opts to conceal her feeling and kept smiling then onwards. The final words "see you soon, Amma" was an assurance to herself that they would meet again. This was also to hide her emotional pain and feelings of fear.

The poet has touched upon some deep-rooted fears of permanent separation from her mother and has highlighted the pain that comes with the idea of ageing and the death of our loved ones. Somehow, towards the end, the poem reflects the spirit of hope, which comes from the line "see you soon, Amma". Moreover, from upright rejection, the poem moves in the direction of a calm acceptance and was beautifully portrayed through the poet's long smile as she watched her mother depart. On a closer look, we might observe a slight hint of bravery and rationalism in the way the poet accepts what is inevitable – and the medium is the self-comforting smile.

Child-mother love and relationship are outlined in a thought-provoking manner. Fear of losing our loved ones, rejection of the inevitable truth and escape, then gradually a quiet acceptance of harsh realities is the core theme of the poem.

PREVIOUS YEARS'
EXAMINATION QUESTIONS
▶ **Short Answer Type Question:**

[1 Marks]

1. The poet Kamala Das brought in the image of 'spilling children' with the intention
   (a) of praising children
   (b) of reminiscing her childhood
   (c) of bringing in a contrast to the mood of the poet.
   (d) of making her mother happy and cheerful

▶ Short Answer Type Questions:

[2 & 3 Marks]

2. What was the poet's childhood fear?

    [All INDIA 2014]

3. How does Kamala Das try to put away the thoughts of her ageing mother? [DELHI 2014]

4. Why has the poet's mother been compared to the 'late winter's moon'? [DELHI 2014]

5. What were the poet's feelings at the airport? How did she hide them? [ALL INDIA 2012]

6. What were Kamala Das's fears as a child? Why do they surface when she is going to the airport? [ALL INDIA 2011]

7. What does the poet's smile in the poem, 'My Mother at Sixty-six' show? [DELHI 2018]

8. Having looked at her mother, why does Kamala Das look at the young children?

    [ALL INDIA 2017]

9. What kind of pain does Kamala Das feel in 'My Mother at Sixty-six'? [DELHI 2017]

10. What are the feelings of the poet about her aged mother with reference to the poem 'My Mother at Sixty Six'? [DELHI 2023]

▶ Extract Based Type Questions

[4 Marks]

11. Read the extract given below and answer the questions that follow : [DELHI 2018]

    Old

    Familiar ache, my childhood's fear,

    but all I said was, see you soon

    Amma,

    all l did was smile and smile and

    smile... ...

    (a) What does the phrase, 'familiar ache 'mean'?

    (b) What was the poet's childhood fear?

    (c) What do the first two lines tell us about the poet's feelings for her mother?

    (d) What does the repeated use of the word, 'smile 'mean?

12. Read the extract given below and answer the questions that follow : [ALL INDIA 2016]

    ....I saw my mother

    beside me,

    doze, open mouthed, her face

    ashen like that

    of a corpse and realised with

    pain...........

    (a) What is ' I '?

    (b) What did 'I' realise with pain?

    (c) Why was the realisation painful?

    (d) Identify and name the figure of speech used in these lines.

13. Read the extract given below and answer the questions that follow : [ALL INDIA 2015]

    and

    looked out at young

    trees sprinting, the merry children spilling

    out of their homes, but after the airport's

    security check, standing a few yards

    away, I looked again at her, wan,

    pale

    as a late winter's moon and felt that

    old

    familiar ache...

    (a) How can the trees sprint?

    (b) Why did the poet look at her mother again?

    (c) What did she observe?

    (d) Identify the figure of speech used in these lines.

14. Read the extract given below and answer the questions that follow : [DELHI 2015]

    I saw my mother,

    beside me,

    doze open mouthed, her face

    ashen like that

    of a corpse and realized with

    Pain

    that she was as old as she

    looked but soon

    put that thought away,

    (a) What worried the poet when she looked at her mother?

    (b) Why was there pain in her realization?

    (c) Why did she put that thought away?

    (d) Identify the figure of speech used in these lines.

15. **Read the extract given below and answer the questions that follow :**   [ALL INDIA 2013]

> Driving from my parent's
> home to Cochin last Friday morning,
> I saw my mother, beside me, doze,
> open-mouthed, her face ashen like that
> of a corpse and realised with pain
> that she was as old as she looked...

(*a*) Where was, the poet driving to?

(*b*) Why was her mother's face looking like that of a corpse?

(*c*) What did the poet notice about her mother?

16. **Read the extract given below and answer the questions that follow :**   [ALL INDIA 2011]

> As a late winter's moon and felt that
> old
> familiar ache, my childhood's fear
> but all I said was, see you soon,
> Amma

(*a*) What does the 'Childhood fear' refer to?

(*b*) What do you mean by familiar ache?

(*c*) What was mother being compared to and why?

17. **Read the extract given below and answer the questions that follow :**   [DELHI 2011]

> ....but soon
> put that thought away and
> looked out at young
> trees sprinting, the merry children spilling
> out of their homes,

(*a*) Which thought did the poet put away?

(*b*) What do the 'sprinting trees' signify?

(*c*) What are 'the merry children spilling out of their homes', symbolic of?

18. Read the extract given below and answer the questions that follow: [DELHI 2019]

> I looked again at her, wan, pale as a late
> winter's moon and felt that old familiar
> ache, my childhood's fear, but all I said
> was, see you soon, Amma, all I did was
> smile and smile and smile ...

(i) Name the poet and the poem.

(ii) What was the poet's childhood fear?

(iii) What is the poetic device used in lines 1-2 ?

(iv) Explain: 'late winter's moon'.

19. Read the extracts given below and answer the questions that follow each of them.   [DELHI 2020]

> Driving from my parent's
> home to Cochin last Friday
> morning, I saw my-mother,
> beside me,
> doze, open mouthed, her face
> ashen like that
> Of a corpse and realised with
> pain
> that she was as old as she
> looked ... ...

(i) Where was the poet driving to ? Who was sitting beside her ?

(ii) What did the poet notice about her mother ?

(iii) Which thought made the poet feel painful ?

(iv) Name the figure of speech used in the expression : 'her face ashen like that of a corpse'.

▶ Extract Based Type Question

[6 Marks]

20. Read the given extracts to attempt the questions with reference to context :   [DELHI 2023]

> but after airport's
> security check, standing a few yards
> away, I looked again at her, Wan,
> pale
> as a late winter's moon and felt that
> old
> familiar ache, my childhood's fear
> but all I said was, see you soon,
> Amma,
> All I did was smile and smile and
> smile -------

(i)   Choose the correct option :

      In the above extract the narrator feels

      (a) satisfied

      (b) fearful

      (c) nostalgic

      (d) regretful

(ii) Identify the word in the extract that means 'Colourless'.

(iii) Complete the following analogy correctly :

      She sang like a bird : Simile

      All I did was smile and smile and smile :

      ____

(iv) Read the following statement and choose the correct option :

      (1) The poet had gone through the security check.

      (2) She did not want to look at her mother.

      (a) (1) is true, but (2) is false.

      (b) (1) is false, but (2) is true.

      (c) Both (1) and (2) are true.

      (d) Both (1) and (2) are false.

(v)   What childhood fear is the poet referring to?

(vi) Fill the blank with appropriate words with reference to the extract :

      Pale as a winter's moon suggests ________.

🔑 Solutions ______________

1. (c) Old, inactive, sad mother contrasted with young, energetic, happy and agile children. [1]

2. A child is always afraid of being separated from his or her parents. Similarly, in the poem, the poet's fear as a child was that of losing her mother or her company. [3]

3. Troubled with the thoughts of her ageing mother. Kamala Das tries to console herself with the view outside the car that was full of youthful vim and vigour. She watches the trees 'sprinting' past her speeding car and the children, full of life and activity, running out of their houses to play. [3]

4. The poet's mother looks pale and worn out, devoid of the brightness, and blush of youth. In the twilight of her life, she appears as lacklustre as the winter moon. [3]

5. The 'wan', 'pale' face of the poet's mother at sixty-six brings an image of decay and death. It brings that old familiar fear of separation back at the airport. She fears the ultimate fate of human beings. But she must put on a brave face. She exercises self-control. She composes herself and tries to look normal. She tries to hide her ache and fear by smiling continuously. [3]

6. The fears of ageing and ultimate death were her fears as a child. She was struck by the realization of her mother in old age. The old age creeping on her mother is a hard fact. [3]

7. The poet was smiling as she didn't want to reveal to her mother that she was actually very sad. She was just disguising it with a fake smile. However, she was, extremely distressed as she feared to lose her mother soon. [3]

8. Kamala Das knew that her mother was getting old and the frightening thought that her mother might die soon filled her with fear. So she looked at the young children as they are full of energy, and represent youth, thus driving away the disturbing thought that her mother was dying. [3]

9. When the poet looks at her mother's face she found that it had become pale and withered. She realised that her mother was at the edge of her life and her end was near. The thought that her mother would be soon separated from her caused unbearable pain and ache in the poet's heart. [3]

10. The poet Kamala Das is a daughter who loves her mother dearly. She compares her mother's ageing with different phrases like a 'corpse' or like 'a late winter's moon'. Her feelings expressed in the poem reflect her anxiousness and insecurity of losing her mother forever. She is worried if she would be able to see her mother alive or not. The poet's smile hides her pain and her fear of losing her. She is repeatedly gripped by the same insecurity and fear of losing her mother. [2]

11. (a) The pain, that her mother was growing old and the fear of separation [1]

    (b) The poet's childhood fear was fear of losing her mother. [1]

    (c) The poet loves her mother a lot and she had a fear of losing her. [1]

(*d*) The word 'smile 'was repeatedly used as the poet hides her feelings from her mother under a smile. [1]

12. (*a*) 'I' in the above extract is the poet or the daughter. [1]

(*b*) The poet realised the approaching death of her mother. [1]

(*c*) The realisation of the poet is painful because her mother now looked as old as she was, her bodily infirmities that come with old age were visible on her face and she was approaching her death. [1]

(*d*) The figure of speech used is a Simile. [1]

13. (*a*) When we look out of a moving vehicle, we see the objects moving in the opposite direction. This motion is referred to as 'sprinting' by the poetess, who when looked out of her moving car, felt as if the trees were running. [1]

(*b*) The poetess looked at her mother again to reassure herself of her mother's presence. [1]

(*c*) The poetess observed that her mother looked pale and weak. [1]

(*d*) The figure of speech is used in these lines are personification and simile. [1]

14. (*a*) The poet was worried about her mother's advancing age. [1]

(*b*) There was a pain in the poet's realisation because her mother now looked as old as she was, her bodily infirmities that come with old age were visible on her face and she was fast approaching her death. [1]

(*c*) The poet put that thought away because she would not be able to go through with her plan of travelling away from home if she continued to dwell on her mother's old age [1]

(*d*) The figure of speech used is a simple, [1]

15. (*a*) The poet was driving from her parents' home to the Cochin airport. [1]

(*b*) Her mother's face looked pale, faded and lifeless, like a dead body. [1]

(*c*) She noticed that her mother was dozing with her mouth open. [1]

16. (*a*) 'The childhood fear' refers to the death of her mother. The fear of death of her mother troubled her. It was the old fear which crept again on seeing her ageing mother. [1]

(*b*) The 'ache' refers to the troubled thoughts related to her mother's death. Seeing her mother growing old and almost withered away due to age, the poet feared to see her no more. The fear of her death was not new as a child, since even she was troubled by this thought. [1]

(*c*) The mother has been compared to 'Late Winters' moon'. Just like winter moon, the mother seemed pale, glow-less and lacking strength and youthful shine. [2]

17. (*a*) The poet put away the painful thought of her mother's ageing and declining health. [1]

(*b*) Sprinting trees signify energy/youth/ activity. [1]

(*c*) They symbolise happiness, youth and vigour. [2]

18. (i) The poem is 'My mother at sixty six' and the poet is Kamala Das. [1]

(ii) The poet's childhood fear is that someday she would lose her mother to death [1]

(iii) The poetic device is simile. [1]

(iv) Late winter's moon is pale and seems lifeless, this is used to signify that the poet's mother has lost vitality and energy, she looks pale and lifeless in her old age. She is in the winter of her life which is compared to the last stage of life. [1]

19. (i) The poetess was driving from her parent's home to Cochin airport on a Friday morning. Poetess's mother was sitting beside her. [1]

(ii) She noticed that her mother was dozing off and she grown old. [1]

(iii) The thought that her mother might not live long. [1]

(iv) Simile [1]

20. (i) The correct option is (b) i.e. fearful [1]

(ii) pale [1]

(iii) Repetition [1]

(iv) (a) (1) is true, but (2) is false [1]

(v) The poet Kamala Das in her poem 'My Mother at Sixty Six' is referring to fear of separation from her mother forever just as a child is always insecure of getting separated from her mother whenever she is not visible or nearby to him/ her. [1]

(vi) the mother's weak and withered face. [1]

2. Keeping Quiet

Summary

Introduction:

The Nobel Prize-winning poet Pablo Neruda invites everyone to suspend all their activities and count to twelve. He further wants us all to calm down and keep still. It would have never been before in the moment of human history when everything becomes standstill for some time. There won't remain the concept of the oppressor and oppressed. In this state of stillness, there won't be any activity like preparation of war or any act which could cause damage to the environment.

However, the poet has no ambiguity regarding how long this state of stillness should prevail. His sole desire is that all the activities should be suspended for some time and not to be stopped forever. According to him, life is all about action and progress whereas inactivity symbolises death. His thinking is that this moment of introspection will lead us in the right direction.

1.   Now we will count to twelve

     and we will all keep still.

     For once on the face of the Earth

     let's not speak in any language,

     let's stop for one second,

     and not move our arms so much.

In these lines, the poet invites everyone to suspend all their activities and count to twelve. He further wants us all to calm down and keep still. He proposes to prohibit us from speaking any language in order to dissolve the boundaries of cultures marred by limitations of languages. The poet asks us to be still for a while, and not make even any arm movement for some time. The underlying intent is to let our thoughts flow free without any hurry.

2.   It would be an exotic moment

     without rush, without engines,

     we would all be together

     in a sudden strangeness.

The poet says that it would be a strange feeling or an exciting experience when the world comes to a standstill, where there will be no rushing of everyday works. The machines would no longer engage us. Everyone will come together but in a strange kind of way, a sudden moment of inactivity, which the world has rarely witnessed.

3.   Fishermen in the cold sea

     would not harm whales

     and the man gathering salt

     would look at his hurt hands.

Here fishermen represent the killers or the oppressors who hardly ever think of others and have become merciless hunters. Here the poet also outlines that the goal is to not only bring brotherhood amongst humans but also peace amongst nature and humankind. Hunters will empathise with their prey and would reflect upon their act of violence. The salt-gatherers will also get some time to introspect about their life who otherwise are trapped in the rat-race of earning their livelihood. Even they can feel the pain and can reflect upon their hurt hands.

4.   Those who prepare green wars,

     wars with gas, wars with fire,

     victory with no survivors,

     would put on clean clothes

     and walk about with their brothers

     in the shade, doing nothing.

Now the poet moves to green wars- war with the environment by creating pollutions, and exploitation of nature for the selfish reasons of mankind. By "wars with gas, wars with fire", he means to speak about the chemical and nuclear wars that humans had fought to harm each other. The poet outlines the irony of the wars, where even the winner experiences a loss, and the victory becomes an excuse in order to end the wars. Neruda asks them to clean their souls of negativity, and walk with their fellow being. He concludes they would shun the path of destruction for the moment when they will be quiet.

5.   What I want should not be confused

     with total inactivity.

     Life is what it is about;

     I want no truck with death.

In these lines, the poet clarifies his idea of "being still". He does not mean total inactivity, as per him total inactivity would mean only not doing any physical activity; however, their minds must be active in introspecting. The poet's message is about life, and he does not want people to link to death.

6.   If we were not so single-minded

     about keeping our lives moving,

     and for once could do nothing,

     perhaps a huge silence

might interrupt this sadness

of never understanding ourselves and

of threatening ourselves with death.

Here Neruda says that the central goal of mankind is to stay alive, and hence everyone needs to work towards it. Making entire life about survival has led to a rat-trap to check all the boxes in life. As per the poet, if people embrace the momentary silence and reflect about themselves, they will realise the sadness of never being able to recognise or appreciate themselves.

7. Perhaps the Earth can teach us

as when everything seems dead

and later proves to be alive.

These lines ask humans to learn from nature because whatever once seems like dead rejuvenates and reclaims life again. In autumn it seems that leaves have left the tree and its life is over, however, as the spring approaches life comes with fresh greenery. The journey on the earth is about life and death and the cycle continues throughout its journey.

8. Now I'll count up to twelve

and you keep quiet and I will go.

With these lines, the poet tries to give a narrator's viewpoint towards the entire poem and ideas facilitated through it, as he starts to quietly leave the scene while counting up to twelve, as the thought process has been triggered and the message has been passed.

PREVIOUS YEARS'
EXAMINATION QUESTIONS

▶ **Short Answer Type Questions:**

[1 Mark]

(Q 1 to 5) : Read the extract given below and answer the questions that follow :[DELHI TERM I, 2022]

What I want should not be

confused

with total inactivity

Life is what it is about;

I want no truck with death.

If we were not so single-minded

about keeping our lives moving

and for once could do nothing

Perhaps a huge silence

might interrupt this sadness

of never understanding ourselves

and of threatening ourselves with death.

1. The poet's intention in the first line is to
   (a) give warning to the readers
   (b) give right direction to the readers
   (c) give choice to the readers
   (d) give a clarification to the readers

2. Select the option that best explains the stand of the poet in the expression : "I want no truck with death".
   (a) He advises people to escape death
   (b) He asserts that death is inevitable
   (c) He assures that he does not advocate death
   (d) He expresses his desire not to die

3. Select the option that aptly describes the tone of the poet in the expression :
   "If we were not so single minded".
   (a) regretful   (b) critical
   (c) encouraging   (d) friendly

4. According to the poet who is to blame for the condition of threatening ourselves with death?
   (a) Stressful life
   (b) Keeping quiet
   (c) Lack of understanding
   (d) State of confusion

5. The tone of the poet in the expression
   "perhaps a huge silence
   might interrupt this sadness" is
   (a) unsure yet optimistic
   (b) sure and confident
   (c) poetic & melodramatic
   (d) hopeful but not confident

6. 'would put on clean clothes.' What does Pablo Neruda mean by 'clean clothes' ?
                                   [DELHI TERM I, 2022]
   (a) white dress to reflect peace
   (b) mind without courage and confidence
   (c) mind without confusion and fear
   (d) mind without hatred and prejudice

▶ **Short Answer Type Questions:**

[2 & 3 Marks]

7. How would keeping quiet affect life in and around the sea?   [ALL INDIA 2017]

8. 'Life is what it is all about'. How is keeping quiet related to life?   [ALL INDIA 2015]

9. What will be counting up to twelve and keeping still help us achieve?   [DELHI 2015]

10. What is the sadness the poet refers to in the poem, Keeping Quiet?   [ALL INDIA 2014]

11. Which is the exotic moment that the poet refers to in 'Keeping Quiet'?   [DELHI 2014]

12. What are the different kinds of wars mentioned in the poem? What is Neruda's attitude towards these wars?   [ALL INDIA 2013]

13. According to the poet, what is it that human beings can learn from Nature?   [ALL INDIA 2012]

14. What is the sadness that the poet, Pablo Neruda refers to in the poem, 'Keeping Quiet?   [ALL INDIA 2011]

15. Do you think the poet, Pablo Neruda advocates total inactivity and death? Why/Why not?   [DELHI 2011]

16 How will 'Keeping Quiet' protect our environment ?   [DELHI 2020]

17. 'There can be life under apparent stillness'. Explain. (Keeping Quiet)   [DELHI 2023]

▶ Extract Based Type Questions:

[4 Marks]

18. **Read the extract given below and answer the questions that follow:**   [ALL INDIA 2016]

> Now we will count to twelve
> and we will all keep still.
> For once on the Face of the Earth
> let's not speak in any language,
> let's stop for one second,
> and not move our arms so much.

(a) What is the significance of the number, twelve?

(b) Which activities does the poet want us to stop?

(c) What does the poet mean by let's not speak in any language?

(d) Describe the pun on the word 'arms'.

19. **Read the extract given below and answer the questions that follow:**   [DELHI 2013]

> Perhaps the Earth can teach us
> as when everything seems dead
> and later proves to be alive.
> Now I'll count up to twelve
> and you keep quiet and I will go.

(a) What does the Earth teach us?

(b) What does the poet mean to achieve by counting up to twelve?

(c) What is the significance of 'keeping quiet?

🔑 Solutions

1. (d) The poet is giving clarification that he is not advocating total inactivity. [1]

2. (c) No association with death. [1]

3. (b) Poet critically asserts that we, human beings, understand lot of things but fail to understand our own self. [1]

4. (c) Failing to understand ourselves. [1]

5. (a) Here 'perhaps' points out not being confident/ unsure but, the end result of introspection might bring positivity which paves way for being optimistic. [1]

6. (d) Feelings of mutual understanding without any bias. [1]

7. Keeping quiet will immensely affect the life at the sea. The fishermen will stop killing whales for some time and the salt gatherers will also get some time to heal their wounded hands. [3]

8. Keeping quiet does not mean absolute sluggishness. It simply means to quit doing all those activities that are destructive and harmful to nature. Mother Earth is also very quiet but it nurtures so much life in it. Similarly, we should also be quiet and do something worthwhile. [3]

9. Counting up to twelve takes a very short time. Keeping still for this brief interval of time gives us a momentary pause to introspect and review the course of action. It is generally observed that most of the ills and troubles of the world are caused by our rush or hurry. Violence is caused by anger. Keeping quiet and still give us necessary respite and ensures peace. [3]

10. The poet refers to the 'sadness' of failing to understand oneself in the monotonous everyday existence. He also finds it sad that the humanity is moving towards its own ruin, owing to its unanalysed actions. He regrets the rush of outdoing others that have made one forget the values of humanity. [3]

11. The author talks about the exotic moment when everyone keeps quiet and still. The moment will be extraordinarily tranquil, with no hustle bustle of the frenzied world. Although it may seem a little strange in the beginning, eventually it will bring us all together. [3]

12. The poet is against wars of all kinds. He wants a total stoppage of war. Green wars against the environment, wars with poisonous gases and wars with fire must be terminated at once. [3]

13. The poet, 'Pablo Neruda' clearly demarcates between 'stillness' and 'total inactivity'. There can be life even in 'utter stillness'. The poet invokes the Earth as a symbol to prove his point. Even in utter stillness, earth 'proves to be alive'. Nature keeps on working in stillness and keep its existence. [3]

14. The poet refers to the sadness we feel as we do not understand ourselves, we also feel sad as we feel that we are heading towards destruction. [3]

15. No, the poet does not advocate complete inactivity and death. He makes it clear that stillness should not be confused with 'total inactivity'. Total inactivity brings death. But the poet has no truck with death. His stillness means halting of harmful and hostile human activities. [3]

16. Keeping quiet will initiate peace and brotherhood among men, halting all destructive activities like waging wars which harm people besides damaging the environment. [2]

17. The Poet Neruda in his poem Keeping Quiet doesn't combine stillness with total inactivity. The poet says that even when a body is still, there is activity in it which proves that there is life in it. The poet says that nature reflects lessons to teach us. The poet takes the example of the earth to prove his opinion. He talks about winter season which seems to be dead and silent but the same follows with spring bringing new life. Thus, he proves his point by saying that even in inactivity there is still liveliness apparent. [2]

18. (a) The number twelve represents the twelve hours marks on the clock to measure time. [1]

(b) The two activities of not speaking in any language and stop all activities for one second. [1]

(c) The people of the world are much indulged in wars, bloodsheds and unnecessary debates. If they keep quiet and not speak in any language, it will ensure Peace. [1]

(d) The word 'arms' in the extract mean both the hands and weapons.' [1]

19. (a) The Earth teaches us that there is life under seeming stillness. [1]

(b) The Poet wishes to wipe out the discord in the world and the reason for the imbalance that exists between man and nature. Ultimately, he wants to ensure the survival of the human race. [1]

(c) Keeping quiet will provide time for introspection and create feeling of oneness among human beings. [1]

3. A Thing of Beauty

Summary

Introduction:

'A Thing of Beauty' is a poem written by John Keats. In this poem, the poet outlines the permanent nature of beauty. The joy from them is everlasting as their beauty is of immortal nature and it only keeps flourishing. It leaves a lasting impression in our mind rather soul. They gives eternal peace just like the shady trees give beautiful dreams and sound sleep. Our world has much pain and suffering while very few people have nobility at their hearts. Every morning preparation of flowery wreath is one of the things which strengthen our bond with nature. Darkness, gloom, trial and tribulations are all washed away from our souls by things of beauty. The poet further lists things of beauty like, the sun, the moon, old and young trees, the daffodils and musk roses. The ballads, the epics and the mythological stories about the heroic and mighty acts of our ancestors are all eternal sources of happiness.

1. A thing.....................................
....
...........................quiet breathing.

Being an admirer of nature, John Keats loved beauty in all forms. According to him beautiful objects gives us everlasting happiness and eternal joys. The beauty of such things only flourishes with time and never fades away rather beauty is of immortal nature. In fact, they make permanent impressions in our memory and it's because of such memories we get sound sleeps and beautiful dreams. In other words this brings us peace, tranquillity and healing to our mental and physical health.

2. Therefore on every...................

    ....

    .... our dark spirits.

In these lines the poet says that every morning when we wake up after sound sleep and beautiful dreams, we weave wreath of flowers as this strengthens our bond to earth and nature more. Mankind suffers from a lot of disappointments, hopelessness, lost faith and negativities. This is due to scarcity of humans with nobility and good deeds. In spite of all these reasons to be saddened we become optimistic as we see these things of beauty. They help us to shun negativity and darkness.

3. Such the sun.............................

    ....

    ....musk rose blooms.

Now the poet moves to list the beautiful things of nature like the sun, the moon, trees no matter old or young they provide shade to one and all, the daffodils, the clear and cool streams which provide relief in hot summers and musk roses are all things of beauty and infuse joys and happiness.

4. And such.....................................

    ....

    .... the heaven's brink.

Keats now moves to literary beauty. The beauty depicted through the ballads, the epics and the mythological stories about the heroic and mighty acts of our ancestors are all eternal sources of happiness. They inspire us to be brave and courageous. Finally, all the beautiful things are compared to water poured from fountain of heaven and are sent by the God himself.

PREVIOUS YEARS'
EXAMINATION QUESTIONS

▶ Short Answer Type Questions

[2 & 3 Marks]

1. How can 'mighty dead' be things of beauty?
    [DELHI 2017]

2. Mention any four things of beauty that add joy to our life.   [ALL INDIA 2017]

3. What does Keats consider an endless fountain of immortal drink and why does he call its drink immortal?   [ALL INDIA 2013]

4. What is the message of the poem, 'A Thing of Beauty'?   [ALL INDIA 2011]

5. Why and how is grandeur associated with the mighty dead?   [DELHI 2011]

6. Do we experience things of beauty only for short moments or do they make a lasting impression? Explain. (A Thing of Beauty)   [DELHI 2023]

▶ Extract Based Type Questions

[4 Marks]

7. Read the extract given below and answer the questions that follow :   [DELHI 2018]

    ...... and clear rills

    That for themselves a cooling covert make

    'Gainst the hot season; the mid forest brake,

    Rich with the sprinkling of fair musk-rose
        blooms ;

    (a) Identify the poem and the poet.

    (b) What is the role of the clear rills?

    (c) How has the mid forest brake become rich?

    (d) Name the figure of speech in 'cooling covert'.

8. Read the extract given below and answer the questions that follow: [DELHI 2016]

    'It loveliness increases, it will never

    Pass into nothingness, but will keep

    A bower quiet for us, and asleep

    Full of sweet dreams, and health,
        and quiet breathing.

    (a) Whose loveliness will keep on increasing?

    (b) Identify the phrase which says that 'it' is immortal.

    (c) What is a 'bower'?

    (d) Why do we need sweet dreams, health, and quiet breathing in our lives?

9. Read the extract given below and answer the questions that follow: [DELHI 2014]

    All lovely tales that we have heard or read;

    An endless fountain of immortal drink.

    Pouring unto us from the heaven's brink

    (a) Name the poem and the poet.

    (b) What is the thing of beauty mentioned in these lines?

    (c) What image does the poet use in these lines?

10. **Read the extract given below and answer the questions that follow:** [DELHI 2013]

> A flowery band to bind us to the Earth,
>
> Spite of despondence, of the inhuman dearth
>
> Of noble natures, of the gloomy days,
>
> Of all the unhealthy and o'er -darkened ways

   (*a*) What are we doing every day?

   (*b*) Which evil things do we possess and suffer from?

   (*c*) What are the circumstances that contribute towards making humans unhappy and disillusioned with life?

11. **Read the extract given below and answer the questions that follow:** [ALL INDIA 2012]

> A thing of beauty is a joy for ever
>
> Its loveliness increases, it will never
>
> Pass into nothingness, but will keep
>
> A bower quiet for us.

   (*a*) A thing of beauty is joy for ever'. Explain.

   (*b*) Why does a beautiful thing pass into nothingness?

   (*c*) What does poet mean by a bower quiet for us?

▶ Long Type Question   [5 Marks]

12. 'Aunt Jennifer's Tigers' and 'A Thing of Beauty', can be read together to show the permanence and everlasting impact of art and of things of beauty. Comment. [DELHI 2023]

🔑 Solutions

1. The grandeur of death lies in the promise of an eternal sleep which continues unperturbed without the usual earthly concerns and strife that plagues us daily. The dead also have a power over us; they do not leave us free but instil themselves in our memory. The death lives on in those who are alive. [3]

2. The poet says that a beautiful thing is a source of everlasting happiness. The four things that add joy to our life are the sun, the moon a bower of trees and a clear stream of water. [3]

3. A fountain of eternal joy and immortality pours into the heart and soul of man. It flows right from the heaven's brink and pours into the human heart. It is like immortal nectar. The immortal drink that nature's endless fountain pours into our hearts, is a source of immense joy for us. [3]

4. The message is that certain things are beautiful and are worth to be treasured. [3]

5. The mighty dead were very powerful and dominating persons during their own times. Their achievements made them mighty and great. Their noble works dazzle our eyes. [3]

6. The phrase 'A Thing of Beauty' is completed by the poet by saying that a thing of beauty is a joy forever in his collection of poems in Endymion. Thus, the things of beauty which exist in nature itself do not only remain with us for a short moment, they give us endless pleasure and joy. The blissful memories of the beauty of nature are a source of everlasting joy and happiness according to the poet. [2]

7. (*a*) It's "A Thing of Beauty" written by John Keats. [1]

   (*b*) Clear rills create shelter for themselves with plants on the banks. It leaves a pleasing experience. [1]

   (*c*) It becomes rich as musk rose blooms. [1]

   (*d*) It's alliteration. [1]

8. (*a*) The loveliness of a thing of beauty will keep on increasing. [1]

   (*b*) 'Never pass into nothingness. [1]

   (*c*) A pleasant shady place under a tree is called bower. [1]

   (*d*) We need sweet dreams, health and quite breathing in our lives to bear problems of life to remove the gloom or to uplift the mood. [1]

9. (*a*) The given lines are from the poem 'A Thing of Beauty' by John Keats. [1]

   (*b*) The things of beauty mentioned in the given lines are the lovely tales of mighty men. [1]

   (*c*) In these lines, the poet uses the image of 'an endless fountain of immortal drink, to describe the beautiful bounty of the Earth. The Earth, like a fountain, gives us numerous beautiful sights like the Sun, the Moon, flowers, rivers and greenery. [2]

10. (*a*) Every day, we renew our bond with nature and it is the beauty of nature that keeps us attached to this Earth. [1]

(*b*) We suffer from a lack of goodness in human nature and 'unhealthy' or evil ways adopted by human beings. [1]

(*c*) The trials and tribulations of life that test our balance to make us despondent in life. [1]

11. (*a*) A thing of beauty is a source of constant joy. Its beauty goes on increasing day by day. It never passes into nothingness. It even gives solace in the dreams. [2]

(*b*) A thing of beauty gives the everlasting impression as it is not subjected to time. [1]

(*c*) He was looking for a shady place to sit and ponder. [1]

12. 'Aunt Jennifers' Tigers' and 'A Thing of Beauty' have certain commonalities in the sense that they reflect how art and beauty releases the fears and sadness and converts it into a never ending joy and bliss. Aunt Jennifer, though is a victim of male chauvinism feels at ease when she paints majestic lions which are so beautifully painted that they seem to be real. Similarly, John Keats in his Poem A Thing of Beauty seen in the nature and its things can remove sadness and lets us forget sadness and fills our heart with ultimate bliss and ease. Conclusively, both the poems somewhere end up saying that beauty provides a serenity which helps in removing melancholy. [5]

4. A Roadside Stand

Summary

Introduction:

Robert Frost was a popular American poet. Although his poetry is simple it has elements of irony. He deals with commonplace incidents and human relations.

A Roadside Stand is a poem about the lives of poor village people who hope to get some money to improve their standard of living. The city people who drive past them seldom cast a glance at them. However, there are dogooders who want to help them. Ironically, they wish to deprive them of their lands on the pretext of helping them. They want to enforce benefits on the poor people.

The poem begins with a farmer having an old house on the edge of a highway. He puts up a roadside stand in front of his house and has home-made squash and wild berries to sell. Thousands of cars speed past him. He hopes that some of the cars will stop and buy his produce. People in the country don't have much money. They wish they had some more money to improve their lot.

Every day he waits for a car to stop at his stand. But the drivers never look left or right, they do not stop. Even if they cast a glance, they look with disdain at the sights painted in an uneducated manner. They believe that the farmers have destroyed the beautiful landscape.

Only three cars stopped at the stand. One of them used the farmer's yard to back and turn around. It furrowed the grass and drove away. Another one stopped to ask the way. And a third one wanted to buy a gallon of petrol. The farmer was annoyed because they did not buy anything and he was unable to sell his petrol.

It is heard that some people want to help the poor farmers. Those greedy people wanted to buy their property for commercial use. They want the farmers to go into the village and live there next to a theater or a store and want to cheat them with sweet talk. They want to ruin their lives by taking to vices.

The speaker is highly concerned about the miserable lives and the living standard of the people. He thinks of a childish solution to the problem that all the poor people should be killed at once so that they can end their misery. But soon he realizes that it is a vain thought. He wishes he was dead so that he was free from sorrows about them.

PREVIOUS YEARS'
EXAMINATION QUESTIONS
▶ Short Answer Type Questions

[2 Marks]

(Answer the following questions in about 30-40 words each)

1. The city folk who drove through the countryside hardly paid any heed to the roadside or the people who ran it. If at all they did, it was to complain. Which lines bring this out? What was their complaint about?

2. What was the plea of the folk who had put up the roadside stand?

3. The government and other social service agencies appear to help the poor rural people, but actually do them no good. Pick out the words and phrases that the poet uses to show their double standards.

4. What is the 'childish longing' that the poet refers to? Why is it a 'vain'?

5. Which lines tell us about the insufferable pain that the poet feels at the thought of the plight of the rural poor?

▶ Extracts for Comprehension

[4 & 6 Marks]

6. Read the lines below and answer the questions that follow :

The little old house was out with a little new shed

In front at the edge of the road where the traffic sped,

A roadside stand that too pathetically pled, It would not be fair to say for a dole of bread, But for some of the money, the cash, whose flow supports,

The flower of cities from sinking and withering faint.

(i) Where was the new shed put up?

(ii) Who put it up there?

(iii) What did the roadside stand plea pathetically for?

(iv) What was unfair to say?

7. Read the lines below and answer the questions that follow:

The polished traffic passed with a mind ahead, Or if ever aside a moment, then out of sorts

At having the landscape marred with the artless paint

Of signs that with N turned wrong and S turned wrong

Offered for sale wild berries in wooden quarts,

Or crook-necked golden squash with silver warts,

Or beauty rest in a beautiful mountain scene,

You have the money, but if you want to be mean,

Why keep your money (this crossly) and go along.

(i) What is polished traffic referred to?

(ii) What was wrong with the signs?

(iii) What were the signs meant for?

(iv) What was said crossly?

8. Read the lines below and answer the questions that follow:

Here far from the city we make our roadside stand

And ask for some city money to feel in hand. To try if it will not make our being expand, And give us the life of the moving-pictures' promise

That the party in power is said to be keeping from us.

(i) Who made the roadside stand?

(ii) Why do they want money for?

(iii) What dreams do they have?

(iv) What do they think the party in power has done to them?

9. Read the lines below and answer the questions that follow:

It is in the news that all these pitiful kin

Are to be bought out and mercifully gathered in

To live in villages, next to the theatre and the store,

Where they won't have to think for themselves anymore,

While greedy good- doers, beneficent beasts of prey,

Swarm over their lives enforcing benefits

That are calculated to soothe them out of their wits,

And by teaching them how to sleep they sleep all day,

Destroy their sleeping at night the ancient way.

(i) How do the do gooders want to help the poor village people?

(ii) What is their calculated move?

(iii) What does the poet think of the good-doers?

(iv) What name was given by the poet to the do gooders?

10. Read the lines below and answer the questions that follow:

Sometimes I feel myself I can hardly bear

The thought of so much childish longing in vain,

The sadness that lurks near the open window there,

That waits all day in almost open prayer For the squeal of brakes, the sound of a stopping car,

Of all the thousand selfish cars that pass,

Just one to inquire what a farmer's prices are.

And one did stop, but only to plow up grass

In using the yard to back and turn around;

And another to ask the way to where it was bound;

And another to ask could they sell it a gallon of gas

They couldn't (this crossly); they had none, didn't it see?

(i) What do you think is the poet's childish longing?

(ii) Why does the farmer setup the roadside stand?

(iii) What made them say crossly "they had none......"?

(iv) Which word in the passage means 'fruitless'?

11. **Read the lines below and answer the questions that follow:**

No, in country money, the country scale of gain,
The requisite lift of spirit has never been found,

Or so the voice of the country seems to complain,

I can't help owning the great relief it would be
To put these people at one stroke out of their pain.

And then next day as I come back into the sane,

I wonder how I should like you to come to me
And offer to put me gently out of my pain.

(i) What do the country people complain? Why do they so complain?

(ii) How does the poet end the misery of those people?

(iii) What does he think when he 'comes back into the sane'?

(iv) Which two words in the extract are opposite of each other?

12. **Read the given extracts to attempt the questions with reference to context :**

[DELHI 2023]

Sometimes I feel myself I can hardly bear

The thought of so much childish longing in vain,

The sadness that lurks near the open window there,

That waits all day in almost open prayer.

For the squeal of brakes, the sound of a stopping car,

Of all the thousand selfish cars that pass,

Just one to inquire what a farmer's prices are,

(i) What is the sentiment expressed in the above extract?

(i) remorse		(ii) regret	
(iii) empathy		(iv) disappointment	
(v) guilt			

Choose the correct appropriate option.

(a) (iii) and (iv)   (b) (ii) and (iii)
(c) (iv) and (v)   (d) (i) and (v)

(ii) Identify the phrase in the extract that suggests 'innocent desires'.

(iii) The roadside stand owners pray for ________.

(a) a relief from the heat

(b) free housing

(c) cars stopping

(d) benefits from pollution

(iv) Complete the following analogy correctly :

He fought like a lion : Simile :: selfish cars :

____

(v) On the basis of the extract, choose the correct option with reference to (1) and (2) given below :

(1) The people who have put up the roadside stand keep waiting for customers.

(2) They become sad when someone turns up.

(a) (1) is true, but (2) is false.

(b) (1) is false, but (2) is true.

(c) Both (1) and (2) are true.

(d) Both (1) and (2) are false.

(vi) Fill the blank appropriately with reference to the extract.

'Squeal of brakes' implies ________.

🔑 Solutions

1. The lines that tell this are:

   The polished traffic passed with a mind ahead,
   Or if ever aside a moment, then out of sorts

   At having the landscape marred with the artless paint

   Of signs that with N turned wrong and S turned wrong

   Their complaint was that the signs with N and S turned wrong spoiled the Beauty of the landscape. [2]

2. The plea of the pople who had put up the roadside stand wanted some money to improve their living standard. They did not want charity, but wanted to offer produce in order to earn money. [2]

3. The so-called do gooders are selfish and greedy. They bring plans to help the poor village people. But in fact they want to grab their lands. The following words / phrases used by the poet shows their double standards:

- Mercifully gathered to live in villages
- Beneficent beasts of prey
- Enforcing benefits
- Greedy good-doers
- Soothe them out of their wits   [2]

4. The childish longing that the poet refers to is the speaker's desire to kill all poor people in order to end their misery. He later realizes that his desire is in vain as it is not feasible and practical. It was a childish idea.   [2]

5. The lines that tell us about the poet's insufferable pain are:

   Sometimes I feel myself I can hardly bear.

   The thought of so much childish longing in vain,
   The sadness that lurks near the open window there.   [2]

6. (i) The new stand was put up in front of a house on the edge of the road.   [1]

   (ii) It was put up there by a farmer who owned the house.   [1]

   (iii) It pled for money in exchange of farmer's produce.   [1]

   (iv) It was unfair to say that he pled for charities.   [1]

7. (i) The polished traffic refers to the glistening cars that sped along the road past the roadside stand.

   (ii) The letters N and S in the signs were painted the wrong way.

   (iii) The signs offered wild berries and golden squash for sale.

   (iv) The farmer cursed wealthy city people for not stopping and buying something from the stand.

8. (i) A farmer has made the roadside stand in front of his house.   [1]

   (ii) They wanted to raise their standard of living.   [1]

(iii) They have seen in movies how people enjoy the luxuries of life in cities.   [1]

(iv) They think the party in power is responsible for their poverty.   [1]

9. (i) They want to buy their land to help them with money.   [1]

   (ii) Their calculated move was to cheat the poor farmers with a sweet talk.   [1]

   (iii) The poet thinks that the good-doers are selfish and mean.   [1]

   (iv) The poet calls them beasts of prey.   [1]

10. (i) The poet's childish longing is to end the misery of the farmers at one stroke.   [1]

    (ii) The farmer set up the roadside stand hoping that the cars would stop and buy things. [1]

    (iii) The car showed no interest in things that he could offer.   [1]

    (iv) vain   [1]

11. (i) The country people complained that they cannot enjoy life.   [1]

    (ii) They don't have much money and their profit is very small.   [1]

    (iii) He thinks, they should be killed to relieve them of their sufferings.

    When the poet regains his wisdom, he thinks it is a vain idea to kill all the poor people.   [1]

    (iv) Pain-Relief   [1]

12. (i) The correct option is (a) i.e. (iii) and (iv) [1]

    (ii) childish longing   [1]

    (iii) The correct option is (c) i.e. cars stopping   [1]

    (iv) Personification   [1]

    (v) (a) (1) is true, but (2) is false   [1]

    (vi) Stopping of cars   [1]

5. Aunt Jennifer's Tigers

Summary

Introduction:

"Aunt Jennifer's Tigers," which appeared in Rich's first collection of poems, is typical of her early work, illustrating the modest poetic ambitions for which she was praised by Auden. Technically, the work displays flawless craftsmanship, with a carefully regulated meter and rhyming couplets. Only later did Rich recognize how formalism functioned as she writes,

"asbestos gloves," enabling her to grasp potentially dangerous materials without putting herself at risk, as in this poem.

Through the poem, 'Aunt Jennifer's Tiger's the poetess outlines the pains and suffering of a woman who has been a victim of failed marriage. She depicts her feelings by creating tigers on a woollen strip of cloth.

Aunt Jennifer's creations are poles apart from her own character. The tigers which are being woven by her move freely in the forest. They boast bright yellow coats with white strips. Tigers are fearless and are ignorant about people as they are confident of their strength and freedom.

Aunt Jennifer is so weak that her feeble fingers can't even pull the otherwise light needle. Though her own married life is sheer failure and she suffers greatly from the hands of her husband, her creations, the tigers are mighty. It seems, Uncle has been ignorant of her feelings and she has been subjected to trials and tortures of marriage. The tiger symbolises the character missing in aunt's own life.

The fear is so deep-rooted in Aunt Jennifer's mind that she feels that even after death and when her body would be lowered to grave, the burden of the ring won't let her free. And, to its contrast, the tigers created by her will remain free, fearless and mighty forever.

1. Aunt Jennifer's.........................

....

.... chivalric certainty.

The tigers of Aunt Jennifer highlight the sufferings of the married life of a woman. Aunt Jennifer too is a victim of the patriarchal mindset of the society. She has also gone through the trials and the tortures of a failed marriage. Her tigers are mighty, fearless and free and are certainly not scared men under the tree as they themselves symbolizes bravery. All the traits that Aunt Jennifer lacked in her life are present in the tigers e.g. they move with great confidence.

2. Aunt Jennifer's fingers ....

....

.... Jennifer's hands.

The terror of her husband is as such that makes her fingers trembles while pulling out the needle from the wool which is very light. Her physical and emotional weakness is at display in these lines. The wedding ring represents the burden of her married life and has become the symbol of her lost freedom.

PREVIOUS YEARS'
EXAMINATION QUESTIONS

▶ Short Answer Type Questions

[2 & 3 Marks]

1. Aunt Jennifer's efforts to get rid of her fear proved to be futile. Comment. [DELHI 2016]

2. What picture of male chauvinism (tyranny) do we find in the poem, Aunt Jennifer's Tigers'?
[ALL INDIA 2016]

3. How are Aunt Jennifer's tigers different from her?
[ALL INDIA 2014]

4. What are the difficulties that aunt Jennifer faced in her life? [DELHI 2014]

5. What lies heavily on Aunt Jennifer's hand? How is it associated with her husband?
[ALL INDIA 2013]

6. What will happen to Aunt Jennifer's Tigers when she is dead? [DELHI 2013]

7. How do 'denizens' and 'chivalric' add to our understanding of the Tigers' attitude?
[DELHI 2011]

8. Explain the irony at the end of the poem, 'Aunt Jennifer's Tigers'. [DELHI TERM II, 2022]

▶ Extract Based Type Questions

[4 Marks]

9. Read the extract given below and answer the questions that follow: [ALL INDIA 2017]

Aunt Jennifer's fingers fluttering through her wool

Find even the ivory needle hard to pull.

The massive weight of Uncle's wedding band

Sits heavily upon Aunt Jennifer's hand.

(a) What is Aunt Jennifer doing with her wool?

(b) Why does she find it difficult to pull her ivory needle?

(c) What does 'wedding band' stand for?

(d) Describe the irony in the third line.

10. Read the extract given below and answer the questions that follow: [DELHI 2017]

Aunt Jennifer's tigers prance across a screen,

Bright topaz denizens of a world of green.

They do not fear the men beneath the tree;

They pace in sleek chivalric certainty.

(a) Why are the tigers called Aunt Jennifer's tigers?

(b) How are they described here?

(c) How are they different from Aunt Jennifer?

(d) What does the word, 'chivalric' mean?

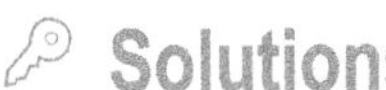

Solutions

1. Aunt Jennifer can't get rid of her fear even after her death. The terrified hands will be ringed with ordeals she was mastered by and she is still dominated by her uncle, in other words, the 'male-dominated society.' [3]

2. Aunt Jennifer lived a life weighed down by gender bias and subjugation to males. All the time she is in the grip of ordeals and terrors. They have crushed her and affected her married life. She had to put up with all the bullying of her dominating husband. The hardships and sufferings were the parts of her married life. She is a victim of male chauvinism. [3]

3. Aunt Jennifer's tigers are proud, free, fearless and sure of themselves. Unlike them, Aunt Jennifer is terrified and oppressed by her chauvinist husband. She lived her life under the constant pressure of duties and responsibilities of a married lady. [3]

4. Aunt Jennifer lived her life in accordance with the rules laid down by her husband. Her life was overburdened by the demands and duties of her married life. It lacked self-expression. Although old and weak, she had to face oppression from her husband. [3]

5. Aunt Jennifer is working with ivory needles and wool. But she can't move her fingers freely in the wool; she finds it hard to pull even the ivory needles easily. The experiences of her past married life are quite bitter. She has unpleasant memories of her married life with her husband. The weight of the wedding band sits heavily upon her hand. [3]

6. Aunt Jennifer's tigers will survive her. She has created the Tigers in a panel. They are made of wool. These objects of wool will survive their creator. The Tigers will go on jumping, proud and unafraid. [3]

7. Like all beasts of prey, the Tigers are the denizens of the forest. They live far away from human settlements. They are called 'chivalric'. This indicates the majestic and honourable position that they occupy in the world of animals. [3]

8. It is ironical that Aunt Jennifer's creations, the tigers, will continue to pace and prance freely, while Aunt herself will remain frightened even after death. Even her death would not liberate Aunt Jennifer from the oppression that she faced. Her fingers would remain 'ringed' with the uncle's wedding band. But the tigers that she made would always remain fearless and bold. [2]

9. (a) Aunt Jennifer is knitting her wool. [1]

   (b) She finds it difficult to pull her ivory needle because of the massive weight of Uncle's wedding band. [1]

   (c) The wedding band is a symbol of her marriage. [1]

   (d) The third line is ironical as marriage means a helping hand but it is described as a massive weight. [1]

10. (a) The Tigers are called Aunt Jennifer's tiger as they are knitted by her, in another word, they are her creation. [1]

    (b) Aunt Jennifer's tigers are described as ferocious, fearless, always harmful, sleek and chivalric. [1]

    (c) The Tigers are depicted as brave, strong, confident and happy. They are fearless beings and the presence of men does not scare them a bit. Contrarily, Aunt Jennifer is burdened by a life which, most probably, others chose for her. [1]

    (d) The word 'chivalric' refers to the confidence of the tigers about their power and brevity in their actions. [1]

1. The Third Level

Summary

Introduction:

Charley is a young man of 31. At multiple instances, he had got lost at the Grand Central Station. . He bumps into new doorways and new corridors and finds himself that leeads him to place where he never wished to go. His psychiatrist friend believes that he has been day-dreaming in order to escape the unhappiness of his present life. But Charley does not believe so. He has been to the third level where he can find means to escape into the past. He, however, is never again able to find the third level. He tells his psychiatrist friend about a very small and peaceful town called Galesburg.. The psychiatrist is infected by Charley's dream. He himself escapes into it. The story is a terrific mixture of reality and fantasy. It is not possible for anyone to time-travel, except in one's dreams. But Sam as well as Charley have experienced it. Charley even finds a letter with a postmark dated July 18, 1894 written by Sam after he has been there for two weeks, it is hard to believe it as true.

Charley, a 31 year old man was married to Lousia. Several times he had lost himself in the Grand Central Station. He always found himself bumping into new doorways and new corridors. Every time he had a new experience. He even had begun to believe that the Grand Central was like a huge tree ever pushing new tunnels and new corridors like the roots under the ground. Once he got into a mile long tunnel and came out in the lobby of a hotel. At another time, he came up into the building of an office.

Although there were only two levels at the Grand Central, Charley believed there certainly were three levels. . He talked about it to his friends. He discussed the same with his psychiatrist friend. The psychiatrist said that it was nothing but day-dreaming, a means of escape from his present unhappy life.. The modern world was full of fear, tension and worries. The third level provided him an escape from that world.

All his friends agreed with the psychiatrist's opinion. They said that his stamp collecting was also a temporary escape.

Charley did not agree with them. According to him, it was his grandfather who started the stamp collection. And in his grandfather's days, life was peaceful. He did not need an escape. Interestingly, President Roosevelt also collected stamps.

One day, Charley got late from his office and wanted to reach him quickly. So he went to the Grand Central to catch a train. He walked down to the first level, and then walked down another flight of stairs. He thought he had reached the second level again. But he got lost. He walked down a corridor. He thought it was wrong. But he walked on downward. He walked down a short flight of stairs. He thought that he had reached the second level again. But actually he had reached the third level.

After reaching there, he saw that the the third level was entirely different and old- fashioned with lesser ticket windows. The information booth was made of wood. The lights were open flame gas lights and on the floor lied brass spittoons. Men had beards and sideburns. Women wore old-fashioned dresses and high buttoned shoes. The railway engine was small with a funnel shaped stack. Everything at the third level looked as if it were a century old. He walked to the newsboy. There he glanced at "The World". The lead story was about President Cleveland. Later Charley found out from the library files that it was printed on June 11, 1894.

Charley wanted to go to Galesburg. He had been there in his childhood days. It was a wonderful town with beautiful trees and houses. . In 1894, it was a heaven of peace and tranquility. People lived a carefree life. So he asked for two tickets to Galesburg. He paid the fare in modern notes which were different from those in 1894. The clerk thought the notes were fake and Charley was trying to cheat him. He threatened to get him arrested Charley immediately turned around and started walking away as fast as possible.

Next day, Charley went to a coin-dealer to purchase old-style notes. He got only two hundred old dollars for three hundred new dollars. Disappointingly, he was never able to find the the corridor that led to the third level.

The act of purchasing old currency worried his wife. So, Charley turned to his stamp collection. One day, among his grandfather's collection of first day covers, he discovered an envelope. The postmark showed that it had been there since July 18, 1894. He opened the envelope but the paper inside was not blank. The letter was from his psychiatrist friend Sam to whom Charlie had always told about Galesburg.

He had already gone there. He urged Charley to continue to look for the third level and join him in the Galesburg of 1894. It was a wonderful place.

Later Charley learnt that Sam had bought eight hundred dollars' worth of old currency. Charley hoped Sam would have set up hay and feed business in Galesburg. And that was what he had always wished to do.

PREVIOUS YEARS'
EXAMINATION QUESTIONS
▷ **Short Answer Type Questions**

[2 Marks]

(Answer the following questions in about 30-40 words each)

1. What does the third level refer to?
2. Would Charley ever go back to the ticket counter on the third level to buy tickets to Galesburg for himself and his wife?
3. Do you think that the third level was a medium of escape for Charley? Why?
4. What do you infer from Sam's letter to Charley?
5. What did the psychiatrist think when Charley told him about the third level?
6. 'The modern world is full of insecurity, fear, war, worry and stress.' What are the ways in which we attempt to overcome them?
7. How did Charley 'reach' the third level of the Grand Central Station ? [DELHI 2020]

▷ **Long Answer Type Questions**

[4 & 6 Marks]

(Answer the following questions in about 125-150 words each)

8. Do you see an intersection of time and space in the story?
9. Apparent illogicality sometimes turns out to be a futuristic projection. Discuss.

10. Philately helps in keeping the past alive. Discuss other ways in which this is done. What do you think of human tendency to constantly move between the past, the present and the future?
11. Compare the interweaving of fantasy and reality in the stories The Third Level and The Adventure.
12. Why did Charley think that Grand Central Station was growing like a tree, pushing out new corridors and staircases like roots?
13. The clerk figured the fare – he glanced at my fancy hat band, but he figured the fare – and I had enough for two coach tickets, one way. But when I counted out the money and looked up, the clerk was staring at me. He nodded at the bills. "That ain't money, mister," he said, "and if you're trying to skin me, you won't get very far," and he glanced at the cash drawer, beside him. Of course the money was old-style bills half again as big as the money we use now a days and different looking. [DELHI 2023]

(i) Why did Charley ask for two tickets?
(ii) Complete the sentence by choosing the correct option :

When Charley offered money to the booking clerk, the latter stared at Charley because the booking clerk

(a) thought it wasn't money.
(b) did not trust Charley.
(c) thought Charley was trying to tease him.
(d) thought that Charley had given him less money.

(iii) Select the option that best describes Charley in this extract. He is

(a) a cheat
(b) gullible
(c) an opportunist
(d) an escapist

(iv) 'If you're trying to skin me' suggests ______.

🔑 **Solutions** ____________________

1. The third level refers to the imaginary third underground level o f the Grand Central Railway Station. [2]
2. No, despite trying hard, Charley failed to go back to the ticket counter on the third level to buy tickets to Galesburg for himself and his wife. [2]

3. Yes, the third level was clearly a medium of escape for Charley. He had a strange day-dream wish to escape all his worries and go to the past. He firmly believed that life, in old days, was peaceful. People in his grandfather's time lived a carefree life. All those charms were lost. The present day world is full of worries, wars, tension and haste. Charley was always lost in his own thoughts. He was unaware of his surroundings. One day he found himself in the lobby of the Roosevelt Hotel and some other time he came up in an office building. Another day, he reached the third level. [2]

4. Sam was a psychiatrist, but like his friend, he also had his share of daydreams. The description of Galesburg given by Charley infected him and he too wished to escape the present world, away from modern day worries. . He did not like to pursue his present profession. He wanted to live in a small town like Galesburg. He wanted to settle as hay, feed and grain businessman. So, he also discovered the 'third level' to escape.

The letter he wrote to Charley bore the postmark of July 18,1894. Probably, it was a first day cover sent to Charley's grandfather by somebody. Since the letter was addressed to Charley by Sam, it meant that Sam had really escaped into the past. He had crossed the boundaries of time and space to reach the Galesburg of 1894. Or else, it was Charley who was day-dreaming. [2]

5. Since there were only two levels at the Grand Central Station, when Charley told the psychiatrist that he had been to the third level, he believed that Charley was day-dreaming. His friend Sam thought that Charley was trying to escape the worries and tensions of the present world [2]

6. A thing about past is that everyone believes it to be better, it is alluring. Man always believes that the past was pleasant, without haste and worries and that people lived a relaxed life. So, people are always fascinated with the past and try to escape from the reality of the present. We do so in different ways. But it is our imagination that pays the major role. We write or read charming stories about the past. Sometimes we read stories of love and adventure. Some people pursue some hobbies like music, stamp collecting, painting, or reading religious scriptures. [2]

7. One evening Charley reached this station and then walked down the second level to catch an early train to his home. While he was on the second level, he strangely happened to notice a doorway down. He followed the steps and reached the third level which was never heard or seen by anyone. [2]

8. H. G. Wells strongly portrays the poet of imagination in his work. According to him, it was possible to travel in time as we can travel in space. He thought that a machine could be invented that could carry us back into the past or the future. If we went into the past, we would find the place different from what it looks like today. Sam's case is the perfect ecample of this. He travelled to Galesburg which was not like as it is today but as it was in 1890s. Similarly, when Charley reached the third level, everything was as it was in 1894. The men, the ticket booth, women dressed in old-fashioned garments, currency notes, and even the naked flames were of 1894. There surely is an intersection of time and space. [6]

9. The gift of imagination is the most beautiful gift that man has ever received. He is a dreamer. Every great invention was an illogical dream to begin with. One of the example is Icarus and his father flying with artificial wings. How illogical! They could not have flown like that. Even though it seems like a dream, it was possible for them to flly like birds.. But today we can fly at great speed. The aeroplane of today is a dreamer's idea of the flying carpet or uran khatola of past imagination. But those illogical things are the realities of today. [6]

10. Past has always fascinated mankind. He looks back and is eager to know how life was like in old times. Not only the past of mankind, but even the distant past of the earth is alluring. Scientists spend fortunes and precious years of their lives to look for fossils to reconstruct the conditions under which those extinct animals lived. Pyramids are ransacked to learn about pharaohs and their times. We preserve ancient monuments to keep the past alive. Our history books tell us about lost civilisations. Coins, pottery, artifacts, statues, temples and other things tell us about the past. These are preserved and displayed in museums. Man is seldom satisfied with the present. So, he looks 'before and after'. [6]

11. Narlikar in his story 'The Adventure' presumes that multiple parallel worlds exist. Professor Gaitonde accidently bumps into an India which is not like the India he has always known. It is not a story about the past, it is about the India that existed alternately. But the history had taken two entirely different routes. Narlikar says that it is not a presumption. It is not what would have happened if the Marathas had won the battle of Panipat. But actually, scientifically, it is possible for a number of worlds to exist simultaneously. On the other hand, 'The Third Level' is a journey into the past, similar to H.G. Well's idea of time machine. It does not believe in the existence of different worlds, but the different fourth dimension.

Such things may be possible to discover someday. The stories are improbable. They interweave fantasy and reality.   [6]

12. As described in the text, the Grand Central Station of New York is huge. It has two levels. Although Charley had been at the Station various times, he always had a new experience each time. He always lost track of the way. . He would bump into new corridors and new staircases.. Once he got into a tunnel a mile long and came up in the lobby of a hotel. Another time he came up in an office building. So he had begun to suspect that the Grand Central was ever pushing up new corridors and new staircases like roots of a tree. Perhaps new corridors and tunnels were trying to reach Times Square and Central Park. But his most amazing experience was when he got lost and somehow reached the third level of the Grand Central. lost his way and reached the third level. He was in a hurry to reach home one evening. He wanted to take a train on the second level. But the corridor led him to the third level, although there is no third level to the Grand Central Station. The strangest thing was that the corridor had led him into the past. Everything, including people, on third level, was about a century old. It was that of 1894.   [6]

13. (i)   Charley asked for two tickets because he had decided to go to Galesburg in 1894's time with his wife Louisa.   [1]

     (ii) The correct option is (a) i.e. thought it wasn't money   [1]

     (iii) The correct option is (a) i.e. a cheat   [1]

     (iv) that the clerk thought about the protagonist 'Charley' to be a cheater and if he dared to cheat, he would be caught very soon.   [1]

2. The Tiger King

Summary

Introduction:

The story starts with Tiger King being born. It was prophesied that the Tiger King would be a great king and would be regarded as the champion among all the elite champions, but eventually meet his end i.e. death. This idea of death was being presented as, "Any child born under the sky, eventually meets his end".

Jilani Jung Bahadur alias The Tiger King, was just 10 days old when he spoke for the first time and as if he was completely grown up. The people around him were wondering that to meet one's end was obvious but the prophecy would be more sensible if they knew the reason for his death. Then the chief of the astrologers told his prince that he was born in the hour of Bull, henceforth the prince would meet his end from a tiger as Tiger and Bull are enemies.

Jilani Jung Bahadur alias The Tiger King belonged to Pratibandapuram State. Pratibandapuram State had numerous forests and had a total of 100 tigers. The King began an expedition to kill all the 100 tigers in his state. He set out on a hunt and killed his first tiger. In doing so, he called upon the chief of the astrologers to show him the dead tiger. On looking at the dead tiger, the chief advised the king that he would have to kill the remaining 99 tigers too and he would have to be very careful with the last tiger. The king now enquired that if he killed all the tigers, what then. For the king's question, the priest stated that if the above stated happened the king would be safe and the priest would tear up all of his books.

For the sake of the king's expedition, there was a ban on hunting tigers in Pratibandapuram State. The fine of not following the new order was very harsh including confiscation of all the riches of a person. In fact several high ranking British Officials were denied poaching tigers in the area, nevertheless, they could hunt any other animal they chose. Several years passed and the king kept on hunting tigers. Sometimes he would miss the mark by an inch and as a result, he also had to fight the tiger was his bare hands. 10 years passed and the king was able to kill 70 tigers in his state. Following his expedition, the king faced a challenge of losing his kingdom, for which he paid a bribe of 3 lakh rupees in the form of three gold rings.

By the time the king killed 70 tigers, Tigers in his state became extinct. Now he came up with an idea to marry a girl from a state having the maximum number of tigers. The Dewan of his state found out the right match and the king married the girl. When the king would visit his father in law, he would kill 4 to 5 tigers in his every visit. Eventually, the king killed 99 tigers in total.

Now only one tiger remained to be killed, following which the king could end his expedition. The search of the 100th tiger went on but the 100th tiger was nowhere to be found. As a result, a tiger was brought from a zoo in Chennai and released in the forest where the king was hunting. The king found the tiger, aimed at him and fired the shot. But at the very same moment, the tiger fell in a pit. The King was elated thinking he had killed all his tigers but the hunters along with the king realized the tiger was not dead. Seeing this one of the hunters killed the tiger.

Everything went back to normal routine. After a few days, the king wanted to celebrate his son's birthday who was going to turn three. For his son's birthday, the king bought a wooden tiger for his son as a present. When he presented it to his son, he got a wooden needle-shaped sliver stuck in his hand. As a result, an infection spread and in three to four days' time, the suppurating sore was ruled out. The best surgeons in the state performed surgeries on the king but the king died. In a way, we can say that the 100th tiger was the one which eventually took the king's life.

PREVIOUS YEARS'
EXAMINATION QUESTIONS
▶ **Short Answer Type Questions**

[2 & 3 Marks]

1. What sort of hunts did the Maharaja offer to organize for the high-ranking British officer? What trait of the officer does it reveal?

[DELHI 2013]

2. Why was the Maharaja so anxious to kill the hundredth tiger? [ALL INDIA 2012]

3. What consideration influenced the Tiger King to get married ? [ALL INDIA 2018, 2017]

4. Why was the Maharaja once in danger of losing his kingdom? [DELHI 2017]

5. When he was only ten days old, a prediction was made about the future of the Tiger King. What was ironic about it? [DELHI 2016]

6. The manner of his (the Tiger King's) death is a matter of extraordinary interest. Comment.

[ALL INDIA 2016]

7. Even today so many among us believe in superstitions. An astrologer predicted about, the 'Tiger King' that he would be killed by a tiger. He, killed one hundred tigers yet was himself killed by a tiger. How did the superstitious belief prevail? [ALL INDIA 2015]

8. Why did the Maharaja order the dewan to double the land tax? [ALL INDIA 2014]

9. Why did the Maharaja ban tiger hunting in the state? [DELHI 2014]

10. How did the Tiger King 'manage to kill' the hundredth tiger? [DELHI 2019]

11. What did the Maharaja and dewan do to avoid the danger of losing the throne?

[DELHI 2023]

▶ **Long Answer Type Questions**

[4 & 6 Marks]

12. Giving a bribe is an evil practice. How did the Tiger King bribe the British officer to save his kingdom? How do you view this act of his?

[DELHI 2015]

13. What was the prediction of the astrologers regarding the ultimate fate of the Tiger King ? How did it come to be true ? Describe with reference to the story. [DELHI 2020]

🔑 **Solutions** ______________

1. The Maharaja declined to enable the British officer to chase tigers in his kingdom, instead, he offered to arrange some other chase, for example, a pig chase, even a mosquito chase. It demonstrates the shallowness falsification of the British authority. [2]

2. The Maharaja had executed ninety-nine tigers. On the off chance that one he kill only one more tiger, he would have no dread left. At that point, he could leave tiger chasing. He thought of the tiger amid the day and longed for it around evening time. [2]

3. To overcome the celestial prophet's prescience, the Maharaja needed to murder a hundred tigers. He had just slaughtered seventy tigers and the tiger populace in his state neared elimination. Consequently, he wished to wed a young lady in the illustrious group of a state with a rich tiger populace, where he would slaughter whatever remained of the tigers. [2]

4. There was a time when the Maharaja was in danger of losing his throne. Once a visitor who was a high ranking British officer, came to Pratibandhpuram. He was exceptionally attached to chasing tigers and capturing them. But the Maharaja declined to give him the permission of doing so as he didn't want him to hunt the tigers. He had forestalled such a high positioning officer from filling his desire. Hence, he remained in threat of losing his kingdom itself. [2]

5. The Chief astrologer predicted that the Tiger King will die one day. Hearing this the ten-days old boy started saying that those who are born will one day die. For this nobody required the predictions of the astrologers. It would make some sense if they could tell the manner of that death. The ten days old boy speaking is itself irony. [2]

6. The Maharaja's life revolved around killing tigers, but ironically, he was killed by a wooden tiger. While playing with his son, the king was wounded and the infection led to his death. Destiny had taken its revenge on the king through the wooden tiger. [2]

7. On his introduction to the world, a fortune-teller had forecasted that the Maharaja's demise would be caused by the hundredth tiger. When the Maharaja learnt of this, he began killing tigers. This demonstrates however individuals put stock in superstition the Maharaja needed to demonstrate the prediction off-base. Subsequent to executing every one of the tigers in his kingdom, he wedded a young lady whose state had an expansive tiger populace. He murdered the tigers in his father-in-law's kingdom as well. He was guaranteed that he had executed a hundred tigers though one was as yet alive. However unexpectedly, his demise was caused by a wooden tiger. While playing with his child and his wooden tiger, an unpleasant sliver penetrated the Maharaja's rear causing a contamination that later prompted his passing. Destiny had delivered its retribution for attempting to overrule it. The superstitious conviction won as the hundredth tiger left to the Maharaja's demise. [2]

8. In the wake of hearing, about vanishings of sheep, the Maharaja set out on a campaign to locate the hundredth tiger, which could be the explanation behind this. Be that as it may, the tiger couldn't be found. In his wrath, the Maharaja ordered the dewan to double the land tax. [2]

9. The Maharaja needed to demonstrate that the State soothsayer's forecast that he would be slaughtered by the hundredth tiger was wrong. Along these lines, he limited the chasing of tigers in all the tiger-rich woods of Pratibandapuram to himself so that he could kill 100 tigers. [3]

10. When Jilani Jung Bahadur was ten days old the chief astrologer predicted that the child that is born will die one day. On this the ten days old prince spoke very clearly that death is inevitable, it would be more helpful if they could tell something about the manner of death. After ths everyone was shocked and the chief astrologer put his hand on his lips and said that the child raises intelligent questions indeed. [3]

11. Maharaja and the Dewan decided to placate and pacify the officer through bribe by sending gifts of expensive diamond rings to the 'duraisani", the wife of the British officer. Thus, he managed to save his throne. [2]

12. The Tiger King sent off a telegram to a renowned British organization of gem dealers in Calcutta to send samples of costly precious stone rings of various outlines. Exactly fifty rings arrived and the Lord sent the whole parcel to the British officer's significant other. The lord and his pastor had expected that the Duraisani would pick maybe a couple of rings and send the rest back. In any case, it worked out that the Duraisani had kept the whole part and answered with a card to say thanks for the endowments. In two days, a bill for three lakh rupees originated from the British gem dealers, which the Maharaja was glad to pay since he

had figured out how to hold his kingdom. **This demonstration of the lord reveals insight into the despicable routine with regards to gift that propagates the endless loop of defilement, particularly considering the way that the ruler had individual interests to ensure instead of the welfare of his kingdom.**   [6]

13. At the birth of the Tiger King, the astrologers predicted that the Crown Prince was born in the hour of the Bull. Since the Bull and the Tiger are both enemies, the King would be unquestionably killed by a tiger.

    When the king came of the age, he killed a tiger and sent for the astrologer who in turn advocated that the killing of one tiger would not be a cause of his death. Killing of the hundredth tiger would lead to king's death. The king was able to kill ninety nine tigers and was anxious for the hundredth tiger. When the king shot the hundredth tiger it collapsed but did not die. The king unaware about the reality and thinking himself safe brought a wooden tiger as the birthday present for his son. It had tiny sliver on its surface. One of those slivers pierced the Maharaja's right hand. The next day, there was a lot of infection in the maharaja's right hand due to that shaving of wood that had pricked his hand. In a period of four days, the infection turned into a wound full of pus and spread all over the king's right arm.In this way the hundredth tiger was the wooden one that killed the king. Thus the prediction proved to be true.   [6]

3. Journey to the End of the Earth

Summary

Introduction:

The worsening condition of our ecology and environment is a major cause of concern. Man, over the years, has been responsible for global waming, which, in turn, is leading to climate change. Glaciers are receding and ice caps are melting. But we seldom realize the real impact of the rise in temperature. A visit to the Antarctica makes it visibly clear. There one can see ice shelves collapsing.

'Students on Ice' is a programme headed by Canadian Geoff Green. The aim of the programme is to make the students understand the impact of global warming. Since they are the future of our mankind, it is essential for them to understand the problem and save our planet from the catastrophe.

The author visited Antarctica on a Russian research ship called Akademik Shokalskiy. He started from Chennai. They had to cross nine time zones, six checkpoints, three water bodies and three ecospheres. The whole journey took him 100 hours. When he landed on the Antarctica, he was spellbound by its vastness, isolation and uninterrupted horizon. He wondered how there could have been a time when India and Antarctica were part of the same land mass - Gondwana.

About 650 million years ago, Gondwana was a very flourishing continent. It was warm and many species of flora and fauna prospered there. At that time, there were no humans living there. Tragically, after the dinosaurs started becoming extinct, Gondwana began to break up. India pushed against Asia and buckled its crust to form the Himalayas. South America drifted to join North America, opening up the Drake Passage. It created a cold current that went round the South Pole. This left the Antarctica cold and isolated.

The Antarctica is now a part of that history. It helps us in understanding the history of human civilization. It helps us to understand the significance of Cordilleran folds and pre-Cambrian granite shields. It helps us to understand about evolution and extinction. Antarctica has remained unspoiled by humans. Its ice-cores hold half-a- million-year old carbon record. It is essential because it helps us in estimating and analyzing the past, present and the future. Although barren, Antarctica is huge expanse of ice. There is no trace of humans. There are no trees, buildings or billboards. There are huge icebergs. There are blue whales. But there are very tiny th in gs to o. T here are no mornings, noons, evenings and nights. It is a 24-hour day. There is silence everywhere. So you lose all earthly sense of time and space there.

Although human civilization is as old as 12,000 years, on the geological clock, it is only a few seconds old. Even in a few seconds, mankind is responsible for creating climatic havoc!. He has built towns and cities. He has wiped out many other species to grab limited natural resources. Man has created a harmful blanket of carbon dioxide by burning fossil fuels. As a result, the global temperature is increasing.

This rise in temperature has caused climatic changes.

It is the most hotly debated question. Many scientists foretell disaster.

Antarctica is the place to see the impact of these changes. Because it has a simple ecosystem, a little change in the environment can trigger a big effect. For example, take the microscopic phytoplankton. They are single celled plants. Through photosynthesis they assimilate carbon to form organic compounds. They sustain the entire food chain in the southern oceans. They regulate the global carbon cycle. Any further depletion of ozone layer will cripple phytoplankton. If they did not function, the entire food chain and global carbon cycle would collapse.

Headed by Canadian Geoff Green, 'Students on Ice' is a programme that has chosen students to take students to the end of the world—Antarctica. He wants to provide young students an opportunity to understand and respect the planet. Students are young. They are ready to learn and act. They can actually see the effect of global warming. They see glaciers retreating and ice shelves collapsing. They cannot remain unaffected. They can see that the threat is real. They are the future policy-makers. They have idealism. They will act.

The research ship Shokalskiy was caught between white stretches of ice, just near the Antarctic Circle, and was unable to go any further. So, the captain decided to turn round and go north. Before taking action, he ordered everybody to gang plank and walk on the ocean. So, all the 52 of them walked on ice. Beneath the ice there was a living ocean. They saw seals running themselves on ice floes. They looked like stray dogs lying in the shade of a banyan tree.

PREVIOUS YEARS'
EXAMINATION QUESTIONS

▶ Short Answer Type Questions
[2 & 3 Marks]

(Answer the following questions in about 30- 40 words each)

1. How do geographical phenomena help us to know about the history of mankind?

2. What are the indications for the future of mankind?

3. Why is Antarctica the place to go to understand the earth's past, present and future?

4. How did Tishani Doshi feel on reaching the Antarctica?

5. What was Gondwana like? How did it change?

6. What prevented the Shokalskiy from going further? What did the captain instruct the passenger to do? (Journey to the End of The Earth)   [DELHI 2023]

▶ Long Answer Type Questions
[6 Marks]

(Answer the following questions in about 125-150 words each)

7. "The world's geological history is trapped in Antarctica." How is the study of this region useful to us?

8. What are Geoff Green's reasons for including high school students in "Students on Ice" expedition?

9. "Take care of small things and the big things will take care of themselves". What is the relevance of this statement in the context of the Antarctic environment?

10. The Antarctica was part of warm and green Gondwana. How did it become cold and isolated?

11. What are phytoplankton ? How are they important to our ecosystem? (Journey to the End of the Earth)   [DELHI 2020]

🔑 Solutions _______________

1. It is by watching and observing geographical phenomena that we can imagine how small changes could have caused a big change over centuries. They help us to understand where we came from and where we might be heading. [2]

2. Global warming is hauntingly real. This can bring about drastic climatic changes. Unless acted upon, the world will not remain the same as we know it, which is a real threat to the future of humankind.   [2]

3. The only place that can reflect on the present, past and future of human civilization is Antarctica because it is the only place where humans are unable to adapt. . So, it remains almost as pure as it used to be millions of years ago. There we can observe how a little change can affect the environment. Besides, half-a-million- year-old carbon records lie trapped in its layers of ice. So, if we want to study the earth's past, present and future, Antarctica is the right place.   [2]

4. Tishani was filled with wonder at Antarctica's immense white expanse, uninterrupted blue horizon and isolation. He wondered how Antarctica and India could have been the part of the same landscape Gondwana. [2]

5. Gondwana was a super continent about 650 million years ago. The climate was warm with flourishing flora and fauna. It was only a million years ago that it was disintegrated into separate countries. [2]

6. The Shokalskiy had managed to wedge herself into a thick white stretch of ice between the peninsula and Tadpole Island which was preventing us from going any further. [1]

The captain instructed all the passengers to climb down the gangplank and walk on the ocean. [1]

7. Present day Antarctica was the center of a huge landmass called Gondwana. It was in existence for it existed about 650 million years ago and thrived for 500 million years. Then, it was not cold. Climate was warm. Thousands of species of flora and fauna lived there. But there were no human beings. Then this landmass disintegrated. After breaking away, India was pushed against Asia and created the Himalayas. South America drifted away to join North America. It was and only is Antarctica that holds the key to the geological history of our world.

It helps us in understanding the significance of Cordilleran folds and pre-Cambrian granite shields, ozone and carbon, evolution and extinction. [6]

8. Human civilisation on earth is only 12000 years old. But during this short period, man has created much confusion here. He has built towns and cities. He has wiped out species to snatch limited resources of this earth for his ever increasing population. By burning fossil fuels, he has created a blanket of carbon dioxide around the world, which, in turn, is increasing the global temperature. The Climate change is a hot debate topic currently, it is being widely searched, researched and analysed. Geoff Green has included students in his expedition to provide them inspiring educational opportunities. Students are the policy makers of tomorrow. They are at an age when they are ready to learn and act and possess the quality of idealism, something that the lder folks lack. [6]

9. Phytoplankton are microscopic single-celled grasses. They synthesize organic compounds using the energy of the sun. These very-very tiny grasses sustain the entire food chain in the southern oceans. Scientists tell us that any further depletion of ozone layer will have a bad effect on the activity of these single celled plants. In turn, the whole food chain will be disrupted. That will endanger the lives of all sea creatures as well as birds in this region. So, if we take care of phytoplankton or the ozone layer, everything else will take care of itself. [6]

10. Around 650 million years ago, there was a giant super continent in the south. Now we name it Gondwana. Antarctica formed the central part of that landmass. In those days, the climate was relatively warmer and human beings had not came into existence. Many species of flora and fauna were there. For 500 million years Gondwana thrived. Bu t, around the time when dinasaurs disappeared and mammals began to develop, Gondwana began to break up. India broke away and pushed herself against Asia and buckled its crust to create the Himalayas. South America drifted to join North America opening up the Drake Passage. This led to the establishment of cold current around the South Pole. On account of this, the Antarctica was left not only isolated but it became frigid and desolate also. [6]

11. Phytoplankton are the grasses of the sea of the Southern Ocean. These are single celled plants and use the sun's energy. With the process of photosynthesis, they supply food and oxygen for all the marine life of the sea. But the global warming can affect the activities of these plants and life of all the creatures depending on them. Global warming also causes the melting of the ice-bergs and collapsing of ice-shelves in the region.

The phytoplankton convert carbon dioxide and water into food using energy from sunlight. If they fail to do so the temperature of the earth would increase. The ozone layer will get depleted and the ultra-rays would reach the earth. This can lead to the death of various organisms. Therefore, it is very important for our eco-system. [6]

4. The Enemy

Summary

Introduction:

Dr. Sadao Hoki used to live in a house on one of the Japanese coasts. Sadao's father was a serious person who would never play or joke with his child. Sadao's father's chief concern was Sadoa's education. Sadao's father sent Sadao to America at the age of 22 to learn medicine. Sadao was 30 years old when he completed his education and on doing so he returned to Japan. Sadao's father cherished his son becoming a famous surgeon in medicine. But Sadao's father passed away.

When Sadao was in America, he met a girl Hana at a professor's house. He fell in love with her at the very exact moment but did not talk to her unless he made sure she was Japanese too. She turned out to be Japanese and their marriage was arranged in a traditional way in Japan. They had a good life and had two children too.

One day Sadao and Hana were in their house and they saw a white man crawling on hands and knees approaching towards their house. While crawling, the man dropped on his face and fainted. Sadao and Hana rushed towards the man to help. Sadao realized that the man suffered from a gunshot wound on his lower back. Sadao rushed and packed the wound with sea moss. He wore a cap which said, "U.S. Navy" from which it was clear that the man was a prisoner of war.

Now seeing a white man, Sadao and Hana were in a dilemma whether to hand over the person to the police or to save him. If they tried to hand him to the police without treatment, he would die and if they did not turn him in, they would be imprisoned. So Sadao decided to operate on the man. The servants of the house did not want to help the white man, so as a result, the servants returned to their usual tasks. Hana took over the job of helping Sadao. Hana herself washed the victim using hot water.

Sadao started operating on the victim with Hana's help. Sadao asked Hana to anaesthetize the victim when required. Sadao realized that the bullet was still in the body and the victim had already lost so much blood, so he pulled the bullet out with a deep and precise cut. Seeing blood all around, Hana could not bear the sight, so she went out of the room and

returned after some time with a bottle and cotton. The victim was still unconscious but muttered in pain when the bullet was taken out. Post-surgery Sadao realized that the American man would live.

Some time passed and now the American man woke up and told them that his name was Tom. Tom was very weak and terrified to see the place where he was in. Hana comforted him by saying that he need not worry and he would be strong again in a few days. 3 days passed and Sadao confirmed that Tom's health was improving. Following this Tom asked Sadao what he would do with Tom. Sadao did not answer as he was still thinking if he did not turn the American in, he would be betraying his country but on the other hand, he also that Tom was just seventeen and very young.

As there was an American prisoner realized hiding in Sadao's house, all the servants were terrified. The servants, in fact, were worried what the people around might think. The servants grew more watchful and decided to leave on the 7th day. Hana maintained her pride and let all the servants go after paying them what was owed. Sadao wanted to see the American on his foot and asked the American to practice walking daily. The American thanked Sadao but he said not to thank him yet. The last stitches of the wound were also eventually pulled out and Sadao told the American that he would be better in about a fortnight.

Sadao went to the General to tell him about the American. The general was old and did not want Sadao to get arrested as Sadao was the only doctor he trusted for his operation. The general worried what if Sadao got imprisoned and killed and the general required Sadao the next day for his operation. So the general advised Sadao that he would send 2 assassins to kill the American in the night. Following this approach, the problem would be solved without any sound.

Sadao told nothing of the general's plans to Hana. Sadao was a bit uncomfortable in getting the American killed, so he prepared a boat with food and necessary supplies to survive on the coast for the American. He advised the American to reach a nearby island on which no one lived and to catch a Korean boat. He also advised the American that if he ran out of supplies, signal him with two flashes. In the meantime, Sadao told the general that the American escaped. The general also forgot about it as he was in a poor health. Sadao never came across two flash signals which confirmed that the American escaped the Japanese territory successfully.

After all this, Sadao thought that when he was in America he found it so much difficult to find a place to live just because he was Japanese and the American people were full of prejudice. He was happy that finally, the two nations were at a head-on war. He also thought why did he let the American escape or why could not he get him killed.

PREVIOUS YEARS'
EXAMINATION QUESTIONS
▶ **Short Answer Type Questions**

[1 Mark]

(Q. 1 to 5) : Read the extract given below and answer the questions that follow :

[DELHI TERM I, 2022]

"You are well", Sadao agreed. He lowered his voice. "You are so well that I think if I put my boat on the shore tonight, with food and extra clothing in it, you might be able to row to that little island not far from the coast. It is so near the coast that it has not been worth fortifying. Nobody lives on it because in storm it is submerged. But this is not the season of storm. You could live there until you saw a Korean fishing boat pass by. They pass quite near the island because the water is many fathoms deep there.'

The young man stared at him, slowly comprehending. 'Do I have to? he asked.'

"I think so", "Sadao said gently." "you understand – it is not hidden that you are here."

1. The arrangements of food and clothing by Dr. Sadao portrays him as
   (a) a kind and compassionate person
   (b) an experienced sailor
   (c) a good event organizer
   (d) a good advisor

2. 'not been worth fortifying' indicates that it____.
   (a) has been left uncared for and neglected
   (b) can be easily spotted by the Korean boats
   (c) will be easy for the white man to enter the island
   (d) is dangerous to stay there alone

3. The speaker's tone in the expression : "Do I have to ?" is
   (a) pleading
   (b) commanding
   (c) irritated
   (d) fear and doubt

4. "But this is not the season of storm." Dr. Sadao tries to
   (a) explain the situation
   (b) assure him of safety
   (c) educate him on climate
   (d) display his knowledge

5. "... it is not hidden you are here."
   Dr. Sadao's intention is :
   (a) to explain why he cannot stay there anymore
   (b) to remind him that he has tried to hide his presence
   (c) to explain that it is necessary and good for both of them
   (d) to assert that his house is not a hiding place

6. Select the option that aptly describes Hana as a wife :   [DELHI TERM I, 2022]
   (a) Hana is very possessive about her husband
   (b) Hana is a very caring and responsible wife
   (c) Hana is a very dominant wife
   (d) Hana is a very fussy and nagging wife

7. She did not wish to be left alone with the white man. This thought of Hana reveals the fact that   [DELHI TERM I, 2022]
   (a) Hana hates white man
   (b) White men are dangerous
   (c) War makes people enemies
   (d) Hana is timid and cautious

8. 'Suppose you were condemned to death and the next day I had to have my operation?' The tone of the General indicates he is
   [DELHI TERM I, 2022]
   (a) worried about Dr. Sadao as he is a good scientist.
   (b) working against the law and order of the country
   (c) uncertain about his health condition
   (d) selfish and dependent on Dr. Sadao for his treatment.

▶ Short Answer Type Questions

[2 & 3 Marks]

9. How did Dr. Sadao ensure that the American sailor left his house but he himself remained safe and secure? [DELHI 2011]

10. What was his father's chief concern about Dr. Sadao? [DELHI 2016]

11. In what condition, did Dr. Sadao find the American soldier at the seashore?

[ALL INDIA 2015]

12. What forced Dr. Sadao to be impatient and irritable with his patient? [ALL INDIA 2013]

13. What was Hana's role in Dr. Sadao's life when he brought home an injured American soldier ? [DELHI 2019]

14. Why was Dr. Sadao not arrested on the charge of harbouring an enemy ? [DELHI 2020]

▶ Long Answer Type Questions

[5 & 6 Marks]

15. Do you think Dr. Sadao's final decision was the best possible one in the circumstances? Why/Why not? Explain with reference to the story 'The Enemy'. [DELHI 2013]

16. How did Dr. Sadao rise above narrow prejudices of race and country to help a human being in need? [DELHI 2013]

17. Dr. Sadao was compelled by his duty as doctor to help the enemy soldier. What made Hana, his wife sympathise with him in the face of open defiance from the domestic staff?

[ALL INDIA 2011]

18. To choose between professional loyalty and patriotism was a dilemma for Dr. Sadao. How did he succeed in betraying neither?

[ALL INDIA 2017]

19. Good human values are far above any other value system. How did Dr. Sadao succeed as a doctor as well as a patriot? [DELHI 2017]

20. Dr. Sadao faced a dilemma. Should he use his surgical skills to save the life of a wounded person or hand an escaped American P.O.W over to the Japanese police? How did he resolve this clash of values? [ALL INDIA 2015]

21. Dr. Sadao was a patriotic Japanese as well as a dedicated surgeon. How could he honour both the values? [DELHI 2015]

22. What was the General's plan to get rid of the American prisoner? Was it executed? What traits of the General's character are highlighted in the lesson 'The Enemy'? [ALL INDIA 2014]

23. After seeing off the enemy soldier, Dr. Sadao must have felt relieved. He was able to uphold the oath that he had taken as a doctor. Dr. Sadao made an entry into his daily diary explaining the dilemma faced by him and how he resolved it.

Imagine yourself to be Dr. Sadao and express his thoughts.

(You may begin like this :

I was able to uphold the oath that I had taken as a doctor ....) [DELHI 2023]

⚷ Solutions

1. (a) The young man was his enemy even then he was making arrangements for his safe departure. [1]

2. (c) The island is not being guarded and so to enter that place would be quite easy. [1]

3. (d) The American was scared that he might again be caught by the force and was doubtful too as he didn't want to leave Dr.Sadao's place where he felt safe. [1]

4. (b) Dr Sadao didn't want to bother the American with any problematic thoughts and wanted to convince him of his safe stay at the island. [1]

5. (a) The doctor was giving him the reason of leaving that place. [1]

6. (b) She didn't leave her husband's side and even helped in treatment of the enemy against her own wish. [1]

7. (d) She was nervous and alert at the same time. [1]

8. (d) He only thought about himself and needed Dr.Sadao for his treatment. [1]

9. Dr. Sadao offered his personal boat with food and extra clothing and advised him to go to a nearby island and escape from there by boarding a Korean fishing boat.

10. Sadao's father's chief concern was his education. He wanted Sadao to go abroad for higher studies and he wanted to see him as the best surgeon in the world.

11. Dr. Sadao saw the man thrown out of the ocean by a wave. He saw him stagger a few steps then fall on all fours. The man crawled before he fell on his face and lay there. Dr. Sadao found that he was wounded and unconscious. He had a gunshot wound on the right side of his lower back that had been reopened when it had struck against the rocks- and was bleeding.

12. Sadao heard Hana spewing in the garden and said that it would be better for her to purge her stomach. He went ahead with his work. He had overlooked that she had never observed a task. In any case, her pain and his powerlessness to go to her without a moment's delay made him restless and bad tempered with the man who lay like dead under his blade.

13. Dr. Sadao was a compassionate person and highly valued his duty as a doctor. He treated the American soldier even though he was an enemy, which shows his love towards humanity. However, he was patriotic towards his country as well and decided to inform the general about his American patient. He had stayed back from war to treat the general. [3]

14. It was against the laws to shelter an enemy. Dr. Sadao had sheltered an enemy soldier but he can't be arrested for harbouring the enemy because his servants did not disclose the secret to the police. [2]

15. For Yes:

   (i) He was duty bound as a doctor to save lives.

   (ii) Political enemies are not personal enemies

   (iii) Tom was a young soldier merely doing his duty.

   (iv) Compassion is a natural instinct.

   For No:

   (i) The fore most duty is towards one's motherland.

   (ii) The soldier after recovering would continue with his job of killing Japanese soldiers.

   (iii) Harbouring enemy soldiers is an offence.

   (iv) After doing his duty as a doctor he could have handed over the soldier to the authorities.

16. Dr. Sadao was a well known Japanese surgeon and researcher. He lived with his significant other, two youngsters and two workers. One day when Dr. Sadao came back from this obligation, he saw a man hit by a projectile. He found that the harmed man was an American wartime captive who had gotten away. A war was going ahead between America and Japan back then and it was wrong to give sanctuary or to help an aggressor. Yet, Dr. Sadao realized that in the event that he didn't do his obligation as a specialist and fix the harmed he would do bad to his honorable calling. In this way, Dr. Sadao worked on the man and did everything he could to save his life. At long last, he thought of giving over the harmed fighter to the army, yet in the meantime, he realized that the army would kill the warrior. Along these lines, he chose to assist the fighter with escaping in a pontoon. This demonstrates Dr. Sadao was a good surgeon as well as an honorable soul who transcended slender prejudice of race and nation to help a person in need.

17. Hana was a passionate woman. Even though she disliked the enemy soldier, she was unable to bring herself to put him back into the sea as he was wounded. Even though the servants opposed the keeping of the man in the house, Hana did not submit. It was her maternal instincts that made her sympathetic to the wounded enemy soldier despite open hostility from the domestic staff.

18. Dr. Sadao was a dedicated doctor . One day an American prisoner crowled to his doorsteps. He was badly wounded. He did not know about the wounded man's identity and was hesitant in letting the man in. But as a doctor, it was his moral duty to save a wounded man. So he treated him.

When he came to know about the real identity of the patient he had in his home, being a patriotic Japanese he informed a senior General about the American. He waited for the assassins to arrive but when they did not show up, he gave a boat to the American and let him escape. In this way Dr. Sadao succeeded in betraying neither his professional loyalty nor his patriotism.

19. As a doctor, Sadao, knew the value of a human life. He risked his own life by saving the American sailor, even though he knew that he could go to prison for hiding a prisoner of war. He cleaned the American's wounds, fed him and nursed him back to health. When the American was feeling healthy, he gave him provisions such as food and a boat, and allowed him to

escape from Japan. As a Japanese citizen, he fulfilled his duty by telling the General about the American. Even though the General forgets to send his assassins, Sadao cannot be blamed for the American's "escape". Thus we can say that Sadao carried out his responsibilities, as a doctor, and as a patriot.

20. A conflict of interests arises in a situation when someone in a position of trust, such as a doctor, has competing interests that make it difficult to fulfil his duties. Dr Sadao was a Japanese surgeon who lived in Japan during the Second World War. He had spent several years in the United States where he had experienced cultural prejudice and bias. He disliked whites and struggled with issues of duty, wartime medicine and racism yet he risks his life to save an enemy, an American and a prisoner of war. He, like a real hero, stood up for what he believed in and did not calculate the repercussions. He struck a balance between his duty towards humanity and his country. He tended the soldier, revealed the truth about him to the General and later helped the soldier escape to safety. He can be viewed as a true hero for his bravery and professional competence.

21. Dr. Sadao Hoki was not only a trained surgeon but also a fervent patriot who dedicated himself to the cause of serving his country in wartime through scientific research. However the dilemma that Sadao faced in lieu of the arrival of the wounded enemy soldier on his doorstep was a clash between his duties as a doctor and that of a citizen of a particular nation' Sadao remarked that if the man had been whole and uninjured, then he would not have faced any difficulty in turning him over to the police. However, the fact that he was wounded complicated this issue because as a doctor, Sadao had taken the oath to put his professional duties first and serve mankind as a whole, without any discrimination on the basis of nationality. But he was able to protect his patriotism by informing the General about the man. In this way, he balanced both of his values by tending the soldier and helping him escape at the end, while having informed General about his presence.

22. The General intended to dispose off the American detainee by sending his own professional killers and afterward expel his body from Sadao's home. The arrangement was not executed on the grounds that the General overlooked his guarantee to send the professional killers. The old General had a long dull face, which appeared to mirror the chilly and ascertained mercilessness of the man as a General. He had an abnormal comical inclination and appeared to create fear in others' 'hearts easily'. In his connection with Sadao, he seemed to be a man who put his self-enthusiasm above everything else. As Sadao is the main individual whom he trusted with his health, he let Sadao free. His chilly and computing streak is shown in the carefulness with which he thoroughly considered the arrangement of executing the American wartime captive whom Sadao had given shelter.

23. Saturday,

25 February 20XX

Dear Diary,

I'm feeling so relieved today as I was able to uphold the oath that I had taken as a doctor. For a doctor a patient must be his priority regardless of his religion, caste, country, or background and today I could do justification with my profession when I could save an enemy's life. There was a time when I got convinced with General's decision of killing the enemy but that would never have given me mental peace. I did right in saving his life and helping him to go back to America. In this noble cause even my better half Hana has also shown indispensable courage and perseverance.

Even when she herself was facing so much of discomfort she still proved to be a compassionate woman. Without her help, I could not have found courage to save the soldier from his approaching death. I am thankful to the Almighty for letting me come out of the dilemma between the head and the heart. It was the toughest decision to choose to be governed by the emotion or the reason. Yet my inner conscience and call of duty won over my mind. Now when I'm back after helping the American soldier to reach to his destination, I'm feeling about the days in America. Still, I wonder what did not allow me to kill the enemy Tom.

Now I'm feeling sleepy as tomorrow again I've to render my services which I'm bound to provide.

Sadao   [5]

5. On the Face of It

Summary

Introduction:

Derry walked slowly and cautiously and entered Mr. Lamb's Garden. He got startled when Mr. Lamb came close to him as Derry thought that there was nobody there in the garden. Mr. Lamb tried to make Derry feel comfortable and said that Derry could pick up crab apples and that he didn't need to go away. Mr. Lamb told Derry that the gate of his garden was always open and he didn't mind anyone who came. He assured Derry that he could stay there and that he didn't need to climb over the wall when Derry told Mr. Lamb that he was not there to steal the apples.

Derry said that people were afraid of him and found his face terrible and ugly as one side of his face was burnt. Sometimes while looking in the mirror he himself got afraid. Mr. Lamb looked at him and said that he was going to get a ladder and a stick so that he could pick crab apples as he makes jelly from them. But Derry wanted to talk about himself and didn't want to deviate from the topic. Derry corrected Mr. Lamb by telling him that his face got burnt because acid ran down on one side of his face when Mr. Lamb thought that his face might have got burnt in a fire.

Mr. Lamb lost his leg and some kids call him "Lamey Lamb". He had got a tin leg. Lamb was old and Derry was young just as one green plant is called weed while other a flower. It was not just a tin leg or a burnt face which could be noticed. There are many more other things such as weeds, sunflowers and crab apples. All these things full of life also deserve our attention and that's why Mr. Lamb enjoyed life and people as much as he could.

Derry suffered from a complex because of his burnt face and always remained withdrawn and defiant. He said that people tried to console him by telling him fairy stories and comforting lies like it didn't matter what you look like. But Derry knew that he would stay as a 'monstrous beast' and he could not change and that no one would ever kiss him except his mother, who also kissed him on his other side of the face. He said that it didn't matter if nobody ever

kissed him. Mr. Lamb asked Derry if it still didn't matter to be kissed by pretty girls who have long haired and large eyes. Would he still not like to be kissed by the people he loved? He said that he won't ever look different and no one would ever kiss and love him, even when he grew as old as Mr. Lamb. He would only have "half a face". To this, Mr. Lamb replied that even though Derry got a "half face" but the world had got a "full face" and that he should look at it.

Derry said that people reminded him that there are even worse people in the world than him and he was obsessed with what people said about him. He might have been blind, dumb or mad by birth. A woman once looked at him and said to another woman, "Look at that, that's a terrible thing" and only a mother could love such a face. He didn't like to be near people as he could stand their uncharitable looks and cruel comments. Mr. Lamb advised Derry to keep his ears shut.

Mr. Lamb reminded Derry that he could not just lock himself up and never leave the room. He then told him a story of a man who was afraid of everything in the world such that he locked himself up in a room and stayed there. A picture fell off a wall onto his head and killed him. To that, Mr. Lamb said that life should be enjoyed just like he did. He liked sitting in the sun and reading books and he was not fond of curtains. Mr. Lamb motivates and inspires Derry by saying that he had got two arms, two legs, eyes and ears, a tongue and a brain. He could do whatever he wanted to do just like other people and that if he chose, he could "get on better than all the rest". Derry asked "How?" and Mr. Lamb replies that Derry could live like he did. Everyone was welcome in Mr. Lamb's garden and the gate was always open. Mr. Lamb said that hatred was more harmful than a bottle of acid when Derry said that there were some people who hated him. Derry then got up to leave promising that he would come back, to which Mr. Lamb said that people just said that generally but never came back.

When Derry reached home, his mother warned him not to go there again and he assured her that there was nothing to worry about as an old man with tin leg lived there who had a very big house and a garden as well where everyone who welcome. He was Mr. Lamb. Next day, Derry ran to Mr. Lamb's garden crying that he had come back. Suddenly, he heard a thud and a crashing sound. The ladder fell back with Mr. Lamb on it. He died. Derry kept on crying, "Lamey-lamb! I did… come back".

PREVIOUS YEARS'
EXAMINATION QUESTIONS

▶ Short Answer Type Questions

[2 & 3 Marks]

1. Comment on the ending of the play 'On the Face of It'. [DELHI 2013]

2. What Peculiar things does Derry notice about the old man, Lamb? [ALL INDIA 2012]

3. How does Mr. Lamb keep himself busy when it is a bit cool? [DELHI 2012]

4. People are insensitive to those who have disabilities. Give instances from the story. [DELHI 2012]

5. Why does Mr. Lamb leave his gate always open? [ALL INDIA 2011]

6. Why does Derry's mother not want him to go back to visit Mr. Lamb ? [ALL INDIA 2018]

7. If you were to give a different ending to the story "On the Face of It", how would you end it? [ALL INDIA 2013]

8. What is common between Derry and Mr. Lamb ? [DELHI 2020]

9. How did Mr. Lamb's conversation and company change Derry's desire to isolate himself from the world? [DELHI TERM II, 2022]

▶ Long Answer Type Questions

[4, 5 & 6 Marks]

10. What is the bond that unites the two-the old Mr. Lamb and Derry the small boy? How does the old man inspire the small boy? [DELHI 2013]

11. The lesson, 'On the Face of It', is an apt depiction of the loneliness and sense of alienation experienced by people because of a disability. Explain. [DELHI 2011]

12. Both Derry and Lamb are victims of physical impairment, but much more painful for them is the feeling of loneliness. Comment. [ALL INDIA 2016]

13. Derry sneaked into Mr. Lamb's garden and it became a turning point in his life. Comment. [DELHI 2016]

14. Both Derry and Lamb are physically impaired and lonely. It is the responsibility of society to understand, and support people with infirmities so that they do not suffer from a sense of alienation. As a responsible citizen, write in about 100 words what you would do to bring about a change in the lives of such people. [ALL INDIA 2014]

15. Derry and Mr. Lamb both are victims of physical impairment, but their attitudes towards life are completely different. Elaborate. [DELHI 2019]

16. Justify the title of the lesson 'On The Face Of It'. [DELHI TERM II, 2022]

17. Mr. Lamb : Well that needn't stop you, you needn't mind.

Derry : It'd stop them. They'd mind me. When they saw me here. They look at my face and run.

Mr. Lamb : They might. They might not. You'd have to take the risk. So would they.

Derry : No, you would, you might have me and lose all your other friends, because nobody wants to stay near me if they can help it.

Mr. Lamb : I've not moved.

Derry : No ....

Mr. Lamb : When I go down the street, the kids shout 'Lamey-Lamb'. But they still come into the Garden, into my house; it's a game. They're not afraid of me. Why should they be? Because I'm not afraid of them, that's why not.'

(i) The kids tease Mr. Lamb but still come into his garden. Why?

(ii) Choose the best option that describes Mr. Lamb.

  (a) headstrong

  (b) pessimist

  (c) negligent

  (d) positive

(iii) Choose the correct option with reference to the extract :

What makes Derry tell Mr. Lamb that if he comes, others would stop coming?

  (a) Mr. Lamb would not let others come

  (b) They would be repulsed by Derry.

  (c) Mr. Lamb will have to choose between him and others

  (d) Derry would flare up

(iv) What does Mr. Lamb mean by 'They might, they might not'?   **[DELHI 2023]**

🔑 Solutions

1. The play has a pathetic however emotional completion. Mr. Lamb who works effectively regardless of his physical inability loses his balance and tumbles down alongside the stepping stool. Derry enters and attempts to speak with Mr. Lamb who does not react. Mr. Lamb's "exit" is the same as visualized by Derry before in the play.

2. Derry conceives that the old man is Peculiar. He says particular things. He makes inquiries which Derry does not get it. There are no drapes at the windows in his home. He enjoys the light and obscurity and hears the breeze with the windows open.

3. There is a brief delay in the discussion. At that point Mr. Lamb changes the subject. He says that when it gets somewhat cooler, he will get the stepping stool and a stick. At that point he will pull down those ready crab apples. He makes jam. He calls these orange shaded and brilliant apple enchantment organic product.

September is a decent time to make jam. He tells the kid that he could encourage him.

4. People generally pity the handicap or react with disgust. For instance, people used to stare at the ugly face of Derry. He even once overhead two women remarking that only a mother could love his face. His own family even always discussed his future. Mr. Lamb also shared his experience being stared at by people and children calling him Lamey Lamb.

5. Mr. Lamb is an old man. Probably he had served in the army where one of his legs was blown off in the war. Now he has a tin leg. He stays in a big house and has a garden. He even-keeps the gate of his garden open to welcome everyone in his garden. Most of his time is spent on reading books or sitting in the garden.

6. Derry's mother claims to have heard many things about Mr Lamb. She has been told and warned by the people that he was not a good person. She asked Derry not to go back there. Derry asked her not to believe all she heard because he was determined to go there.

7. A happing ending will narrate the story as, both Mr. lamb and Darry happily collect crab apples and lived together. Darry got inspire from Mr. lamb and start following the message of accepting life as it comes.

8. Derry was a boy whose face was burnt because of acid and Mr. lamb was an old person who had a tin leg because his leg was blown off by a bomb in the war. the common thing in both of them was that they both were physically impaired   **[2]**

9. Mr. Lamb was a physically handicapped man with tin leg. He lived alone but never showed signs of loneliness. Mr. Lamb was not repulsed by Derry. He accepted Derry as he was and never pitied him. Also, he did not react to Derry's rudeness, He did not force Derry to stay and listen to him. But when he happened to strike a conversation with Derry, he made him realise that handicaps are not obstacles,

He opened the world to him. He highlighted Derry's strengths too. He shared his own life experiences and motivated him by the story of the Beauty and the Beast. He told him to wait, watch and listen and never expected him to do anything against his wish.   [2]

10. Mr. Lamb turned Derry into a confident boy from a different one. Both were physically handicapped but with different perspectives towards life. In the beginning

Derry was a defiant and withdrawn boy who hated meeting people. Their stares, jibes and pity made him frustrated. He suffered a lot due to his burned face and was a pessimist Mr. Lamb transformed his vision of life and decided to live it on his own terms and conditions. Mr. Lamb discussed his own life with Derry to make him understand that he should be open-minded. He told him that God had made all the things and one should not keep oneself in a room forever. He also kept his garden gate open and welcomed all.

Moreover, Derry could open up the layers of his heart and complexes in front of Mr. Lamb which unburdened his heart. He got a new ray of hope in his life, the light of life enlightened his soul to live it as it was. He also taught Derry to use whatever God had given to him. Derry was disheartened to find out about his death.

To meet Mr. Lamb, he defied his mother and his return to Lamb's garden showed his appreciation for living life as shown by Lamb. He learnt the lesson of optimism.

11. The play entitled, "On the Face of It" is written by Susan Hill. It is a problem play dealing with the issue of the disabled people. It does not deal with actual pain or inconvenience due to a physical impairment which distresses a disabled person. It rather deals with the behaviour of the people all around him. The play had two disabled persons, deny a young boy of fourteen who bears a burnt face, and Mr. Lamb an, old man who has got a tin leg. A disabled person is regarded as an outcast.

People do sympathise with him. However, they are not accepted in the mainstream of life. The disabled person feels bolted from the human society. The feelings of alienation are truly depressing than the actual pain or inconvenience because of physical impairment. A physically impaired person wants others to regard him as a human being and not as an object of pity.

12. In the story, both Derry and Lamb are physically impaired and lonely. Such people can live their lives with respect and honour, if they are not ridiculed and punished with heartless pity. These people expect empathy, rather than sympathy, from others. If everyone looks down at them with a pessimistic approach, they may never be able to come out of their sorrow: consequently, they may recline to their own secluded worlds. As responsible citizens, we should understand the tremendous mental and emotional pressure these people go through. Instead of reminding them of their disabilities, we should give them the chance to live a normal life because being lonely is extremely painful mentally.

13. One day, Derry sneaked into Mr. Lamb's garden. Derry was withdrawn and defiant. He did not like being with people. Once, he got acid all down on one side of his face. The acid burnt it all away. This created a complex in his mind. He considered his face as the most terrible thing in the world. When he looked in the mirror and shows it, he was afraid of himself. He thought that people were afraid of him. He didn't like being near them.

Only his mother kissed him and that too on the other side of his face. People looked at his face and passed uncharitable remarks. Mr. Lamb was also a physically challenged man. He had got a tin leg. But Mr. Lamb had a positive attitude towards life. He liked to talk and have company. He was open and never shut himself in.

Mr. Lamb's meeting with Derry brought a turning point in Derry's life. He gave confidence to Derry. He persuaded him that he can get better than the rest of the people. He should stop hating people. Hatred burns oneself inside. Derry should take life as it was. This left a deep impression on Derry. He came back to Mr. Lamb only to find him dead. But Mr. Lamb brought a change in Derry's life." He developed the confidence to face the world in a more positive way.

14. Derry's one side face had been burnt by acid and that was his main problem. He suffered from a tremendous amount of inferiority complex. He remained conscious of the fact that his face was ugly and terrible. He tried to escape from the people. He allowed himself to be alone. on the other hand, Mr. lamb lived with spirit of accepting life as it comeshe always carry a positive attitude towards life, things and people. He doesn't find comfort in escaping. Children call him "Lamey-Lamb" and tease. Despite of losing one of his leg in the war he is full of life and enjoy it to his fullest. Sitting in sun, reading books and growing weeds and flower are some of his hobbies that he enjoys the most.

15. Derry and Lamb both were victims of mishaps. Mr. Lamb had a tin leg while Derry had a half burnt face. However their attitude towards life was completely different. Derry was pessimistic, depressed and hated other living beings. He felt that no one will ever love him except his mother as he had once heard a woman saying the same while walking down the street. He felt that he could not achieve anything and would never make any friends. His parents worried as to what will happen to him after they are gone. In contrast to Derry's attitude, Lamb did not let his tin leg hold him back. He was an optimistic, affectionate and energetic person. He made jelly for kids, welcomed everyone into his life and inside his house. He saw weeds the same as flowers and believed 'handsome is as handsome does'. [6]

16. According to the dictionary, "On the Face of it" is an informal expression used to say that something seems to be good or true, but this opinion may be changed when you know more about it.

This definition of the expression should leave us in no doubt about the appropriateness of the title. An individual may be quite different from what we think of him or what he or she may apparently appear to be at the first glance. There is an imperative need for us to view others by removing our glasses of prejudice, hatred, hearsay and dislike.

In the story, On the face of it, Mr. Lamb appears to be mysterious, lonely, lame old fellow who lives in a neighbourhood house with a huge garden, but in reality he is very kind, generous, loving and altruistic. Similarly, although Derry has an ugly looking scary face, he is a fine lad of fourteen with a deep longingness for love. There is nothing wrong with Mr. Lamb and Derry. What is wrong is the way people in their lives and around view them and treat them.

In the story, On the face of it, there is so much of diversity, so many differences and divisions between the people and other species of the world but underneath is oneness, sameness – all of them are created by God and all of them need to live and grow together with love and mutual acceptance. As the play progresses, the characters' views about each other and our impression of them changes for the better. Thus, Susan Hill has quite appropriately entitled her play "On the Face of it". [4]

17. (i) The kids loved Mr.Lamb and were not afraid of him. They knew that he won't mind even if they tease him by calling 'Lamey-Lamb'. [1]

(ii) The correct option is (d) i.e. positive [1]

(iii) The correct option is (b) i.e. they would be repulsed by Derry. [1]

(iv) Mr. Lamb means that it's not necessary that if the people or the children will look at Derry's face; they would mind coming close to him. It might be that they run away, or they might not run away. Mr. Lamb wants Derry to think optimistically and not be pessimistic. [1]

6. Memories of Childhood

Summary

I. The Cutting of my Long Hair- Zitkala-Sa

Introduction:

The first day in the land of apples was bitter cold and the ground was covered with snow. There was a large bell ringing for breakfast and the annoying clatter of shoes which disturbed the peace. There was a constant clash of harsh voices and an undercurrent of many voices murmuring an unknown tongue. The narrator felt that her soul's peace and freedom were lost.

The girls were marching into the dining hall. She noticed Indian girls in clinging dresses and stiff shoes. She found the dresses immodest. The boys entered the dining hall from the opposite door. She felt uncomfortable. The narrator pulled her chair and sat down when the first bell rang but noticed that all the others were still standing. She got confused. Then there was the second bell and all were seated. She was keenly watched by a strange pale-faced woman. On the third bell, everybody picked their knife and fork and began eating.

Judewin, the narrator's friend gave her a terrible warning in the late morning that she overheard the pale-faced woman talking about cutting their long and heavy hair. But among her people, mourners wore short hair while cowards wore shingled hair. Judewin decided to submit but the narrator decided to struggle and rebelled.

She ran to a large room with three big white beds and hid under one of them. She heard the footsteps quickening nearby and voices growing louder. She was dragged from under the bed and taken down the stairs where she was tied-fast to a chair. Her long and heavy hair was shingled like that of a coward. She screamed and resisted but no one came to comfort her. Now, she felt like she was one of many little animals driven by a herder.

II. We too are Human beings - Bama

Bama was in the third class and she hadn't yet heard people talking openly about untouchability, but had already seen and humiliated by what it was. Although the distance between her school to her home could be covered in 10 minutes, she usually took about 30 minutes to an hour to reach home because she would watch all the fun and games that were going on the road. She would look at the shops and the bazaars. She would also look at the snake charmers and the monkeys performing. There were some other attractions as well as Maariyaatta temple, Pongal celebrations, the Statue of Gandhiji and some snacks stalls. All these attracted her attention on her way home.

In the bazaar, street plays or a puppet show or a stunt performance were shown. The political parties would arrive and make speeches through their mikes. There were coffee clubs and she would also see people selling vegetables fruits and sweets and chopping onions or almonds being blown away by the wind. All these activities fascinated Bama on the way back from school.

One day while walking home from school she saw a landlord seated on a piece of sacking spread over a stone ledge near her street. An elderly person in the community was carrying a packet of Vada with strings and gave it to the landlord without touching him or the contents of the packet. She was amused to see such a wise and old man carrying the packet in a funny manner. She narrated the whole incident to her elder brother in a comic way. Her brother explained to her that they were treated as untouchables and people thought that if they touched anything or any person it would become impure since they belonged to a low caste.

Bama was angry at hearing this. She felt sad and disgusted about it. She wanted to Rebel against the caste system which made this distinction between human beings. She was so filled with rage that she wanted to touch those vadas herself.

Her brother, Annan, told her that since they were born in a low caste community they were never given any respect or dignity. He further told her that the only way to get out of this situation was to study hard and become educated. Once they were educated no one would ask their cast. She started studying hard and always topped the class. Many people became her friends. What Annan told her that day left a deep impression on her and changed her life.

PREVIOUS YEARS'
EXAMINATION QUESTIONS

1. What advice did Annan Offer Bama?
   [ALL INDIA 2011]

2. What did Zitkala-Sa feel when her long hair was cut? [DELHI 2011]

3. At the dining table why did Zitkala-Sa begin to cry when others started eating?
   [ALL INDIA 2016]

4. Why was Zitkala-Sa in tears on the first day in the land of apples? [ALL INDIA 2014]

5. Which words of her brother made a deep impression on Bama? [DELHI 2014]

6. What were the articles in the stalls and shops that fascinated Bama on her way back from school? [ALL INDIA 2013]

7. Zitkala-Sa's experience in 'Memories of Childhood' is that of a victim of the caste system. What kind of discrimination does Bama's experience depict? What are their responses to their respective situations?
   [ALL INDIA 2013]

8. It may take a long time for oppression to be resisted, but the seeds of rebellion are sowed early in life. How did Zitkala-Sa face oppression as a child and how did she overcome it ?
   [ALL INDIA 2018]

9. In India, the so-called lower castes have been treated cruelly for a long time. Who advised Bama to fight against this prejudice, when and how? [ALL INDIA 2017]

10. Untouchability is not only a crime, it is inhuman too. Why and how did Bama decide to fight against it? [DELHI 2017]

11. Why did Bama stroll in the market place instead of hurrying back home? Describe the sights she enjoyed seeing there.
    [DELHI 2019]

12. What did Judewin tell the narrator? What was the effect? [DELHI 2023]

13. Both Bama and Zitkala-Sa were from marginalised communities. They challenged the system to bring dignity into their lives. Justify. [DELHI 2023]

Solutions

1. He said to her, "Study with care and learn all you can. If you are always ahead in your lessons, people will come to you of their own accord and attach themselves to you. Work hard." By this he motivated and inspired her.

2. She felt angry and like an animal driven by a herder. She was helpless like a puppet.

3. The narrator felt quite uncomfortable at the dining table. A small bell was tapped. She pulled her chair out and sat on it. She was the only, one seated there. A second bell was sounded. All of them were seated. A pale face woman watched her keenly. Then everyone started eating. All these activities confused her. She felt quite uncomfortable and began to cry.

4. On the first day in the land of apples, Zitkala-Sa was in tears because her hair was cut mercilessly. Relentlessly moaning for her mother, she kicked wildly and cried out loud, continuously shaking her head in resistance.

5. While describing, what happened while returning home, Bama's senior sibling disclosed to her that in spite of the fact that individuals don't get the chance to choose the family they are naturally introduced to, they can outsmart the insults incurred upon them in the event that they are well perused and successful. This left a profound impact on her.

6. These incorporated the performing monkey, the snake charmer's snake, the cyclist who had continued biking for three days, the turning wheel, the Maariyaata sanctuary and the immense chime hanging there. She additionally saw the Pongal offering being cooked before the sanctuary.

7. Social discrimination had been experienced by both Bama and Zitkala-Sa. Zitkala-Sa had to face a horrible experience. She was dragged out. She kicked and scratched wildly to resist but it was of no use. They carried her downstairs and and tied her fast in a chair. She tried to get rid of the grip and cried loud while shaking her head but all in vain.

   On the other hand, one day Bama saw an unusual thing. She saw that an old man was carrying a packet of eatables by a string without touching it for the landlord. The old man belonged to a lower caste and his landlord belonged to a higher caste. Bama was very touched by this incident. Bam and Zitakal-Sa fought against the discrimination, caste system, and untouchability, through this excursion of defiance. Bama effectively implemented her sibling's recommendation to finally top in her class. While Zitkala-Sa keeps on rebeling by reprimanding the disasters of racial preference through her works, Bama decided on a more unpretentious approach to convey forward her quiet yet viable oppositions.

8. Since the day the writer was away from her mom, she had endured outrageous insults. Individuals had gazed at her. She had been hurled all around like a wooden mannequin. Her cover had been removed from her shoulders. She felt that she was indecently dressed. She was so stunned and persecuted that she felt like sinking to the floor. Afterwards, her delicate sandals were taken away. These were the customary footwear of the neighbourhood Indian American. They were supplanted by squeaking shoes. She saw other Indian young ladies in solid shoes and firmly staying dresses. The little young ladies wore sleeved cook's garments and shingled hair. The most exceedingly awful insult she endured was the removing her long hair. The quitter's shingled hair made her groan with anguish. She believed she was not an individual but rather one of the little creatures driven by a herder. The efficient disintegration of their way of life and discourtesy to ladies was very severe. She couldn't defeat these in her youth, however, the seeds of disobedience were sowed.

9. Annan had told Bama about the class discrimination when she had narrated her an incident of man who was carrying a small packet held by a string. The man went to the landlord, bowed in front of him and handed him the packet. Bama found the situation to be funny. Annan then told Bama that there was nothing funny about it and that the higher class had always treated the lower class in this way. The upper class believed that the lower class should not touch them. Although they were allowed to do anything within their community. Annan told Bama to concentrate on her studies and not think about it much. Then only they could throw discard away all the indignities.

10. Bama first encountered untouchability when she saw an elder of her caste walking along the street from the direction of the bazaar. Initially, the vision made her laugh but then she saw the elder walk up straight to the landlord, bow low and extend the packet towards him, cupping the hand that held the string with his other hand. Bama's brother Annan explained her the whole incident in detail. He explained that since they were born into the community of the marginalised, they were never given any honour, dignity or respect. They had all been stripped of the basic rights of any person. But if they studied and made progress then they could shake off all these indignities. So he advised his sister to study with care and learn all she could. If she was always ahead in her lessons then people would come to her of their own accord and attach themselves to her. These words that Annan had spoken to Bama made a very deep impression on her and spurred her to study hard with all her breath and being. She stood first in her class and many of the children from upper caste became her friend. In this way, she rebelled against the injustice of untouchability.

11. The distance from Bama's school to her house could be covered in ten minutes, However it took her thirty minutes to one hour to reach home. This was because she took her time observing the activities going on in the market place. The performing monkey, the snake that the snake charmer kept in the box, the cyclist who had not gotten off his bike for three days, Maariyaata temple, the huge bell hanging there, the Pongal offerings, the dried fish stall by the statue of Gandhi, the sweet stall, the hunter gypsy with his wild lemur in his cages ad at times speeches of various political parties are some of the things Bama enjoyed during her stroll. She found it very funny how an elder from her village was walking with a plastic packet held by strings which was sadly an act of discrimination against his caste. [6]

12. Judewin, who knew a few words of English, told Zitkala-Sa that she had overheard the pale-faced woman saying that Zitkala-Sa's long hair would be cut. Judewin advised her to submit and resign to her fate but Zitkala-Sa disagreed with her and decided to resist and stand-up against it. [2]

13. The struggle for identity and the oppression faced by the marginalised communities is the common thread between the lives of Bama and Zitkala -Sa. Both were school going children when they witnessed rough treatment being meted out to themselves or their community. Both the episodes prove that injustice in any form does not escape notice even by children. Zitkala-Sa revolts and resists against the school authorities with all her might because she does not want her hair to be shingled like that of a coward's. She reacts strongly and says that she would not give up without struggling. Bama too realises the oppression that her community faces. She puts up a fight by bringing laurels to her community through her scholarly achievements after her brother Annan advises her to study with care and to stay ahead of others in her lessons so that they could throw away all those indignities. Thus, she also proves herself and challenges the oppression against her, leading to saving not only his own dignity but also the self-respect of her whole community. Both the girls refused to bow down to exploitation and oppression and fought the social discrimination that their communities had to face. Thus, Bama who is now a well-known author and Zitkala-Sa both live without fear. [5]